Fodor's 90
The Carolinas
& the
Georgia
Coast

W9-CBD-808

Parts of this book appear in *Fodor's The South '90*.

Fodor's Travel Publications, Inc.
New York and London

ISBN 0-679-01755-0

Fodor's The Carolinas & the Georgia Coast

Editors: Larry Peterson, Jacqueline Russell
Contributors: Suzanne Brown, Edgar and Patricia Cheatham, John English, Jon Gross, Ellen Knox, Denise Nolty, Eileen Robinson Smith, Arthur Rosenblatt, Carol L. Timblin
Art Director: Fabrizio La Rocca
Cartographer: David Lindroth
Illustrator: Karl Tanner
Cover Photograph: Southern Stock Photos

Design: Vignelli Associates

Special Sales

Fodor's Travel Publications are available at special discounts for bulk purchases (100 copies or more) for sales promotions or premiums. Special editions, including personalized covers, excerpts of existing guides, and corporate imprints, can be created in large quantities for special needs. For more information write to Special Marketing, Fodor's Travel Publications, 201 East 50th St., New York, NY 10022. Inquiries from the United Kingdom should be sent to Fodor's Travel Publications, 30–32 Bedford Square, London WC1B 3SG.

MANUFACTURED IN THE UNITED STATES OF AMERICA
10 9 8 7 6 5 4 3 2 1

Contents

Maps

Foreword

This is an exciting time for Fodor's, as we continue our program to rewrite, reformat, and redesign all 140 of our guides. Here are just a few of the ambitious new features:

★ Brand-new computer-generated maps locating all the top attractions, hotels, restaurants, and shops

★ A unique system of numbers and legends to help readers move effortlessly between text and maps

★ A new star rating system for hotels and restaurants

★ Restaurant reviews by major food critics around the world

★ Stamped, self-addressed postcards, bound into every guide, to give readers an opportunity to help evaluate hotels and restaurants

★ Complete page redesign for instant retrieval of information

★ FODOR'S CHOICE—Our favorite museums, beaches, cafes, romantic hideaways, festivals, and more

★ HIGHLIGHTS—An insider's look at the most important developments in tourism during the past year

★ TIME OUT—The best and most convenient lunch stops along the shopping and exploring routes

★ A mini-journal for travelers to keep track of their own itineraries and addresses

We wish to thank Cheryl Hargrove at Travel South for her assistance in the preparation of this guidebook.

While every care has been taken to assure the accuracy of the information in this guide, the passage of time will always bring change, and consequently, the publisher cannot accept responsibility for errors that may occur.

All prices and opening times quoted here are based on information available to us at press time. Hours and admission fees may change, however, and the prudent traveler will avoid inconvenience by calling ahead.

Fodor's wants to hear about your travel experiences, both pleasant and unpleasant. When a hotel or restaurant fails to live up to its billing, let us know and we will investigate the complaint and revise our entries where the facts warrant it.

Send your letters to the editors of Fodor's Travel Publications, 201 E. 50th Street, New York, NY 10022.

Highlights '90 and Fodor's Choice

Highlights '90

Georgia

Eight to ten million visitors a year are expected to visit the newly opened Underground Atlanta, a $142-million entertainment and shopping complex in the heart of Five Points in downtown Atlanta. Comprised of three levels, one of which is underground, the complex features nearly 100 specialty retailers, 20 food court vendors, and 22 restaurants and nightclubs. There are two large public plazas, 1,250 parking spaces in two garages, and a variety of special attractions. The six-block, twelve-acre complex will cater to the convention trade.

To ease the traffic problems that may arise from visitors to Underground Atlanta, a cloverleaf connecting Interstates I-75, I-85, and I-20 was completed in 1989.

The Atlanta International Museum of Art and Design will be opening its doors in Peach Tree Center, downtown Atlanta.

North Carolina

New on the **Raleigh-Durham** hotel scene are Embassy Suites Hotel, Fairfield Inn, Hampton Inn, Hospitality Inn-Stony Brook, Quality Suites Hotel, Red Roof Inn, and Sundown Inn–North. The Fearrington House in **Chapel Hill** is a new bed-and-breakfast inn. The Reynolds House, a lavish 60-room home of the late tobacco king R.J. Reynolds, will close for renovations in September of 1990 and reopen in late 1991.

Kitty Hawk Aerotours, which leaves from the First Flight Airstrip, has expanded its operation to include charter flights to Norfolk through a subsidiary called Outerbanks Airways.

Spirit Square, the arts center in **Charlotte,** is under renovation and is expected to reopen in 1990. The Public Library, which includes a mural of a Romare Bearden painting, reopened on North Tryon Street in mid-1989 and the Afro-American Cultural Center, a black arts center with galleries, a theater, and bookstore, is housed in a restored building that formerly served as the Little Rock AME Zion Church.

New to Charlotte in the past year are The Dunhill Hotel, Compri, Embassy Suites, and Days Inn Hotel.

April 1, 1989, saw the opening of the Richard Petty Museum in the stock-racer's home town of **Level Cross.** The museum, open to the public Monday through Saturday, displays race cars, trophies, awards, and personal mementos.

At press time, despite a direct hit from **Hurricane Hugo,** everything in Charlotte was open for business as usual—albeit minus several of the city's huge old trees that were uprooted by the force of the storm.

South Carolina

The South Carolina State Museum in **Columbia** is a 50,000-square-foot facility in the process of expanding. Housed in a building that served as the first electric textile mill in 1894, the museum displays, among other exhibits, a replica of the first locomotive built in America for both passengers and freight service. The Charles H. Townes Center celebrates the achievement of the South Carolina Nobel laureate who pioneered the laser. Other achievements of South Carolina residents can be found in the History Hall, which chronicles 14,000 years of the state's history, and the Palmetto Gallery, which exhibits works of South Carolina artists. The art gallery features a variety of changing exhibits and will begin the year with a Scholastic Art Show.

The Koger Center for Performing Arts, one of the South's finest new performing arts complexes, opened its doors in January, 1989. Connected with the University of South Carolina in Columbia, the center, which cost $15 million to complete, contains 2,256 seats on three levels. Programs in 1990 will include performances by the London Philharmonic, the Warsaw Ballet, the New York City Opera, the Moscow Philharmonic, Taj Mahal, and the Boston Chambers Players.

In late September 1989, **Hurricane Hugo** cut a vicious swath through South Carolina, hitting the greater Charleston area and some of the barrier islands dead-center. Property damage was greatest along the shore and in residential and rural areas close to the coast, where clean-up and rebuilding efforts are expected to last for some time.

Charleston's historic district was spared serious damage, and within a month of the storm, the city had returned pretty much to normal, with power fully restored and some 90% of all area businesses reopened. Outside Charleston, **Magnolia Plantation and Gardens** lost some trees but reopened only a few weeks after the storm. Heavily damaged **Cyrpess Gardens** lost two buildings and is closed until an unspecificed date in 1990.

Hugo virtually bypassed **Hilton Head Island** and **Beaufort County,** though the **Isle of Palms** was devastated, and **Wild Dunes Resort** there is not expected to reopen for some time. **Kiawah Island** and **Seabrook Island** resorts were damaged but reopened by the end of 1989. Along the **Grand Strand,** which includes **Myrtle Beach,** damaged beaches are being renourished and hotels are reopening every day, though some of the seasonal properties closed following Hugo, using the fall to make repairs and prepare for their scheduled spring reopenings. All but one of the area's 63 golf courses are open. In hard-hit **Georgetown County** south of Myrtle Beach, much cleaning remains to be done along the inlets. The **Litchfield Inn** is still closed, but Georgetown itself is intact and accommodations there are open.

Fodor's Choice

No two people will agree on what makes a perfect vacation, but it's fun and helpful to know what others think. We hope you'll have a chance to experience some of Fodor's Choices yourself while visiting the Carolinas and Georgia. For detailed information about each entry, refer to the appropriate chapters within this guidebook.

Georgia

Special Moments Cold beers and camaraderie at Manuel's Tavern, Atlanta

The view from the lounge atop the Westin Peachtree Plaza Hotel, Atlanta

Sights, scents, and sounds of the DeKalb Farmer's Market, Atlanta

The choir singing at Ebenezer Baptist Church, Atlanta

Intellectual schmoozing at the Oxford Bookstore's Cup and Chaucer, Atlanta

St. Patrick's Day in Savannah

Taste Treats Southern-style vegetables at Mary Mac's Tea Room, Atlanta

Beignets and coffee at Hueys, Atlanta

Fried chicken and soul food at Deacon Burton's, Atlanta

Barbecued spareribs from Wall's, Savannah

Scenic Drives Buckhead residential area during Dogwood Festival, Atlanta

Festivals Peachtree Road Race on July 4th, Atlanta

Piedmont Arts Festival in Piedmont Park, Atlanta

Dining The Dining Room at the Ritz-Carlton, Atlanta *(Very Expensive)*

LaGrotta Ristorante Italiano, Atlanta *(Expensive)*

Elizabeth on 37th, Savannah *(Inexpensive–Expensive)*

Buckhead Diner, Atlanta *(Inexpensive)*

Mrs. Wilke's Boarding House, Savannah *(Inexpensive)*

Lodging The Cloister, Sea Island *(Very Expensive)*

Ritz-Carlton Downtown, Atlanta *(Very Expensive)*

Eliza Thompson House, Savannah *(Expensive)*

Jesse Mount House, Savannah *(Expensive)*

Museums High Museum of Art, Atlanta

Nightlife The hip rock scene at Club Rio, Atlanta

Dancing at Johnny's Hideaway, Atlanta

Blues and beers at Blues Harbor, Atlanta

Early breakfast at the Majestic, Atlanta

North Carolina

Special Moments Standing under the Gothic arches of Duke Chapel

Shooting the rapids on the Nantahala

Recalling the life of Carl Sandburg at Flat Rock

Observing 19th-century living at Old Salem

Taste Treats Moravian sugar cake at Winkler's Bakery, Old Salem

Barbecue, red slaw, and hush puppies at Lexington Barbecue, Lexington

Festivals Brevard Music Festival

North Carolina Shakespeare Festival, High Point

Mountain Dance and Folk Festival, Asheville

Dining Jonathan's Uptown, Charlotte *(Very Expensive)*

The Marketplace, Asheville *(Expensive–Very Expensive)*

The Angus Barn, Raleigh *(Expensive)*

Claire's, Blowing Rock *(Expensive)*

The Jarrett House, Dillsboro *(Moderate)*

Justine's, Wilmington *(Moderate)*

Lodging Green Park Inn, Blowing Rock *(Expensive–Very Expensive)*

The Greenwich, Greensboro *(Expensive)*

Grove Park Inn and Country Club, Asheville *(Expensive)*

Oakwood Inn, Raleigh *(Expensive)*

Brookstown Inn, Winston-Salem *(Moderate–Expensive)*

The Morehead, Charlotte *(Moderate–Expensive)*

South Carolina

Special Moments Riding a mule-drawn farm wagon at the Plantation Stableyards in Middleton Place

Collecting shells and sand dollars on the beach at Kiawah Island

Boat tour among spring blooms reflecting in the black waters at Cypress Gardens

Relaxing in a rocking chair overlooking luxury yachts in the Harbour Town marina, Sea Pines on Hilton Head

Taste Treats She-crab soup at Henry's in Charleston

Benné-seed wafers from Olde Colonial Bakery in the open-air market, Charleston

Oysters wrapped in Smithfield ham at the Old Fort Pub, Hilton Head Plantation

Festivals Charleston Historic Foundation's Festival of Houses

Spoleto Festival USA and Piccolo Spoleto, Charleston

Dining Henry's, Charleston *(Expensive)*

The Rusty Anchor, Charleston *(Expensive)*

The Shaftesbury Room, Charleston *(Expensive)*

Lodging Mills House Hotel, Charleston *(Very Expensive)*

Omni Hotel, Charleston *(Very Expensive)*

Planters Inn, Charleston *(Very Expensive)*

Myrtle Beach Hilton and Golf Club, Myrtle Beach *(Very Expensive)*

Hotel Inter-Continental Hilton Head, Hilton Head Island *(Very Expensive)*

Museums Charleston Museum, Charleston

Gibbes Art Gallery, Charleston

Patriots Point Naval and Maritime Museum, north of Charleston

Brookgreen Gardens, Murrells Inlet

The Rice Museum, Georgetown

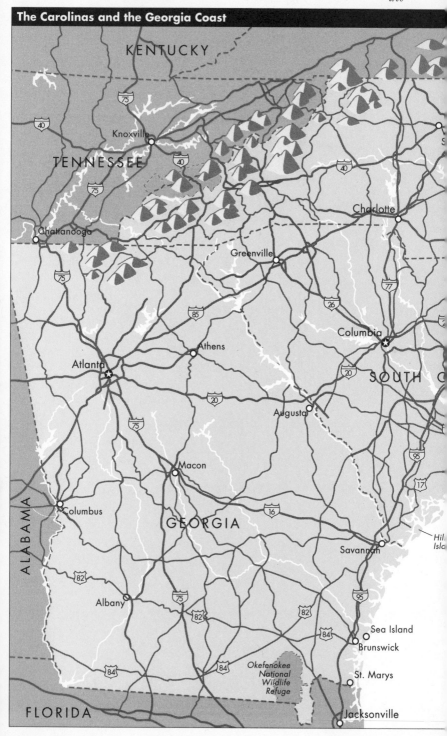

The Carolinas and the Georgia Coast

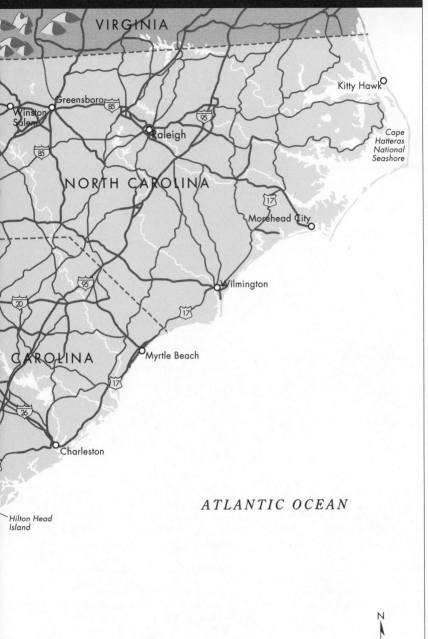

VIRGINIA

Kitty Hawk

Greensboro

Winston
Salem

*Cape
Hatteras
National
Seashore*

Raleigh

NORTH CAROLINA

Morehead City

Wilmington

CAROLINA

Myrtle Beach

Charleston

*Hilton Head
Island*

ATLANTIC OCEAN

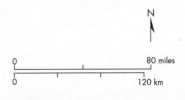

N

0   80 miles

0   120 km

World Time Zones

MONDAY
SUNDAY

International Date Line

+12 +13   -9   -4   -3

25

3

7

-10   -5   -4

4   14 15
                             13
-11   -7   16
5 -8   8   9   17
         -10   -6
6   10   18
     2   11

12

                    19   22

                 -5
                    20   -4   -3

+11   23

+12   -3
1   24
                       21

+11   +12 - -11   -10   -9   -8   -7   -6   -5   -4   -3   -2

Numbers below vertical bands relate each zone to Greenwich Mean Time (0 hrs.).
Local times may differ, as indicated by lightface numbers on the map.

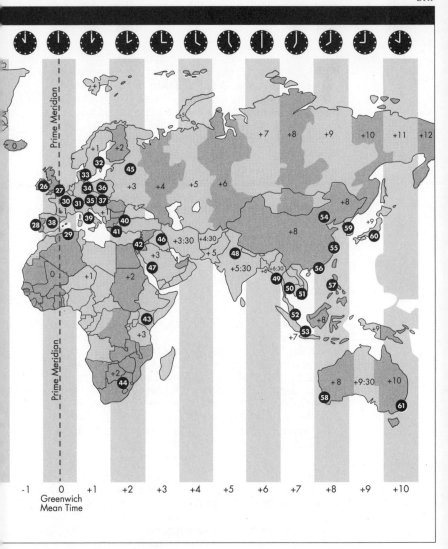

Mecca, **47**
Mexico City, **12**
Miami, **18**
Montreal, **15**
Moscow, **45**
Nairobi, **43**
New Orleans, **11**
New York City, **16**

Ottawa, **14**
Paris, **30**
Perth, **58**
Reykjavík, **25**
Rio de Janeiro, **23**
Rome, **39**
Saigon, **51**

San Francisco, **5**
Santiago, **21**
Seoul, **59**
Shanghai, **55**
Singapore, **52**
Stockholm, **32**
Sydney, **61**
Tokyo, **60**

Toronto, **13**
Vancouver, **4**
Vienna, **35**
Warsaw, **36**
Washington, DC, **17**
Yangon, **49**
Zürich, **31**

Introduction

Throw away all the clichés about the Carolinas and coastal Georgia. Very few of them fit anymore and the others probably never did. It took the world a long time to discover that this area is not tobacco road but, rather, energetic, nature-rich, and quietly dignified. It's a thriving area with very little bustle—there is drive without push.

This area has never been "dirt-poor." Its agriculture is, by many standards, "soil-rich." Things grow here, almost in spite of themselves. Everywhere but on the sandy strip of coastal islands, trees dominate the region's landscape. Pines are the overwhelming favorites of nature here, growing solid and thick over the mountaintops and tall and graceful in the sandy soils of the eastern coastal plain. They camouflage the bare limbs of the hardwoods in winter and add vivid green contrast to the flame of autumn just before Thanksgiving.

Closer to sea level, almost everything can—and does—grow in one part or another of the area. Even in tidy suburban backyards, honeysuckle can scent a summer night so powerfully that one is often tempted to "let it grow" just because it smells so nice. (Few succumb to this notion twice—like its antitheses, poison ivy, kudzu, and Spanish moss, it spreads faster than you'd believe.) Jonquils and forsythia begin their yellow show long before the vernal equinox, followed by azaleas and camellias, and, finally, magnolias with their lemon fragrance. Daylilies sprout along roadsides, and English ivy climbs trees with alacrity. And these are things that grow without a farmer's help!

Cotton is no longer agricultural king here, and tobacco is losing its place as crown prince. They are being replaced by peanuts, soy beans, cucumbers, grapes, Christmas trees, and peaches. (You have never *really* tasted a peach until you have had one grown in the surrounding Sandhills orchards and bought from a roadside stand.) More and more cornfields are appearing across the Piedmont, as are herds of dairy cows, feeding on the lush grassy fields. Pickle production is up, along with that of peanut butter and a new product, wine.

There are four seasons here—spring is wet and fall is dry, but they are just about the loveliest spring and fall to be found in the continental United States. The hardwood trees bud in March and the profusion of flowers, both wild and cultivated, is breathtaking. Everyone comes outdoors to look, to feel, and to wake up. Golfers, tennis players, gardeners, and sunbathers appear with renewed energy. The rains are warm and usually brief. Fall is even prettier, with leaf colors that rival the gold of the sun. Outdoor activity continues until at least the end of November, when the leaves finally fall.

That leaves summer and winter—surely too hot or too cold to enjoy? Definitely not—air-conditioning is a fact of life in the humid summers, when the sun bakes the air until thunderheads pile up. But the beaches, the myriad lakes, and the local swimming pools beckon even the nonswimmers, and mountains, a cool haven, are less than a day's drive from anywhere. In winter the mountains are often snowy while the rest of the area is just chilly. Skiers scurry to the slopes, but those who remain in the low country probably can't remember where they put their boots after last year's one day of snow. If and when that snowfall comes to the low country (as it usually does a couple of times each year) everything comes to a halt—schools close and meetings are cancelled, and local disc jockeys recount their harrowing journey into the station through a couple of inches of serious snow. (Low-country people do not handle driving in the snow at all well, and local governments have no snow removal equipment. If it snows be content to stay where you are.) It's almost a holiday when winter weather truly comes to the Southeast. Adults and children alike find the merest rise in land contour an excuse to go sledding "before it's gone tomorrow." A sprinkle of snow along the coast draws crowds.

Not too long ago the geography books described this area as "agricultural." We've told you what grows here, but what is more important now is what is *made* here—fabrics and pharmaceuticals, bath towels and beer, furniture and films, chemicals, electronic components, lumber, tobacco products, and nuclear power. Most of the current boom is, of course, concentrated in the metropolitan centers, but its effects are rapidly creeping into the rural areas. Tourism is a major industry all over and is widely supported. Officials in charge of such things have already awakened to the need for long-range planning to maintain the quality of the environment. Visitors are welcomed warmly, and there are plenty of accommodations available, but development is being programmed to avoid destruction of natural resources as well as overcrowded beaches. Even in the dense-built Grand Strand at Myrtle Beach in South Carolina one doesn't have to step over recumbent bodies to reach the water. And on most of the beaches, at the height of the summer season, a lonesome dawn stroll is still possible.

Winston Churchill once said that "change is not necessarily progress." It *is* here, with one exception—the people. If there should come a change in the courteous, friendly, and helpful attitudes of these charming inhabitants of North and South Carolina and the Georgia Coast, it would be a shame. The men are courtly—not antifeminist, but apt to address a woman as "young lady" regardless of her age.

And the women, although generally not antifeminist, are nonetheless, soft-spoken. The children learn "ma'am" and "sir" when they're toddlers, and all of this politeness is contagious. Service people (the plumber, the shoe clerk, the auto mechanic) go far out of their way to be accommodating, and they know you'll understand if things move just a *mite* slower here than in some other places. There are smiling faces everywhere, and "Hey, how are you?" sounds genuine. The pace is steady but relaxed; the ambience is open and friendly; the geniality is authentic. Once you've been here, you'll be quick to respond to "y'all come back, y'heah."

1 Essential Information

Before You Go

Visitor Information

Contact each of the following state travel bureaus for free tourist information. If you wish to speak to a travel representative, you must call the bureau directly; for a free travel information packet, call the toll-free "800" number.

Georgia Department of Industry and Trade (Tourism Division, Box 1776, Atlanta, GA 30301, tel. 404/656–3590 or 800/VISIT GA).
North Carolina Division of Travel and Tourism (430 N. Salisbury, Raleigh, NC 27611, tel. 919/733–4171 or 800/VISIT NC).
South Carolina Division of Tourism (Box 71, Columbia, SC 29202, tel. 803/734–0122).

Tour Groups

If you prefer to have someone else drive while you sit back and enjoy the ride, you might do well to consider a package tour. Although you will have to march to the beat of a tour guide's drum rather than your own, you are likely to save money on airfare, hotels, and ground transportation while covering a lot of territory. For the more experienced or adventurous traveler, there are a variety of special-interest and independent packages available. Listed below is a sample of available options. Check with your travel agent for additional resources.

When considering a tour, be sure to find out exactly what expenses are included (particularly tips, taxes, side trips, additional meals, and entertainment), ratings of all hotels on the itinerary and the facilities they offer, cancellation policies for both you and for the tour operator, and if you are traveling alone, what the single supplement is. Most tour operators request that bookings be made through a travel agent; there is no additional charge for doing so.

General-Interest Tours **Cosmos/Tourama** (150 S. Los Robles Ave., Suite 860, Pasadena, CA 91101, tel. 818/449–0919 or 800/556–5454) offers a tour called "The Old South and the Golden Isles" which winds its way from Atlanta to Charleston, with a stopover on Jekyll Island, among other spots.

Maupintour (Box 807, Lawrence, KS 66044, tel. 913/843–1211 or 800/255–4266) takes a step back in time with "Historic Savannah and Charleston."

Special-Interest Tours **Adventure:** *Wilderness Southeast* (711 Sandtown Rd., Savannah, GA 31410, tel. 912/897–5108) runs rugged trips through places like the Okefenokee Swamp in Georgia and the Everglades in Florida.

Package Deals for Independent Travelers

American Fly AAway Vacations (tel. 817/355–1234 or 800/433–7300) offers city packages with discounts on hotels and car rental. Also check with **Delta Air Lines** (tel. 404/765–2952 or 800/241–6108) and **Eastern Airlines** (tel. 305/873–3000) for packages. **American Express** has similar city packages, with half-day sightseeing tours (tel. 800/241–1700).

Tips for British Travelers

Government Tourist Office
The United States Travel and Tourism Administration (22 Sackville St., London W1X 2EA, tel. 01/439–7433) will send brochures and advise you on your trip to the American South.

Passports and Visas
You will need a valid 10-year passport. You do not need a visa if you are staying for less than 90 days, have a return ticket, and are flying with a participating airline. There are some exceptions to this, so check with your travel agent or with the United States Embassy (Visa and Immigration Dept., 5 Upper Grosvenor St., London W1A 2JB, tel. 01/499–3443). No vaccinations are required.

Customs
Visitors 21 or over can take in 200 cigarettes or 50 cigars or 3 pounds of tobacco; 1 U.S. quart of alcohol; duty-free gifts to a value of $100. Be careful not to try to take in meat or meat products, seeds, plants, fruits, etc. Avoid illegal drugs like the plague.

Returning to Britain, you may bring home: (1) 200 cigarettes or 100 cigarillos or 50 cigars or 250 grams of tobacco; (2) two liters of table wine with additional allowances for (a) one liter of alcohol over 22% by volume (38.8° proof, most spirits), (b) two liters of alcohol under 22% by volume, or (c) two more liters of table wine; (3) 50 grams of perfume and a quarter-liter of toilet water; and (4) other goods up to a value of £32.

Insurance
We recommend that you insure yourself to cover health and motoring mishaps. **Europ Assistance** (252 High St., Croydon, Surrey CRO 1NF, tel. 01/680–1234) offers comprehensive policies. It is also wise to take out insurance to cover loss of luggage (though check that this isn't already covered in an existing homeowner's policy). Trip-cancellation insurance is another wise buy. **The Association of British Insurers** (Aldermary House, Queen St., London EC4N 1TT, tel. 01/248–4477) will give advice on all aspects of vacation insurance.

Tour Operators
Albany Travel (190 Deansgate, Manchester M3 3WD, tel. 061/833–0202) offers a 16-day North-South Discovery tour, including Washington, Williamsburg, Charleston, and Savannah, for around £1,000. **Poundstretcher** (Hazelwick Ave., Three Bridges, Crawley RH10 1NP, tel. 0293/518022) offers a three-center holiday in Atlanta, New Orleans, and Orlando, with prices for seven nights (including airfare) beginning at £855.

Airfares
If you are traveling independently, your best bets for a low-price air ticket are APEX fares. APEX round-trip fares to Birmingham start at £513, to Atlanta £399, to New Orleans £377, to Nashville £333, and to Richmond £388. Check with the major airlines: **American Airlines** (tel. 01/834–5151), **British Airways** (tel. 01/897–4000), **Continental Airlines** (tel. 0293/776464), **Delta Airlines** (tel. 0800/414767), **Pan American Airlines** (tel. 01/409–3377), and **Virgin Atlantic Airways** (tel. 0293/38222).

If you can afford to be flexible about when you travel, try the small ads in daily or Sunday newspapers for last-minute flight bargains, but check that all airport taxes are included in the price quoted.

When to Go

Spring is probably the most attractive season in this part of the United States. Cherry blossoms are followed throughout the region by azaleas, dogwood, and camellias from April into May, and apple blossoms in May.

Seasonal and special events occur throughout the year. Festivals (folk, craft, art, and music) tend to take place in the summer, as do sports events. State and local fairs are held mainly in August and September, though there are a few in early July and into October. Historical commemorations are likely to occur at any time of the year.

Climate In winter, temperatures average in the low 40s in inland areas, in the 60s by the shore. Summer temperatures, modified by mountains in some areas, by sea breezes in others, range from the high 70s to the mid-80s, now and then the low 90s.

The following are average daily maximum and minimum temperatures for sample Southern cities.

Atlanta, Georgia								
Jan.	52F	11C	May	79F	26C	Sept.	83F	28C
	36	2		61	16		65	18
Feb.	54F	12C	June	86F	30C	Oct.	72F	22C
	38	3		67	19		54	12
Mar.	63F	17C	July	88F	31C	Nov.	61F	16C
	43	6		70	21		43	6
Apr.	72F	22C	Aug.	86F	30C	Dec.	52F	11C
	52	11		70	21		38	3

Raleigh, North Carolina								
Jan.	52F	11C	May	79F	26C	Sept.	83F	28C
	32	0		56	13		61	16
Feb.	56F	13C	June	86F	30C	Oct.	72F	22C
	34	1		63	17		49	9
Mar.	61F	16C	July	90F	32C	Nov.	61F	16C
	38	3		68	20		38	3
Apr.	72F	22C	Aug.	88F	31C	Dec.	52F	11C
	47	8		67	19		31	−1

Charleston, South Carolina								
Jan.	58F	14C	May	81F	27C	Sept.	83F	28C
	43	6		67	19		72	22
Feb.	69F	15C	June	86F	30C	Oct.	76F	24C
	45	7		74	23		61	16
Mar.	67F	19C	July	88F	31C	Nov.	67F	19C
	50	10		76	24		52	11
Apr.	74F	23C	Aug.	88F	31C	Dec.	59F	15C
	58	14		76	24		45	7

Current weather information on 235 cities around the world—180 of them in the United States—is only a phone call away. To obtain the **Weather Trak** telephone number for your area, call 800/247–3282. The local number plays a taped message that tells you to dial the three-digit access code for the destination you're interested in. The code is either the area code (in the United States) or the first three letters of the foreign city. For a list of all access codes, send a stamped, self-addressed envelope to Cities, Box 7000, Dallas, TX 75209. For further information, phone 214/869–3035 or 800/247–3282.

Festivals and Seasonal Events

The Southern states hold a wide variety of festivals and special events through out the year. The following is a sample. For more complete listings of events, contact the Division of Tourism in each state.

January **Georgia:** A *Rattlesnake Roundup* is held in Whigham. *Savannah Marathon* and *Half Marathon* are run. *Martin Luther King, Jr., Week* is celebrated in Atlanta.

North Carolina: *The Charlotte Observer Marathon* and *Runner's Expo* take place in Charlotte.

South Carolina: Orangeburg invites the country's finest coon dogs to compete in the *Grand American Coon Hunt*. Charleston hosts a colorful *Oyster Festival*.

February **Georgia:** *Georgia Day Event* is held in Savannah. A two-day *Arts and Crafts Georgia Festival* is held in Kennesaw.

North Carolina: Asheville welcomes visitors to its annual *Winterfest Arts and Crafts Show*.

South Carolina: *Black Heritage Celebration* continues all month in North Charleston. Greenville rings with the *Festival of American Music*. The *Southern Gospel Music Festival* is held in Fort Mill.

March **Georgia:** *Rattlesnake Roundup* is held in Claxton. Macon hosts its *Cherry Blossom Festival*. The *Okefenokee Spring Fling* is held in Waycross. And *St. Patrick's Day* is especially colorful in Atlanta and Dublin.

North Carolina: An 18th-century military encampment and Revolutionary War battle reenactment bring history to life on the *Anniversary of the Battle of Guilford Courthouse* in Greensboro. Mooresville hosts the annual *Old Time Fiddlers' and Bluegrass Convention*. Amateur and professional golfers compete in the *K-Mart Greater Greensboro Open*.

South Carolina: *Springfest* lasts all month on Hilton Head Island. Charleston welcomes visitors to its *Festival of Houses*, its *Founder's Festival*, and *The American Seafood Challenge*.

April **Georgia:** *Atlanta Dogwood Festival* is held throughout the capital. *River Days* are celebrated at River Front Park in Albany. The *Rose Festival* is in Thomasville, and the *Masters Golf Tournament* is held in Augusta.

North Carolina: Fayetteville dresses up for its *Dogwood Festival*. Wilmington hosts the *North Carolina Azalea Festival*. Late in the month, Charlotte holds its annual *Springfest* and Chadburn its annual *North Carolina Strawberry Festival*.

South Carolina: *Allendale County Spring Cooter Festival* is held in Allendale. The *World Grits Festival* is held in St. George. *Riverfest* is held in Columbia.

May **Georgia:** *Arts-on-the-River Weekend* is held in Savannah. Athens hosts the *New Jazz Festival*. Special events mark *Memorial Day* weekend on Jekyll Island and in Savannah.

North Carolina: *Tarheel Association of Storytellers' Festival* is held in Winston-Salem. Nags Head is the location for the annual *Hang Gliding Spectacular*.

South Carolina: *Spoleto Festival USA* in Charleston is one of the world's biggest arts festivals. Running concurrently with Spoleto is *Piccolo Spoleto*, which showcases local and regional talent. *Mayfest* takes place in Columbia.

June **Georgia:** Stone Mountain Village holds an annual *Festival of the Arts*. *COA Blueberry Festival* is held in Alma.

North Carolina: The *Kitty Hawk Triathlon* includes hang gliding, windsurfing, and sailing at Nags Head. Asheville hosts the annual *Highland Heritage Art and Craft Show*.

South Carolina: *Sun Fun Festival* is held in the Grand Strand. *Colonial Life Days* are reenacted in Charleston. Hampton hosts the *Hampton County Watermelon Festival*.

July **Georgia:** In Atlanta, there's the *Independence Festival* and the popular *Peachtree Road Race*. Major *July Fourth* celebrations are held in Savannah and Columbus.

North Carolina: In Asheville, clog and figure dancing are part of the *Shindig-on-the-Green*. Among the many Independence Day celebrations is Winston-Salem's *Fourth of July Torchlight Procession* at Old Salem. Mid-July in Winston-Salem is the *Andy Griffith Show Celebration/Mayberry Convention*. Kill Devil Hills hosts the *Wright Kite Festival*.

South Carolina: *July Fourth* is commemorated in several communities, including Clemson, Conway, Greenville, and Gilbert. The *South Carolina Peach Festival* is held in Gaffney. Myrtle Beach hosts *Art in the Park*.

August **Georgia:** A *Beach Music Festival* is held on Jekyll Island. *Sea Island Festival* is centered in St. Simons. *Labor Day Bluegrass Festival* is held in Fort Yargo State Park, and the *Green Corn Festival* is in Calhoun.

North Carolina: Asheville holds the annual *Mountain Dance and Folk Festival* and, later in the month, the *Annual Summerfest Art and Craft Show*. Kill Devil Hills celebrates *National Aviation Day*. The *North Carolina Apple Festival* is held in Hendersonville.

South Carolina: *Palmetto Upstate Festival* is in Woodruff. *South Carolina Peanut Party* is held in Pelion. The *Waccamaw Riverfest* is a citywide event in Conway.

September **Georgia:** *Oktoberfest* begins in Helen, and the *Hot Air Balloon Festival* is held there also. Atlanta hosts the *Fine Arts and Crafts Festival* in Piedmont Park. In Old Town Sharpsburg there's the *Fall Festival*, and in Carollton, the *Autumn Leaves Arts and Crafts Festival*.

North Carolina: The annual *Woolly Worm Festival* takes place in Banner Elk.

South Carolina: *South Carolina Apple Festival* is held in Westminster. Hilton Head Island hosts the *American Festival of Fitness and Sport*. Chesterfield celebrates its *Fall Festival*.

October **Georgia:** *Cotton Days Festival* begins in Marietta. Athens hosts the *North Georgia Folk Festival*. The annual *Fall Bluegrass Festival* is held in Blue Ridge. *National Pecan Festival* is held in Albany. Savannah celebrates its *Oktoberfest*, and *Heritage Holidays* are commemorated in Rome.

North Carolina: The annual *Indian Summer Art and Craft Show* is held in Asheville. Wilmington is the scene of the spooky *Halloween Festival*.

South Carolina: *Moja Arts Festival* in Charleston celebrates African, American, and Caribbean cultures. *Halloween* festivities are especially colorful in Charleston, Greenville, and Georgetown.

November **Georgia:** *Mistletoe Market* is held in Albany. Savannah holds its *Festival of Trees. Cane grinding parties* are thrown in Tifton and Juliette.

North Carolina: The annual *High Country Christmas Art and Craft Show* is held in Asheville.

South Carolina: *Christmas Connection* enlivens Myrtle Beach, as does *Dickens Christmas Show and Festival*.

December **Georgia:** *Sugarplum Festival* is held at Stone Mountain Village. Atlanta hosts its *Holiday Tour of Homes* and the *Peach Bowl and Parade*. Special Christmas celebrations are held in Savannah, at Callaway Gardens, and on Jekyll Island.

North Carolina: Historic homes are open to visitors during the *Candlelight Tour of Chapel Hill*. Winston-Salem re-creates a Moravian Christmas during *Old Salem Christmas*. The *Historic Oakwood Candlelight Tour* is held in Raleigh. *First Night Charlotte* is a New Year's Eve festival on the Town Square.

South Carolina: Christmas in Charleston lasts all month and the *Elgin Catfish Stomp* takes place in Elgin.

What to Pack

Pack light because porters and luggage trolleys are hard to find. Luggage allowances on domestic flights vary slightly from airline to airline. Most allow three checked pieces and one carry-on. Some give you the option of two checked and two carry-on. In all cases, check-in bags cannot weigh more than 70 pounds per piece or be larger than 62 inches (length + width + height) and must fit under the seat or in the overhead luggage compartment.

Generally, the South has hot, humid weather during the summer and sunny, mild weather in the winter. For winters in the southernmost tier of states, pack a lightweight coat, slacks, and sweaters. The northern tier of Southern states can be very cold and damp in the winter. Snow is not unusual, so be prepared. For summer visits, keep the high humidity level in mind and pack cotton and natural fabrics that breathe. You'll need an umbrella for sudden summer showers, but leave the plastic raincoats behind because the humidity makes them extremely uncomfortable. Take a jacket or sweater for summer evenings, or for restaurants that have air-conditioning going full blast. Always take insect repellent during the summer because the mosquitoes come out in full force after sunset.

Cash Machines

Virtually all U.S. banks belong to a network of ATMs (automatic teller machines), which accept bank cards and spit out cash 24 hours a day in cities throughout the country. There are eight major networks in the United States, the largest of which are Cirrus, owned by MasterCard, and Plus, affiliated with Visa. Some banks belong to more than one network. These cards are not automatically issued; you have to ask for them. If your bank doesn't belong to at least one network, you should consider moving funds, for ATMs are becoming as essential as check cashing. Cards issued by Visa and MasterCard may also be used in the ATMs, but the fees are usually higher than the fees on bank cards, and there is a daily interest charge on the "loan," even if monthly bills are paid on time. Each network has a toll-free number you can call to locate machines in a given city. The Cirrus number is 800/4–CIRRUS; the Plus number is 800/THE–PLUS. Check with your bank for fees and for the amount of cash you can withdraw on any given day.

Traveling with Film

If your camera is new, shoot and develop a few rolls before leaving home. Pack some lens tissue and an extra battery for your built-in light meter. Invest about $10 in a skylight filter and screw it onto the front of your lens. It will protect the lens and also reduce haze.

Film doesn't like hot weather. If you're driving in summer, don't store film in the glove compartment or on the shelf under the rear window. Put it behind the front seat on the floor, on the side opposite the exhaust pipe.

On a plane trip, never pack unprocessed film in check-in luggage; if your bags get X-rayed, you can say goodbye to your pictures. Always carry undeveloped film with you through security and ask to have it inspected by hand. (It helps to isolate your film in a plastic bag, ready for quick inspection.) Inspectors at American airports are required by law to honor requests for hand inspection; abroad, you'll have to depend on the kindness of strangers.

The old airport scanning machines—still in use in some Third World countries—use heavy doses of radiation that can turn a family portrait into an early morning fog. The newer models—used in all U.S. airports—are safe for anything from five to 500 scans, depending on the speed of your film. The effects are cumulative; you can put the same roll of film through several scans without worry. After five scans, though, you're asking for trouble.

If your film gets fogged and you want an explanation, send it to the National Association of Photographic Manufacturers (600 Mamaroneck Ave., Harrison, NY 10528). They will try to determine what went wrong. The service is free.

Car Rentals

Outside of south Florida, New Orleans and Atlanta are the South's biggest car rental centers. **Hertz** (tel. 800/654–3131), **Avis** (tel. 800/331–1212), **National** (tel. 800/328–4567), **Budget** (tel. 800/527–0700), **Thrifty** (tel. 800/367–2277), **American International** (tel. 800/527–0202), **Sears** (tel. 800/527–0770), and **Dollar** (tel. 800/421–6868) have airport locations in Atlanta, Charleston, Columbia, and Raleigh. Mid-size cities like Augusta have at least three or four of the above companies, plus local and regional firms. Expect to pay $35–$45 daily for a subcompact in larger cities, with 75–100 free miles daily. **Alamo** (tel. 800/327–9633) offers some of the region's lowest rates, though it does not have offices in all cities. Unlimited free mileage these days seems to be the exception rather than the rule. Be careful renting a car for a multistate Southern trip: many rental companies tack in-state driving restrictions onto their unlimited-mileage specials.

Local and regional companies sometimes skirt the over-25 age restriction and credit-card requirements of many large companies; sometimes they have lower rates, too. Raleigh has **Enterprise** (tel. 800/325–8007), **Able-Leith** (tel. 919/832–2921), **Triangle** (tel. 919/851–2555), and **Choice** (tel. 919/832–2121). Charleston has **Alamo, Holiday Payless, Enterprise,** and **Freedom** (tel. 803/554–9829). Columbia, SC, has **Not A Lemon Rent-A-Car** (tel. 803/782–2640).

It's always best to know a few essentials *before* you arrive at the car-rental counter. Find out what the collision damage waiver (usually an $8–$12 daily surcharge) covers and whether your corporate or personal insurance already covers damage to a rental car (if so, bring a photocopy of the benefits section along). More and more companies are now also holding renters responsible for theft and vandalism damages if they don't buy the CDW; in response, some credit-card and insurance companies are extending *their* coverage to rental cars. These include Dreyfuss Bank Gold and Silver MasterCards (tel. 800/847–9700), Chase Manhattan Bank Visa cards (tel. 800/645–7352), and Access America (tel. 800/851–2800). Find out, too, if you must pay for a full tank of gas whether you use it or not; and make sure you get a reservation number.

Traveling with Children

Publications   *Family Travel Times,* an 8- to 12-page newsletter published 10 times a year by Travel with Your Children (80 Eighth Ave., New York, NY 10011, tel. 212/206–0688). Subscription includes access to back issues and twice-weekly opportunities to call in for specific advice.

Great Vacations with Your Kids: The Complete Guide to Family Vacations in the U.S., by Dorothy Ann Jordon and Marjorie Adoff Cohen (E.P. Dutton, 2 Park Ave., New York, NY 10016; $9.95), details everything from city vacations to adventure vacations to child-care resources.

Bimonthly and monthly publications filled with events listings, resources, and advice for parents and available free at such places as libraries, supermarkets, and museums include *Atlanta Parent* (Box 8506, Atlanta, GA 30306, tel. 404/325–1763) and *Youth View* (1401 W. Paces Ferry Rd., Suite A-217, Atlanta, GA 30327, tel. 404/231–0562). For a small fee you can usually have an issue sent to you before your trip.

Hotels   **Guest Quarters Suite Hotels** (tel. 800/424–2900) offer the luxury of two-room suites with kitchen facilities, plus children's menus in the restaurants. The hotels also allow children under 18 to stay free in their parents' suite. Most **Days Inn** hotels (tel. 800/325–2525) charge only a nominal fee for children under 18 and allow those 12 and under to eat free (many offer efficiency-type apartments, too).

The Hyatt Regency Ravinia (4355 Ashford-Dunwoody Rd., Atlanta, GA 30346, tel. 404/395–1234 or 800/228–9000) shows special attention and offers discounted meals to children in its Cafe Ravinia. **The Ritz-Carlton, Buckhead** (3434 Peachtree Rd., Atlanta, GA 30326, tel. 404/237–2700 or 800/241–3333) pampers children with everything from stuffed lions in their cribs to coloring-book menus in *The Cafe.* A children's program is scheduled during the summer at both **The Cloister** (Sea Island, GA 31561, tel. 912/638–3611 or 800/732–4752) and **Sea Palms Golf and Tennis** (5445 Frederica Rd., St. Simons Island, GA 31522, tel. 912/638–3351 or 800/841–6268).

The Outer Banks of South Carolina harbors a number of resorts with elaborate children's programs and facilities: **Kiawah Island Resort** (Box 12910, Charleston, SC 29412, tel. 803/768–2121 or 800/6–KIAWAH), **Hyatt Regency Hilton Head** (Box 6167, Hilton Head Island, SC 29938, tel. 803/785–1234 or 800/228–9000), **Inter-Continental Hilton Head** (135 S. Port Royal Dr., Hilton Head Island, SC 29928, tel. 803/681–4000 or 800/327–0200), **Marriott's Hilton Head Resort** (130 Shipyard Dr., Hilton Head Island, SC 29928, tel. 803/842–2400 or 800/334–1881), and **Palmetto Dunes Resort** (Box 5606, Hilton Head Island, SC 29938, tel. 803/785–1161 or 800/845–6130).

Condo Rentals
See *The Condo Lux Vacationer's Guide to Condominium Rentals in the Southeast,* by Jill Little (Vintage Books/Random House, New York; $9.95).

Home Exchange
See *Home Exchanging: A Complete Sourcebook for Travelers at Home or Abroad,* by James Dearing (Globe Pequot Press, Box Q, Chester, CT 06412, tel. 800/243–0495 or 800/962–0973 in CT).

Getting There
On domestic flights, children under 2 not occupying a seat travel free. Various discounts apply to children 2–12. Reserve a seat behind the bulkhead of the plane, which offers more legroom and can usually fit a bassinet (supplied by the airline). At the same time, inquire about special children's meals or snacks, offered by most airlines. (See "TWYCH's Airline Guide," in the February 1988 issue of *Family Travel Times*, for a rundown of the services offered by 46 airlines.) Ask the airline in advance if you can bring aboard your child's car seat. (For the booklet "Child/Infant Safety Seats Acceptable for Use in Aircraft," contact the Community and Consumer Liaison Division, APA-400 Federal Aviation Administration, Washington, DC 20591, tel. 202/267–3479.)

Baby-sitting Services
Check with the hotel concierge about child-care arrangements.

Hints for Disabled Travelers

The Information Center for Individuals with Disabilities (20 Park Plaza, Room 330, Boston, MA 02116, tel. 617/727–5540) offers useful problem-solving assistance, including lists of travel agents that specialize in tours for the disabled.
Moss Rehabilitation Hospital Travel Information Service (12th St. and Taber Rd., Philadelphia, PA 19141, tel. 215/329–5715) provides information on tourist sights, transportation, and accommodations in destinations around the world. The fee is $5 for each destination. Allow one month for delivery.

Mobility International (Box 3551, Eugene, OR 97403, tel. 503/343–1284) has information on accommodations, organized study, etc., around the world.

The Society for the Advancement of Travel for the Handicapped (26 Court St., Brooklyn, NY 11242, tel. 718/858–5483) offers access information. Annual membership costs $40, $25 for senior travelers and students. Send a stamped, self-addressed envelope.

The Itinerary (Box 1084, Bayonne, NJ 07002, tel. 201/858–3400) is a bimonthly travel magazine for the disabled.

Access to the World: A Travel Guide for the Handicapped, by Louise Weiss, is useful but out of date. Available from Facts on File (460 Park Ave. S, New York, NY 10016, tel. 212/683–2244). *Frommer's Guide for Disabled Travelers* is also useful but dated.

Greyhound-Trailways (tel. 800/531–5332) will carry a disabled person and companion for the price of a single fare. **Amtrak** (tel. 800/USA–RAIL) requests 24-hour notice to provide redcap service, special seats, and a 25% discount.

Travel Industry and Disabled Exchange (TIDE, 5435 Donna Ave., Tarzana, CA 91356, tel. 818/343–6339) is an industry-based organization with a $15-per-person annual membership fee. Members receive a quarterly newsletter and information on travel agencies and tours.

Hints for Older Travelers

The **American Association of Retired Persons** (AARP, 1909 K St. NW, Washington, DC 20049, tel. 202/662–4850) has two programs for independent travelers: (1) *The Purchase Privilege Program,* which offers discounts on hotels, airfare, car rentals, and sightseeing; and (2) the *AARP Motoring Plan,* which offers emergency aid and trip-routing information for an annual fee of $29.95 per couple. AARP also arranges group tours, through two companies: **Olson-Travelworld** (5855 Green Valley Circle, Culver City, CA 90230, tel. 800/227–7737) and **RFD, Inc.** (4401 W. 110th St., Overland Park, KS 66211, tel. 800/448–7010). AARP members must be 50 or older. Annual dues are $5 per person or per couple.

When using an AARP or other identification card, ask for a reduced hotel rate at the time you make your reservation, not when you check out. At restaurants, show your card to the maître d' before you're seated, since discounts may be limited to certain set menus, days, or hours. When renting a car, remember that economy cars, priced at promotional rates, may cost less than cars that are available with your ID card.

Elderhostel (80 Boylston St., Suite 400, Boston, MA 02116, tel. 617/426–7788) is an innovative 13-year-old program for people 60 and older. Participants live in dorms on some 1,200 campuses around the world. Mornings are devoted to lectures and seminars, afternoons to sightseeing and field trips. The all-inclusive fee for two- to three-week trips, including room, board, tuition, and round-trip transportation, is $1,700–$3,200.

National Council of Senior Citizens (925 15th St. NW, Washington, DC 20005, tel. 202/347–8800) is a nonprofit advocacy group with some 4,000 local clubs across the country. Annual membership is $10 per person or $14 per couple. Members receive a monthly newspaper with travel information and an ID card for reduced-rate hotels and car rentals.

Mature Outlook (Box 1205, Glenview, IL 60025, tel. 800/336–6330), a subsidiary of Sears Roebuck & Co., is a travel club for people over 50, with hotel and motel discounts and a bimonthly newsletter. Annual membership is $7.50 per couple. Instant membership is available at participating Holiday Inns.

Travel Tips for Senior Citizens (U.S. Dept. of State Publication 8970, revised Sept. 1987) is available for $1 from the Superintendent of Documents, U.S. Government Printing Office, Washington, DC 20402.

Golden Age Passport is a free lifetime pass to all parks, monuments, and recreation areas run by the federal government. People over 62 should pick them up in person at any national park that charges admission. A driver's license or other proof of age is required.

Further Reading

For background reading on Southern writers, take along Paul Buiding's *A Separate Country: A Literary Journey through the American South*. Chet Fuller's *I Hear Them Calling My Name* is a first-person narrative of a black journalist traveling through the South.

Eugenia Price's novels *Savannah* and *The Beloved Invader* are little known outside the South but provide a keen sense of place in a historical-romance frame. Look also for *Cold Sassy Tree*, by Olive Ann Burns.

Several good epic/romance/adventure novels are *North and South*, by John Jakes; *The Glass Flame*, by Phyllis A. Whitney; Ben Ames Williams's *House Divided; So Red the Rose*, by Stark Young; *Gone With the Wind*, by Margaret Mitchell; and *Savannah Purchase*, by Jane A. Hodge.

For engaging Southern fiction at its best, take along a few of the following: *A Christmas Memory*, by Truman Capote; *To Kill a Mockingbird*, by Capote's childhood neighbor, Harper Lee; *Edisto*, by Padgett Powell, a young boy's coming-of-age story, set near Savannah and Charleston; Carson McCullers's *Member of the Wedding;* Toni Morrison's *Song of Solomon; The Color Purple*, by Alice Walker; William Faulkner's *The Sound and the Fury*, set in the mythic Mississippi county of Yoknapatawpha; and the short-story collections of Georgia's Flannery O'Connor and Mississippi's Eudora Welty.

2 Georgia

Atlanta

by John English
and William
Schemmel

A transplanted
Georgian since
1970, John English
teaches journalism
at the university in
Athens, Georgia.
Native son Bill
Schemmel is a
freelance writer
based in Atlanta.

"Her patron saint is Scarlett O'Hara," writer James Street
once said of Atlanta, "and the town is just like her—shrewd,
proud and full of gumption—her Confederate slip showing under a Yankee mink coat."

It's true that the Yankee influence has long given Atlanta its
vitality, while its Southern traditions have made it one of
America's most livable cities.

But make no mistake: Atlanta is located in the heart of the
South. The state of Georgia continues to celebrate Confederate
Memorial Day as a holiday every April. *The Atlanta Constitu-
tion's* Sunday section of regional news is still called "Dixie
Living." And one of the top tourist attractions in this metropo-
lis is the Cyclorama, a diorama depicting the famous Battle of
Atlanta, which leveled the city during what locals call the "War
Between the States."

Despite the mystique of *Gone With the Wind*, which Margaret
Mitchell cranked out in a still-remaining apartment house at
10th and Peachtree streets, Atlanta has never really been part
of the moonlight and magnolias myth common in many antebellum cities of the Old South.

Atlanta's chief asset has always been the accessibility of its location. From its earliest days, it was an important freight
center, and it is still a major distribution center for trains,
trucks, and planes. The city has long been called the "Crossroads of the South" because three interstates (I–85, I–75,
and I–20) converge near downtown and because Atlanta's
Hartsfield Airport has become the hub of the entire Southeast.
There is an old local saying that goes, "It makes little difference
whether you wind up in heaven or hell; in either case, you still
have to pass through Atlanta."

In short order, Atlanta boasted other important assets. It became a banking center, and Peachtree Street is often tagged
the "Wall Street of the South." In recent years, the city moved
into the global arena with the opening of foreign banks and
consulates and trade offices. Direct flights to Europe, South
America, and Asia have stimulated new international business.

No mention of Atlanta would be complete without talking
about its reputation as a "city too busy to hate." For the past
three decades, Atlanta has been linked to the civil rights movement. It was Ralph McGill, the crusading editor of the
Constitution, who guided the city through the civil rights
struggle with unfaltering pragmatism. He insisted that folks
simply do what needed to be done because it was right. In the
1960s, Atlanta quietly integrated its school system. The fact
that peaceful desegregation and a soaring economy seemed to
go hand in glove was not lost on anyone. Yet McGill was still a
controversial figure during this critical period. It was often
said that 50% of the local citizenry could not eat breakfast before reading Ralph McGill's daily column and that the other half
couldn't eat after reading his column!

Among the accomplishments of Atlanta's black community was the Nobel Peace Prize that Martin Luther King, Jr., won in 1964. In 1972, Andrew Young was reelected the first black congressman from the South since Reconstruction. After serving as Ambassador to the United Nations during President Jimmy Carter's administration, Young was elected mayor of Atlanta.

In recent years, Atlanta has been ranked among the best places in the country to live. Some would attribute these high ratings to the area's pleasant year-round climate; but others insist that Atlanta just has the right mix of people who have worked together to build a pleasant community.

Arriving and Departing

By Plane Hartsfield International Airport, off I–85 and I–285, 13 miles south of downtown, is one of the world's busiest jet complexes. Airlines servicing it include **Aeromexico, Air Jamaica, American, Bahamasair, British Airways, Cayman Islands Airways, Continental, Delta, Eastern, Japan Airlines, KLM, Lufthansa, Northwest, Sabena, Swissair, TWA, United,** and **USAir.**

Between the Airport **Atlanta Airport shuttle vans** (tel. 404/766–5312) operate every
and Center City half hour between 6 AM and 11:30 PM. The trip ($7 one way) takes about 20 minutes and stops at major hotels. Vans also go to Emory University and Lenox Square ($10 one way). **Northside Airport Express buses** (tel. 404/455–1600) operate from 6 AM to midnight between the airport ($9.75–$15 one way).

If your luggage is light, you can also take **MARTA**'s (Metropolitan Atlanta Rapid Transit Authority, tel. 404/848–4711) high-speed trains between the airport and downtown and other locations. Trains operate 5:30 AM–1:30 AM. The trip downtown takes about 13 minutes and the fare is 85¢.

Taxi fare between the airport and downtown hotels is fixed at $13.50 for one person; $7 each for two people; $5 each for three people. Taxis aren't one of Atlanta's strong suits, so be certain your driver is familiar with your destination.

By Train Amtrak's *Crescent* (tel. 800/USA–RAIL) operates daily to New Orleans, Washington DC, and New York from Atlanta's Brookwood Station (1688 Peachtree St.).

By Bus Hop a bus to Atlanta via **Greyhound/Trailways Bus Lines** (81 International Blvd., tel. 404/522–6300).

By Car Atlanta is the hub of four interstate highways: I–85, running northeast to southwest from the South Carolina to the Alabama border; I–75, north–south from Tennessee to Florida; I–20, east–west from South Carolina to Alabama; and I–285, the Perimeter Highway, circling the metropolitan area for 65 miles.

Getting Around

By Bus The **Metropolitan Atlanta Rapid Transit Authority (MARTA,** tel. 404/848–4711) operates a modern, efficient bus system. The fare is 85¢, and exact change is required.

By Subway MARTA's clean, luxurious rapid-rail subway trains link downtown with most major landmarks. The rail system's two lines connect at the **Five Points Station** downtown, where information on public transportation is available at the **Ride Store**

Georgia

TENNESSEE

NORTH CAROLINA

SOUTH CAROLINA

Dalton

Chattahoochee National Forest

Rome

Chattahoochee National Forest

Lake Sidney Lanier

Allatoona Lake

Marietta

Atlanta

College Park

La Grange

Athens

Oconee National Forest

Oconee National Forest

Lake Sinclair

Oconee R.

Macon

Clark Hill Lake

Augusta

Ogeechee R.

59

411

75

575

285

75

341

20

85

185

129

29

85

72

411

20

25

301

0   40 miles

0   60 km

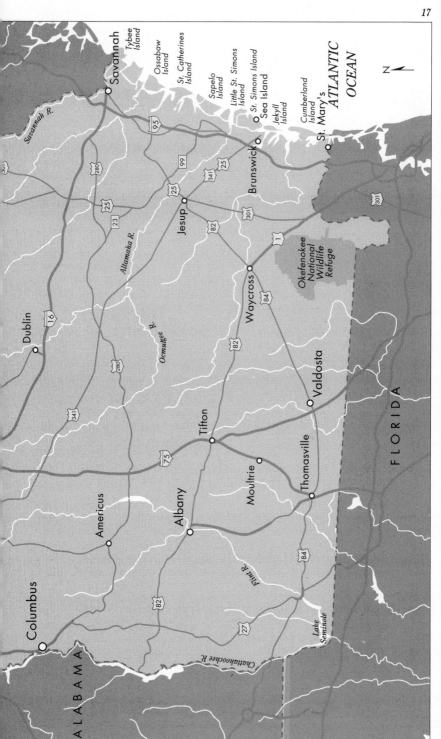

(weekdays 7 AM–7 PM). Trains run 5 AM–1:30 AM, and parking (85¢ all day) can be found around most suburban stations. The fare is 85¢ one way, and exact change is required. Transfers, valid on buses or trains, are free.

By Taxi   Taxis start at $1 and go up 20¢ for each 1/5 of a mile or 40 seconds of waiting time. Each additional person costs 50¢. When traveling in the Downtown, Convention Zone a flat rate of $3 for one person or $2 per person will be charged for any destination within the zone.

Guided Tours

Orientation Tours   **Alpha-Omega Tours** (tel. 404/584–7712) is a small, local company offering customized tours of the city's historic landmarks and places of interest. Tours are in a 47-passenger motor coach. Guides are personable and knowledgeable.

Burton's Tours (tel. 404/525–3415), owned by the city's most famous soul-food chef, covers black historical landmarks like the Martin Luther King, Jr., National Historic District and the Atlanta University Center area. Tours are in motor coaches, with guides full of anecdotes about the city's past and present.

Special-Interest Tours   **Atlanta Carriage Co.** (tel. 404/584–9960) gives 30-minute horse-drawn carriage tours through downtown Atlanta ($25 a couple). The congested streets may lack the romantic charm of Savannah and Charleston, but with a little moonlight, a little champagne, who knows?

Walking Tours   **The Atlanta Preservation Center** (401 Flatiron Bldg., tel. 404/522–4345) offers a half-dozen walking tours of historic areas and other places of interest from April through October ($3 per person). The tour of the Fox Theatre, with backstage looks at the city's elaborate 1920s picture palace, is especially recommended.

Important Addresses and Numbers

Tourist Information   To plan your trip write to the Department of Tourism (233 Peachtree St. NE, Suite 2000, Atlanta 30303). When you are in Atlanta, the Convention and Visitors Bureau has three visitor information centers stocked with maps and brochures: **Peachtree Center Mall** (233 Peachtree St. NE, tel. 404/521–6633), **Hartsfield International Airport** (Airport Welcome Center, tel. 404/767–3231), and **Lenox Square Mall** (3393 Peachtree Rd. NE, tel. 404/266–1398).

Emergencies   Dial 911 for assistance. For hospital emergencies both **Grady Memorial Hospital** (80 Butler St., tel. 404/589–4307) and **Georgia Baptist Medical Center** (300 Boulevard NE tel. 404/653–4000) have 24-hour emergency room service.

Pharmacy   **Treasury Drug** (1061 Ponce de Leon Ave. NE, tel. 404/876–0381).

Exploring Atlanta

Orientation   Atlanta's beltway is most often called "the Perimeter," but it's also known as "The Big O around the Big A," or simply I–285. The interstate's completion in 1969 reaffirmed the city's relentless development to the north. In fact, so many office parks, shopping centers, and multifamily housing developments have cropped up along the northern arc of I–285, that the name of one typical project, "Perimeter Center," may no longer just be an oxymoron. In the southern arc is the massive Atlanta Hartsfield International Airport.

Most of metro Atlanta is located within Fulton and DeKalb counties, but the southern part of the city is in Clayton County. Cobb and Gwinnett counties are in the burgeoning northern sector.

Some visitors are confused by Atlanta's lack of a strict grid system of streets or by its confluence of streets into five-point intersections. One generous explanation is that Atlanta's streets were originally cow paths and Indian trails, which were paved, renamed, and given lights; others blame topography and the meandering Chattahoochee River.

Atlanta is a city shaped like a cursive capital *I*. At the bottom is the downtown area, and at the top is the Lenox Square-Phipps Plaza area. Along the shank of the *I* runs the city's main thoroughfare, the famed Peachtree Street. Actually, Peachtree Street runs only about three miles north from downtown, then changes its name, without notice, to Peachtree Road. Past the Lenox Square area, the grand avenue becomes Peachtree Industrial Boulevard, a name that befits its environment. (Newcomers to the city should be forewarned that there are some three dozen arteries with "Peachtree" in their names, so one must be wary of pretenders.)

Seven distinct sections of the city are plotted along Atlanta's "big I": downtown, midtown, Ansley Park, Brookwood Hills, Peachtree Hills, Garden Hills, Buckhead, and Peachtree Park, which includes the Lenox area.

Numbers in the margin correspond with points of interest on the Downtown Atlanta and Atlanta Vicinity maps.

Downtown The ideal way to get acquainted with Atlanta is to begin with its past. Atlanta is not a historic city like Savannah or Boston, yet its history can be traced to the mid-19th century. A good ❶ way to start is with a saunter through **Oakland Cemetery.** Buried here are many of Georgia's notable politicians and businessmen. There is also a Jewish section and a section for Confederate soldiers. Margaret Mitchell, author of *Gone With the Wind* and a favorite daughter of the city, and golfer Bobby Jones are interred here. *248 Oakland Ave., tel. 404/577–8163. Free tours on weekends. Open daily sunrise–sunset.*

Continue to the Martin Luther King, Jr., National Historic District on Auburn Avenue, a couple of blocks north on Boulevard. Dr. King's white marble tomb with its eternal flame is ❷ located next to the **Ebenezer Baptist Church** (407 Auburn Ave.). For three genera-tions the King family preached here. During the civil rights struggle in the 1960s, and after Dr. King was awarded the Nobel Peace Prize in 1964, Ebenezer Baptist was recognized as the spiritual center of the movement. After King's assassination in 1968, his widow, Coretta Scott ❸ King, established the adjoining **Center for Nonviolent Social Change.** It contains a museum with King memorabilia, a library and a souvenir gift shop, and frequently sponsors educational programs for the community. *449 Auburn Ave., tel. 404/ 524–1956. Admission free. Open weekdays 9–5:30, weekends 10–5:30.*

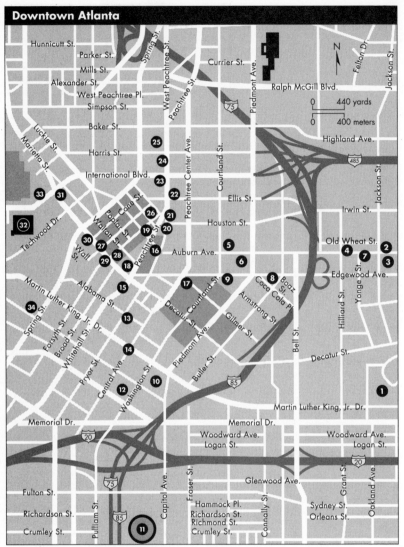

Downtown Atlanta

Hunnicutt St.
Parker St.
Mills St.
Alexander St.
West Peachtree Pl.
Simpson St.
Baker St.
Harris St.
International Blvd.
Currier St.
Ralph McGill Blvd.
Highland Ave.
Luckie St.
Marietta St.
Techwood Dr.
Peachtree Center Ave.
Courtland St.
Ellis St.
Houston St.
Auburn Ave.
Irwin St.
Old Wheat St.
Edgewood Ave.
Hilliard St.
Yonge St.
Coca Cola Pl.
Boaz St.
Armstrong St.
Gilmer St.
Bell St.
Decatur St.
Martin Luther King, Jr. Dr.
Alabama St.
Decatur St.
Courtland St.
Piedmont Ave.
Butler St.
Martin Luther King, Jr. Dr.
Spring St.
Forsyth St.
Broad St.
Whitehall St.
Pryor St.
Central Ave.
Washington St.
Memorial Dr.
Memorial Dr.
Woodward Ave.
Logan St.
Woodward Ave.
Logan St.
Fulton St.
Richardson St.
Crumley St.
Pulliam St.
Capitol Ave.
Fraser St.
Hammock Pl.
Richardson St.
Richmond St.
Crumley St.
Connally St.
Glenwood Ave.
Sydney St.
Orleans St.
Grant St.
Oakland Ave.

440 yards
400 meters

Atlanta Daily World, **6**	
Atlanta-Fulton County Public Library, **26**	
Atlanta Historical Society, **46**	
Atlanta Life Insurance Company, **5**	
Atlanta Newspapers Inc., **30**	
Bank South Building, **27**	
Baptist Student Center, **9**	
Buckhead, **43**	
Candler Building, **20**	
Capital City Club, **25**	
"Castle", The, **37**	
Center for Nonviolent Social Change, **3**	
Citizens and Southern National Bank, **28**	
City Hall, **12**	
CNN Center, **31**	
Dr. King's birthplace, **4**	
Ebenezer Baptist Church, **2**	
Federal Reserve Bank, **30**	
Five Points MARTA, **15**	
Flatiron Building, **19**	
Fox Theater, **35**	
Fulton County Stadium, **11**	
Georgia Governor's Mansion, **45**	

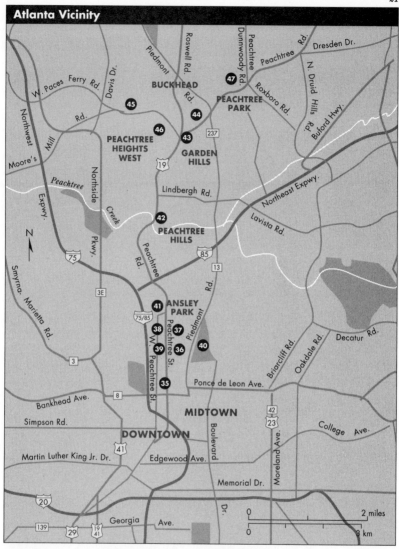

Atlanta Vicinity

BUCKHEAD

PEACHTREE
PARK

PEACHTREE
HEIGHTS
WEST

GARDEN
HILLS

Lindbergh Rd.

PEACHTREE
HILLS

ANSLEY
PARK

Ponce de Leon Ave.

MIDTOWN

DOWNTOWN

Bankhead Ave.

Simpson Rd.

Martin Luther King Jr. Dr.

Edgewood Ave.

Memorial Dr.

Georgia   Ave.

0   2 miles
0   3 km

Georgia-Pacific
Building, **21**

Georgia State
Capitol, **10**

Heath Gallery, **44**

High Museum
of Art, **39**

Hurt building, **17**

IBM Tower, **36**

Municipal Market, **8**

National Park Service
Rangers Station, **7**

New Georgia
Railroad, **14**

Oakland Cemetery, **1**

Omni, **32**

Peachtree Battle
Shopping Center, **42**

Peachtree Center, **24**

Phipps Plaza, **47**

Piedmont Park, **40**

Rhodes Hall, **41**

Richard B. Russell
Federal building, **34**

Ritz-Carlton, **22**

Statue of Henry
Grady, **29**

Underground
Atlanta, **13**

Westin-Peachtree
Plaza Hotel, **23**

William Oliver
building, **18**

Woodruff Arts
Center, **38**

Woodruff Park, **16**

World Congress
Center, **33**

❹ A few doors up the street is **Dr. King's birthplace** (501 Auburn Ave.). The home, a Victorian structure in the Queen Anne style, is managed by the National Park Service and is open to the public daily.

Auburn Avenue is the heart of the black community's business
❺ district. The landmark **Atlanta Life Insurance Company,** founded by Alonzo Herndon, was located in modest quarters at 148 Auburn Avenue until the new modern complex was opened in 1980 at no. 100.

❻ At 145 Auburn Avenue is the **Atlanta Daily World** building, home of one the nation's oldest black newspapers. The church with the "Jesus Saves" sign on its steeple is the Big Bethel African Methodist Episcopal Church. Nearby is the **Royal Peacock Night Club,** a hot spot for black entertainers.

For a history of Auburn Avenue, stop in at the **African American Panoramic Experience** to see the permanent exhibit, as well as their other collections and displays. *135 Auburn Ave., tel. 404/521–2654. Admission: $2 adults, $1 children. Open Mon.–Tues., Thurs.–Fri. 10–5; Wed. 10–6; Sat. 10–4; Sun. noon–4.*

If you're interested in a free, guided walking tour of the so-called Sweet Auburn neighborhood, you can arrange one at the
❼ **National Park Service Rangers Station** (440 Auburn Ave., tel. 404/331–3919) located across from the King Center.

❽ Closer to town, on Edgewood Avenue, is the **Municipal Market,** a thriving produce market where you can buy every part of the pig but the oink. At 125 Edgewood Avenue is the site of the first bottling plant for the Coca-Cola Company; today the site is oc-
❾ cupied by the **Baptist Student Center** for the adjoining campus of **Georgia State University.** Mosey through the urban GSU
❿ campus toward the gold dome of the **Georgia State Capitol building** (206 Washington St.). If you read the state historical markers on the grounds, you'll realize that Atlanta has been virtually rebuilt since General Sherman's urban renewal program more than a century ago. The dome of the capitol is covered with gold leaf, originally mined from Dahlonega, in north Georgia. In addition to housing politicos, it also contains a Georgia history museum, which is open to the public. *Georgia State Capitol, tel. 404/656–2844. Free guided tours of the legislative chambers and museums are given weekdays at 10 and 11 AM and 1 and 2 PM.*

⓫ Behind the capitol is the **Fulton County Stadium,** where the Atlanta Braves and Falcons play. Across the street from the
⓬ capitol is Atlanta's **City Hall** (68 Mitchell St.). When this 14-story neo-Gothic structure with its lavish marble interior was first built in 1926, wags dubbed it "The Painted Lady of Mitchell Street."

Up Central Avenue to Upper Alabama Street is an entrance to
⓭ the city's newest attraction, **Underground Atlanta** (tel. 404/522–1793). This reincarnated six-block entertainment-shopping district, opened in June 1989, now accommodates some 100 specialty retail shops, 20 food-court vendors and 22 restaurants and nightclubs on two levels. The entertainment area, Kenny's Alley, hopes to be a sophisticated version of New Orleans's Bourbon Street, with bars and night spots offering comedy acts, a variety of music (Dixieland, country, pop, folk, jazz) and

dancing. Don't miss the ship decor at Dante's Down the Hatch on Lower Alabama Street.

The center of the $142-million joint venture between the city and The Rouse Co. will be the Peachtree Fountains Plaza, with its distinctive 138-foot light tower. Across the street is an information center and on-site security unit. Two parking garages are on Martin Luther King, Jr. Drive. The new Underground is almost three times larger than the first renovation, which opened in 1969 and closed in 1980.

Two other special attractions will become part of Underground during 1990. A pavilion, called **The World of Coca-Cola** will display historical memorabilia from corporate archives and have interactive exhibits at a four-story, $10-million facility located across the Depot Plaza on Central Avenue. **Atlanta Heritage Row,** on Upper Alabama Street within Underground Atlanta, will feature a multimedia presentation in a 100-seat theatre. Six historical vignettes will tell the story of the city's past and present spirit.

At the Central Avenue entrance to the Underground Atlanta complex is the **New Georgia Railroad** (1 Martin Luther King, Jr., Dr., tel. 404/656–0769). The vintage locomotive and antique passenger coaches make an 18-mile loop around the city three Saturdays a month. One Saturday each month they travel to **Stone Mountain Park and Village,** a suburb that's grown up around the largest granite outcropping in the world, with a monumental Civil War sculpture carved on its side (*see* What to See and Do with Children, below). *Trips at 10 and 2. Loop fare is $10; Stone Mtn. $12.50. Both trips $5 children 3–12. Loop trips are nonstop and take about an hour.*

The **Five Points MARTA** station (Corner of Peachtree and Wall Sts., downtown) is the city's major crossroads, the one tied to the economic lifeblood of the city, with its surrounding bank towers and offices of high-powered law firms. This is pinstripes and power-lunch territory.

On the corner of Peachtree and Alabama streets, outside the station, notice the old-fashioned gas street light, with its historical marker proclaiming it as the **Eternal Flame of the Confederacy.**

At **Woodruff Park** (Corner of Peachtree St. and Park Pl.), named after the city's great philanthropist, Robert W. Woodruff, the late Coca-Cola magnate, you can see a virtual cross section of Atlanta life. During lunchtime on weekdays, the park is filled with executives and secretaries, street preachers, politicians, Georgia State University students, and an array of other characters. If you want to join in, pick up lunch at one of the franchises or Chinese eateries around the park and find an empty bench. For people-watching, the scene rarely gets better than this.

Not much of old Atlanta still exists downtown, although a few turn-of-the-century buildings remain. These elaborately decorated structures stand in sharp contrast to the severe modernism of the skyscrapers of recent decades. **The Hurt Building** (45 Edgewood Ave.) features intricate architectural details, grillwork, and an elaborate marble staircase. **The William Oliver Building** (32 Peachtree St.) is an Art Deco gem. Walk through its lobby and admire the ceiling mural, brass

⑲ grills, and elevator doors. **The Flatiron Building** (at the Peachtree and Broad Sts. triangle) dates from 1897 and is the city's oldest high rise. Perhaps the most prestigious address in the

⑳ legal profession is the **Candler Building** (127 Peachtree St.), which is notable for its decorative details, including marble friezes. Its elegant lobby reeks of Old Atlanta Money, Power, and Influence.

㉑ The towering **Georgia–Pacific Building** (133 Peachtree St.) occupies hallowed ground, the precise site of the old Loew's Grand Theatre, where *Gone With the Wind* premiered back in 1939. One of the architectural oddities about this red marble high rise is that from certain angles the building appears to be two-dimensional or flat against the sky. There's a small branch of the **High Museum of Art** *inside the building. Tel. 404/577–6940. Admission free. Open weekdays 11–5.*

㉒ On the adjacent corner is the downtown **Ritz-Carlton Hotel** (181 Peachtree St.), a stylish place for a cocktail or afternoon high tea.

Next to **Macy's** department store (180 Peachtree St.), is the

㉓ **Westin–Peachtree Plaza Hotel** (210 Peachtree St.), at 73 stories the world's tallest hotel. Designed by Atlanta architect John Portman, the round tower with its trademark exterior elevator features a postmodern interior and a revolving bar/restaurant offering the best panoramic view of the city and the surrounding countryside.

㉔ In the next block, on both sides of the street, is **Peachtree Center**, a city within the city, also designed by John Portman. This complex of buildings, with its connecting skywalks, includes the massive **Merchandise Mart;** the twin office towers of Peachtree Center, with an underground arcade and plaza; **the Apparel Mart;** and the **Hyatt Regency Hotel.** The Hyatt, with its bunkerlike exterior, low entrance, and soaring atrium, earned its place in history by being the first of its type back in 1967.

Within Peachtree Center, the **Atlanta International Museum of Art and Design** shows crafts from around the globe. *245 Peachtree Center Ave., tel. 404/876–3600. Admission free. Open Mon.–Sat. 11–6.*

㉕ The **Capital City Club** (7 Harris St.), is another haunt of the city's power brokers. Its modest size makes it a holdout in the neighborhood, which attests to its clout.

㉖ Back down at the Georgia-Pacific intersection, pause at **Margaret Mitchell Park,** with its cascading waterfall and stately columned sculpture. Across the street, heading south, is the **Atlanta-Fulton County Public Library** (126 Carnegie Way), which houses a large collection of *Gone With the Wind* memorabilia.

Head down Forsyth Street five blocks, to Marietta Street. Notice the renovated **Healy Building** (57 Forsyth St.), an early skyscraper in Commercial style with Tudor decoration.

㉗ Through the lobby is a pretty rotunda. The **Bank South Building** (55 Marietta St.) was briefly Atlanta's tallest building, from 1955 until 1964, when it was superseded by the National

㉘ Bank of Georgia Building. Around the corner is the **Citizens and Southern National Bank** (35 Broad St.), embellished with an exquisite marble floor and bronze banking tables.

㉙ At the corner of Marietta and Forsyth streets is a bronze **statue of Henry Grady,** the post–Civil War editor of *The Atlanta Constitution* and early champion of the so-called "New South." Farther down Marietta Street are the offices of the **Atlanta**
㉚ **Newspapers Inc.** Next door is the **Federal Reserve Bank** (104 Marietta St.). Tours of its monetary museum can be arranged (tel. 404/521–8500).

㉛ Two blocks away, at the corner of Marietta Street and Techwood Drive, is the **CNN Center** (1 CNN Center, 100 International Blvd.), the home of media mogul Ted Turner's Cable News Network. If you want to gawk at the high-tech world of "tee-vee" land and get a behind-the-scenes look at newscasters in action, take a 45-minute tour. The tour begins with a ride up the world's longest escalator to an eighth floor exhibit on Turner's global broadcasting empire. The film version of *Gone With the Wind,* which Turner now owns, plays continuously at the **CNN Cinemas** (tel. 404/577–6928). *Tel. 404/827–2400. Tours: $4 adults, $2 senior citizens and children 5–12. Open weekdays 10–5, weekends 10–4.*

㉜ Behind the CNN Center is the **Omni** (100 Techwood Dr.), where the Atlanta Hawks play and other special events such as
㉝ rock concerts are staged. The **World Congress Center** (285 International Blvd.), where Jimmy Carter held his rally the night he was elected president, and where the Democratic National Convention was held during the summer of 1988, is also nearby.
㉞ A short distance away is the **Richard B. Russell Federal Building** (Spring St. between Mitchell and Martin Luther King, Jr. Dr.), where former President Carter has an office. Its lobby has a tile mosaic that is worth seeing.

Midtown A couple of miles north, up Peachtree Street, is midtown. The
㉟ **Fox Theatre** (660 Peachtree St., tel. 404/881–1977) is a classic movie palace, built in the 1920s in Moorish-Egyption style.

Time Out If you want authentic Southern home-style cooking, don't miss **Mary Mac's Tea Room** (tel. 404/875–4337), just a few blocks from the Fox. Owner Margaret Lupo serves tasty plate lunches with cornbread. *224 Ponce de Leon Ave., tel. 404/875–4337. No credit cards accepted. Inexpensive.*

Peachtree Street at 10th Street used to be the heart of the hippie scene in Atlanta during the early 1970s. New construction has leveled vast areas of this district, but its residential blocks still include large 1920s bungalows and mansions converted into multiunit apartments. Gentrification has brought the Yuppie crowd into the area, so trendy and ethnic eateries and bars have followed.

㊱ Down 14th Street is Atlanta's newest, tallest, and most elegant skyscraper, the **IBM Tower** (1201 W. Peachtree St.). This postmodern high rise, which is visible from many parts of the city, was designed with a Gothic motif by Philip Johnson.

㊲ On 15th Street, across from the Woodruff Arts Center, is an imposing old stone home known as **The Castle** (87 15th St.), which preservationists are struggling to hold on to.

㊳ The **Woodruff Arts Center** (1280 Peachtree St.) is home to the renowned **Atlanta Symphony** and the **Alliance Theatre,** which has more subscribers than does any other regional theater in the country. The Alliance has two venues: a main stage, where mainstream works are produced for general audiences, and a studio downstairs, which does offbeat productions for a more broad-minded public.

㊴ Next door is the white-enamel **High Museum of Art,** a high-tech showplace whose permanent collection is strong on the decorative arts and African folk arts. *1280 Peachtree St., tel. 404/892–4444. Admission: $2 adults, $1 students and senior citizens; free on Thurs. Special exhibits often have an additional charge. Open Tues. 10–5, Wed. 10–9, Thurs.–Sat. 10–5, Sun. noon–5.*

㊵ A few blocks off Peachtree Street is **Piedmont Park,** the outdoor recreation center of the city. Here you'll find tennis courts, a swimming pool, and paths for biking, hiking, and jogging.

The Botanical Garden, located on 30 acres inside the park, has five acres of formal gardens, a 15-acre hardwood forest with walking trails, a serene Japanese garden and a new conservatory, which features unusual, flamboyant and threatened flora from both tropical and desert climates. Don't overlook the whimsical dragon topiary at the entrance. *Tel. 404/876–5858. Admission: $4.50 adults, $2.25 children and senior citizens, free on Thurs. afternoons. Open Tues.–Sat. 9–6, Sun. noon–6.*

㊶ North on Peachtree Street is **Rhodes Hall,** headquarters of the **Georgia Trust for Historic Preservation.** A permanent exhibit focuses on Atlanta architecture of earlier eras. *1516 Peachtree St., tel. 404/881–9980. Admission $2.50. Open weekdays 11–4.*

In the Brookwood Hills area, across I–85, Peachtree Street becomes **Peachtree Road,** and turns into a strip of popular dining places. You'll also note that flowering peach trees once again thrive along various stretches of the road.

㊷ The **Peachtree Battle Shopping Center,** on your right, has Atlanta's largest bookstore, **Oxford Books** (2345 Peachtree Rd., tel. 404/262–3333).

Buckhead Past Peachtree Hills and Garden Hills is **Buckhead,** the heart of
㊸ affluent and trendy Atlanta. Many of Atlanta's finest restaurants and most popular watering spots are in this area. The
㊹ city's major art galleries are here, too. Start at **Heath Gallery** (416 E. Paces Ferry Rd.) and pick up a guidebook for the location of other galleries.

㊺ A short drive out West Paces Ferry Road will bring you to the **Georgia Governor's Mansion.** Built some 20 years ago, in Greek Revival style, the house features Federal-period antiques in its public rooms. *391 W. Paces Ferry Rd., tel. 404/261–1776. Open for free guided tours Tues.–Thurs. 10–11:30 AM.*

㊻ In the same area is the **Atlanta Historical Society.** Of interest on the 26-acre site are the **Swan House,** an Italianate villa filled with European furnishings and art; the **Tullie Smith Plantation,** an 1830s farm house; and **McElreath Hall,** an exhibition space for artifacts from Atlanta's history. *3101 Andrews Dr., tel. 404/261–1837. All inclusive admission: $4.50 adults, $4 senior citizens, and $2 children. Open Mon.–Sat. 9–5:30, Sun. noon–5.*

If you want to gaze at the lovely lawns, gardens, and mansions of Atlanta's well-to-do, drive around in this area, especially along Tuxedo, Blackland, and Habersham roads. Follow the green-and-white "Scenic Drive" signs past an impressive array of Greek Revival, Spanish, Italianate, English Tudor, and French château showplaces.

At the intersection of Peachtree Street and Lenox Road is ❹❼ **Phipps Plaza,** which includes such fashionable shops as Lord & Taylor, Saks Fifth Avenue, Abercrombie & Fitch, Gucci, and Tiffany. On the other corner is the **Ritz-Carlton Buckhead,** which features Atlanta's only five-star restaurant, **The Dining Room** (*see* Dining). If you intend to splurge, this is the place.

Atlanta for Free

Alonzo F. Herndon Home. Founder of the Atlanta Life Insurance Co., the nation's second-largest black-owned insurance company, Alonzo Herndon built this 15-room mansion in 1910. A museum contains furnishings, artwork, photographs, memorabilia. *587 University Pl., tel. 404/581-9813. Open Tues.-Sat. 10-4.*

Concerts. On summer Sunday evenings, the **Atlanta Symphony Orchestra** performs free concerts for thousands of patrons who spread blankets and picnic suppers on the former golf course at Piedmont Park (Piedmont Ave. between 10th and 14th Sts.).

Emory University Museum of Art and Archeology. The pristine interior of this Beaux Arts building on the Emory campus was designed by architect Michael Graves. Exhibits range from an Egyptian mummy to contemporary art. *Emory University, Kilgo Cir., tel. 404/727-7522. Open Tues.-Sat. 10-4:30, Sun. noon-5.*

Telephone Museum. The advances of the telephone over the last century are chronicled in 10 exhibit areas. *Southern Bell Center, Plaza Level, 675 W. Peachtree St. NE, tel. 404/529-7334. Open weekdays 11-1.*

Georgia Governor's Mansion (*see* Exploring).

What to See and Do with Children

The "Weekend" tabloid section of Saturday's *Atlanta Journal-Constitution* has a listing called "Kids," which highlights special happenings around the city for young people.

Fernbank Science Center. The large planetarium here is the only one in the nation owned by a public school system. The museum exhibits focus on geology. A forest behind the center is a treasure itself. *Admission: $2 adults, $1 children. 156 Heaton Park Dr. NE, tel. 404/378-4311. Open Tues.-Fri. 8:30-10, Mon. 8:30-5, Sat. 10-5, and Sun. 1-5.*

Center for Puppetry Arts Museum. The large display of puppets from all over the world is designed to teach visitors about the craft. *1404 Spring St., tel. 404/873-3391. Admission: $2. Open Mon.-Sat. 9-4.*

SciTrek. A new science and technology museum has some 100 hands-on exhibits in four halls—Simple Machines; Light, Color, and Perception; Electricity and Magnetism; and Kidspace, for 2-7 year-olds. *395 Piedmont Ave. NE, tel. 404/522-5500. Admission: $5 adults, $3 children, under 3 free. Open Tues.-Sun. 10-5.*

Six Flags Over Georgia is Atlanta's major theme park, with over 100 rides, musical revues, performing tropical birds and dolphins; and concerts by top-name artists. *I–20W at Six Flags Dr., tel. 404/948–9290. Admission: (all-inclusive one-day pass) $18.20 adults, $11.20 children 42″ tall and seniors 55 and older; $3 parking fee. Opens 10 AM daily in summer and weekends year round; closing times vary. Take MARTA's West Line to Hightower Station and connect with the Six Flags bus (No. 201).*

Stone Mountain Park is the largest granite outcropping on earth. The Confederate Memorial on the north face of the 825-foot-high, five-mile-around monolith is the world's largest sculpture. A 3,200-acre park includes a skylift to the mountaintop, a steam locomotive train ride around the base, an antebellum plantation, an ice skating rink, golf course, swimming beach, campground, paddlewheel steamboat, and Civil War museum. *U.S. 78, Stone Mountain Freeway, tel. 404/498–5600. Admission: $4 per car, additional fees for attractions. Open daily 6 AM–midnight.*

Zoo Atlanta has made a spectacular recovery from a rash of bad publicity (poor management and treatment of animals) a few years ago. An ongoing $35-million renovation program has already resulted in a new Birds of Prey Amphitheater, Flamingo Lagoon, and African Rain Forest. *Grant Park, 800 Cherokee Ave., tel. 404/622–7627. Admission: $3 adults, $2 children 4–11. Open weekdays 10–5, weekends 10–6.*

Off the Beaten Track

Deacon Burton's Grill. The holy grail of Atlanta soul food, this is the place to savor the authentic flavors of glorious Southern fried chicken, chitlins, fried fish, barbecue, turnip greens, cornbread, and cobblers. The chef and maitre d' is "Deacon" Lyndell Burton, an ageless wizard of the iron frying pan. *1029 Edgewood Ave. (across from Inman Park MARTA Station), tel. 404/525–3415. As the sign over the register says, The Credit Manager Is Out, Please Pay Cash. Inexpensive.*

Carter Presidential Center. The museum and archives focus on Jimmy Carter's political career. But it sponsors other activities as well—projects on world food issues, children, foreign affairs conferences. Its Japanese garden is also a serene spot to unwind. *One Copenhill Ave. NE, tel. 404/331–3942. Admission: $2.50 adults, $1.50 senior citizens, children under 16 free. Open Mon.–Sat. 9–4:45, Sun. noon–4:45. Cafeteria open 11–4.*

Shopping

Atlanta's department stores, specialty shops, and flea markets are magnets for shoppers from across the Southeast. Most stores are open Monday–Saturday 10 AM–9:30 PM, and Sunday noon–6 PM. Many downtown stores close on Sunday. Sales tax is 6% in the city of Atlanta and Fulton County and varies in suburban counties.

Shopping Districts The downtown shopping area is anchored on the south by **Rich's Department Store** (45 Broad St., tel. 404/586–4636) and on the north by **Macy's** (180 Peachtree St., tel. 404/221–7221). Both carry top-name apparel and merchandise, but the fashion-conscious prefer Macy's. Smaller stores include **Brooks Brothers** (134 Peachtree St., tel. 404/577–4040) and **Muse's** (52 Peachtree St., tel. 404/522–5400), the latter a long-established local favorite for conservative men's and women's clothing.

At the intersection of Peachtree and Lenox roads, eight miles north of downtown, is Atlanta's high-fashion shopping district. **Lenox Square Mall** has branches of **Neiman Marcus, Macy's, Rich's,** and 300 other specialty stores and restaurants. **Phipps Plaza** houses branches of **Saks Fifth Avenue, Lord & Taylor, Gucci,** and **Tiffany.**

Specialty Shops
Antiques There's a large cluster of antiques shops and flea markets around the intersection of Peachtree and Broad streets in north suburban Chamblee (not to be confused with the Peachtree/Broad streets junction in downtown Atlanta). The many stores include **Broad Street Antique Mall** (3550 Broad St., tel. 404/458–6316) and **Whipporwill Co.** (3519 Broad St., tel. 404/455–8357).

If "junking" is your pleasure, you'll reach nirvana in the area around the intersection of Moreland and Euclid avenues, which is loaded with vintage clothing stores, used record and book shops, and some stores that defy description.

Books Atlanta's largest selection of books and newspapers is at **Oxford Book Store** (Peachtree Battle Shopping Center, 2345 Peachtree Rd., tel. 404/262–3332) and **McGuire's Bookshop** (1055 Ponce de Leon Ave., tel. 404/875–7323). Books are not the only inducement to visit the Oxford Bookstore; along the store's narrow balcony is a coffee shop wonderfully named **The Cup and Chaucer.**

Food **DeKalb Farmers Market** (3000 E. Ponce de Leon Ave., Decatur, tel. 404/377–6400) has 106,000 square feet of exotic fruits, cheeses, seafood, sausages, breads, and delicacies from around the world. Closed Monday.

Participant Sports

Bicycling **Piedmont Park** (Piedmont Ave. between 10th and 14th Sts.) is closed to traffic and popular for biking. **Skate Escape** (across from the park at 1086 Piedmont Ave., tel. 404/892–1292) has rental bikes and skates. The **Southern Bicycle League** (tel. 404/294–1594) has regularly scheduled tours.

Golf The best public courses are **Stone Mountain Park** (U.S. 78, 16 mi east of downtown, tel. 404/498–5600), **Chastain Park** (216 W. Wieuca Rd., tel. 404/255–0723), and **Sugar Creek** (2706 Bouldercrest Rd., tel. 404/241–7671). Carts and rental clubs are available at all three.

Health Clubs Health clubs open to the public include **Midtown Gym** (1107 Peachtree St., tel. 404/892–0287) and branches of the **YMCA** (tel. 404/588–9622). Hotels with health clubs open to guests include the **Westin Peachtree Plaza** and the **Atlanta Marriott Marquis** (*see* Lodging).

Jogging Joggers quickly learn that this is a very hilly city, shaded by many trees. **Piedmont Park** is a traffic-free place perfect for running. Contact the **Atlanta Track Club** (3097 Shadowlawn Ave., tel. 404/231–9064) for other running zones.

Swimming **Piedmont Park** (tel. 404/892–0117) has the city's largest public pool. **White Water Park** (250 North Cobb Pkwy. (U.S. 41), Marietta, tel. 404/424–9283) has a huge wave pool, several water slides, picnic areas, lockers, and showers.

Tennis **Bitsy Grant Tennis Center** (2125 Northside Dr., tel. 404/351–2774) is the area's best public facility. **Piedmont Park** (tel. 404/872–1507) has clay courts only (no locker facilities).

Spectator Sports

Much of Atlanta's reputation as a big-league city must be credited to Hank Aaron, who not only broke Babe Ruth's long-standing home run record but did it in Atlanta playing for the Braves. The National League's **Atlanta Braves** play home games at Atlanta–Fulton County Stadium (521 Capitol Ave., tel. 404/577–9100). The National Basketball Association's **Atlanta Hawks** play home games at the Omni Coliseum (100 Techwood Dr., tel. 404/681–3605). The National Football League's **Atlanta Falcons** play home games at Atlanta–Fulton County Stadium (521 Capitol Ave., tel. 404/261–5400).

Dining

by Christine Lauterbach

Atlanta offers a full range of eating options worthy of its new image as a dynamic international city. From a million–dollar diner to a humble meat–and–three, one can find almost anything in the capital of the New South: prestigious kitchens run by Michelin chefs, fashionable bistros in reclaimed neighborhoods, a multitude of ethnic restaurants, and more fried chicken outlets than anywhere else in the country. But despite the best efforts of the convention and hospitality industry, the Old South is conspicuously absent.

The dining public is value oriented and prices are still low in Atlanta. A full plate means a lot to the average consumer and it is the rare restaurant that does not meet this expectation. The local taste for things sweet and fried cannot be discounted. Try to catch the flavor of the South at breakfast and lunch in modest establishments and to reserve your evenings for more ambitious culinary exploration.

The most highly recommended restaurants in each price category are indicated by a star ★.

Category	Cost*
Very Expensive	over $45
Expensive	$35–$45
Moderate	$25–$35
Inexpensive	under $15

per person without tax (6%), service, or drinks

Downtown
Very expensive
★

City Grill. This posh but breezy new restaurant has made the most of its grand location in the recently renovated historic Hurt building. The bustle of success greets you at the door while bucolic murals and stunning high ceilings help create a feeling of glamour. The menu is traditional American: steaks, chops, and grilled fish. There are a few weaknesses, but you

Dining
City Grill, **8**
Dailey's, **9**
Delectables, **5**
Mick's, **11**
Nikolai's Roof, **13**
Savannah Fish
Company, **4**
The Abbey, **14**
Thelma's, **2**

Lodging
Atlanta Hilton &
Towers, **13**
Atlanta Marriott
Marquis, **10**
Barclay, **3**
Colony Square, **12**
Hyatt Regency, **6**
Omni, **1**
Ritz-Carlton, **7**
Westin Peachtree
Plaza, **4**

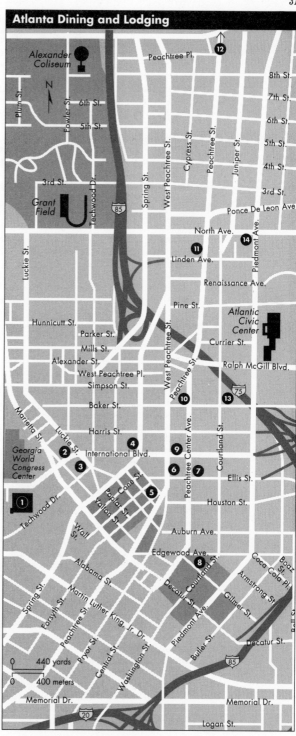

Atlanta Dining and Lodging

can't go wrong with the splendid lamb chops, the fresh salmon or any of the delicious vegetable specialties such as cauliflower soufflé. Club-style service is by a well-trained staff. *55 Hurt Plaza, tel. 404/524-2489. Valet parking. Jacket recommended. Reservations required, weeks ahead for weekend dining. AE, CB, DC, MC, V. No lunch weekends.*

Nicolai's Roof. Once Atlanta's best restaurant, it has been living on its reputation ever since. Rounds of flavored vodka, cossacks rattling off a verbal menu, and complicated dishes under silver cloches make for an impressive show in this Russian-inspired restaurant. Piroshki and borscht (both excellent) are followed by fancy Continental preparations, especially game. The menu changes monthly but you'll find reliable dessert soufflés. *Top of the Atlanta Hilton, 255 Courtland St. tel. 404/659-2000. Jacket and tie requested. Reservations must be made 2 to 3 weeks in advance for a weeknight, 2 to 3 months on weekends. AE, CB, DC, MC, V. Dinner only (two formal seatings 6:30 and 9:30).*

Expensive **Savannah Fish Company.** Have a drink in the revolving lounge at the top of the hotel, but come down to the ground floor for a smashingly good and simple meal of fresh fish, grilled or sautéed without ado. Entrees are served with a bamboo steamer of fresh vegetables. Ignore overpriced appetizers and enjoy the house's saffron and fennel flavored fish stew. Pass up generic cakes for the simple Savannah fried puffs sprinkled with sugar and served with three sauces. There's a hint of Asian simplicity in the pared-down decor. *Westin Peachtree Plaza, Peachtree St. at International Blvd., tel. 404/589-7456. Jacket optional. Reservations accepted for lunch only. AE, CB, DC, MC, V.*

Moderate **Dailey's.** There's always something going on at the bar and in the two dining rooms of this enormous converted warehouse. Downstairs is casual fun. Upstairs there's spectacular decor (merry-go-round horses, enormous shop lamps, both in perfect scale with the imposing space) and more serious dining: veal with Pommery mustard, amberjack au poivre, crisp duck, generous salad, and fried rolls). The menu is recited, the service flashy. Revved-up versions of pastry classics are paraded before the adoring eyes of the crowd on an astounding dessert bar. *17 International Blvd., tel. 404/681-3303. Dress: casual. No reservations; expect a wait. AE, CB, DC, MC, V. No lunch weekends.*

Inexpensive **Delectables.** One of downtown's best kept secrets, don't let the
★ location (inside the Central Public Library) or the format (cafeteria) deter you. This is a very sophisticated little operation serving ravishing salads, wholesome soups, yummy cookies, and freshly baked cakes. Sandwiches are fair. You can enjoy your meal immersed in jazz music and sunshine, on the patio. *Public Library, corner of Margaret Mitchell Sq. and Carnegie Way (enter through Carnegie Way), tel. 404/681-2909. Dress: casual. No reservations. No credit cards. Lunch and coffee break only. Weekdays only.*

Harold's Barbecue. It's a short distance from downtown, but worth the ride. Legislators, political groupies, and small fry from the Capitol sit side by side, wolfing down delicious chopped pork sandwiches, huge platters of freshly sliced meat, and overflowing bowls of Brunswick stew. Don't miss the crackling bread. The knotty pine, tacky art, and management haven't changed in 25 years. *171 McDonough Blvd. near the Federal Penitentiary, tel. 404/627–9268. Dress: casual. No reservations. No credit cards. Closed Sun.*

Thelma's. Honest-to-goodness soul food is served in a squat cinder block building with a cafeteria counter and cramped dining room. Go early at lunchtime to beat the crowds lining up for baked chicken, okra cakes, twice-cooked potatoes, and some of the best flavored greens around town at this cheerful family-run eatery. *190 Luckie St., tel. 404/688–5855. Dress: casual. No reservations. No credit cards. Breakfast and lunch only. Closed weekends.*

The Varsity. Part of Atlanta's collective past, people from all walks of life are likely to run into this enormous, sprawling diner to get one of the famous chili dogs, a glorified hamburger, or a gigantic order of fresh and delicious—but greasy—onion rings. Line up behind the locals and pay close attention to the lingo: "One naked dog, walking and a bag o' rags," will get you a plain hot dog and some french fries. Connoisseurs drink orange frosties. Folks in a hurry get curb service. *61 North Ave., tel. 404/881–1706. Dress: casual. No reservations. No credit cards. Open late.*

Midtown
Very Expensive

The Abbey. Dining in a church, attended by mock–friars, and listening to a harpist plucking away above the altar could be the ultimate in tourist tacky, but it isn't, somehow. The church is a pleasant old building, the chef is young and ambitious, and the wine list is exceptional down to its many selections by the glass or half-bottle. Warm goat cheese salad, poached oysters with pepper confetti, and grilled grouper with zucchini pasta show that high volume and fine food are not mutually exclusive. Ponderous service, however, can drag the meal beyond reason. *163 Ponce de Leon Ave., tel. 404/876–8831. Jacket and tie recommended. Reservations recommended. AE, CB, DC, MC, V. Dinner only.*

Moderate–Expensive
★

Chefs' Café. Living in a symbiotic relationship with the budget lounge in which it is located, this casual San Francisco-style bistro has taught Atlanta to enjoy fashionable food without high-pressure trappings. The menu changes with the seasons but grilled fish, fresh pasta, and creative garnishes can always be found. Grilled eggplant, warm Georgia goat cheese, crab cakes, and roasted lamb sandwich with cilantro mayonnaise are among the specialties. Lunch and Sunday brunch rank high for value. There's an excellent small wine list. *2115 Piedmont Rd. in La Quinta Inn, tel. 404/872–2284. Jacket optional. Reservations recommended. AE, MC, V. Closed Mon. lunch.*

★ **Indigo.** Sizzling and trendy, the creative coastal cuisine proves it can be taken seriously. The owner is a former fashion editor with a great eye for catchy details. Lime and cilantro flavor many of the dishes. Conch fritters, lamb turnovers, grilled oysters with chipotle peppers and tequila, and fish and fresh herbs in a twist of parchment are particularly recommended. Don't miss the refreshing Key lime pie or the sautéed bananas with run and lime. There's brown paper on the tables and gliders on the sidewalk. It's always crowded, but waiting for a table can become part of the fun. *1897 N. Highland Ave., tel. 404/876–0676. Dress: casual. No reservations. AE, MC, V. Dinner only. Closed Sun.*

★ **Partners.** Next door to Indigo, it is also owned by Alix Kenagy. Upbeat and noisy, the creative decor is an appropriate backdrop for an excellent light menu that includes freshly made ravioli with a different stuffing and sauce every day, Cajun mixed grill, Vietnamese chicken cakes, and nostalgic, old-fashioned desserts. An appealing small wine list is full of good values. *1399 N. Highland Ave., tel. 404/875-0202. Dress: casual. No reservations; expect a wait. AE, MC, V. Dinner only. Closed Sun.*

Sierra Grill. Quite trendy, with sparse, witty Southwestern decor, the creative cuisine here involves much grilling and smoking. In-depth knowledge of chili peppers gives many of the dishes a zippy, joyous flavor. Smoked chicken quesadillas, stuffed trout in corn husks, and grilled vegetables are representative of the best options. *1529 Piedmont Rd., tel. 404/873-5630. Dress: informal. No reservations. AE, MC, V. Closed Sun., closed Sat. lunch.*

Inexpensive **Mick's.** Casual and hip, with a well-researched and implemented menu, this restaurant serves the kind of food America never stopped loving: yummy burgers, great chicken sandwiches, big cream pies. The menu also includes fresh pasta, grilled vegetable plates, and soda fountain specials. Great people-watching opportunities abound in a pertly renovated old drugstore. *557 Peachtree St., tel. 404/875-6425 (two other locations: 3393 Peachtree St., tel. 404/262-6425; 4505 Ashford-Dunwoody Rd., tel. 404/394-6425). Dress: casual. No reservations. AE, CB, DC, MC, V. Open late.*

Buckhead **Bone's.** In this brash, New York-style steakhouse, the rich and
Very Expensive powerful rub egos and compare lifestyles over steaks, chops, lobster, and potatoes baked in a crust of salt. Most patrons wear jackets, but if your idea of fun is spending big bucks in a sport shirt, they won't turn you down. *3130 Piedmont Rd., tel. 404/874-0904. Jacket and tie suggested. Reservations recommended. AE, CB, DC, MC, V. No lunch weekends.*

★ **The Dining Room, in The Ritz-Carlton Buckhead.** This is the best restaurant in town and among the country's ten greatest. Under Chef Guenter Seeger, haute cuisine is not flashy or ostentatious. Strictly limiting himself to the freshest regional products, Seeger doesn't like calling attention to the culinary process. The menu, handwritten every day, is likely to involve local sun-dried sweet potatoes (in ravioli), Vidalia onions (with lobster and lobster coral sauce), or persimmons (a mousse with muscadine sorbet and Georgia golden raspberries). Quivering creamy textures (especially fresh duck liver or any kind of seafood) are the result of the chef's own cooking magic. Don't ask for your food to be well-done. Surrender to this imperious genius and the exquisite, discreet service. *3434 Peachtree Rd., tel. 404/237-2700. Jacket and tie requested. Reservations required, several days ahead for weekend dining. AE, CB, DC, MC, V. Dinner only. Closed Sun.*

Hedgerose Heights Inn. Chef Heinz Schwab has equal amounts of talent and common sense. Born in Switzerland, trained in prestigious resort hotels, he now runs a beautiful restaurant in the classic European sense. Pirozki with an impeccable Béarnaise; minced veal in cream with roesti potatoes; and venison, buffalo, duck, and goose liver pâté rolled in minced truffles are some of the dishes he perfected when he headed the kitchen at Nikolai's Roof. His dessert soufflés are among the most luscious in town. Salt can be a problem in some of specialties. The service may be intimidating and the tables are very close together in the pretty, soft dining room. *490 E. Paces Ferry Rd.,* *tel. 404/233–7673. Jacket required. Reservations required (two seatings). AE, CB, DC, MC, V. Dinner only. Closed Sun. and Mon.*

★ **103 West.** An ornate facade and porte cochère add to the proud image of Atlanta's poshest, most palatial restaurant. Antique tapestries, watered silks, and glorious details fill the dining rooms. The kitchen matches this lavish classicism. Here's the place to gorge on crab cakes with beurre blanc, sweet basil and red pepper rouille; or fresh veal sweetbreads with madeira sauce and fresh grapes on a bed of wilted spinach. Glamour dishes include smoked mountain trout with lump crab meat, venison with wild mushrooms and mustard fruit, and an amazing "Grand Dessert" sampler. *103 W. Paces Ferry Rd., tel. 404/233–5993. Jacket and tie required. Reservations required. AE, CB, DC, MC, V. Dinner only. Closed Sun.*

The Coach & Six. This has been one of Atlanta's most famous and most idiosyncratic restaurants for nearly three decades. No place can make you feel more like an outsider, yet no place provides a better opportunity to see the Atlanta that was, and still is, a mercantile boom-town. Marvelous New York-style rolls, raw vegetables, olives, cheese toast, and spinach pie are presented before the meal even begins. The menu focuses on steaks, roasts, chops, and fresh fish. There's also an impressive pastry cart. The service aims for formality but is sometimes uncaring. *1776 Peachtree Rd., tel. 404/872–6666. Jacket and tie required. Reservations required, well in advance for weekends. AE, CB, DC, MC, V. No weekend lunch.*

★ **La Grotta.** Despite its odd location in the basement of an apartment building, this is one of the best-managed dining rooms in town. Magnetic, dynamic Sergio Favalli is a superb host and the waiters are on their toes. The kitchen experiments cautiously with new concepts and trendy ingredients, but old Northern Italian favorites remain at the core of the menu. Don't miss the cold grilled wild mushrooms, the baby quails over polenta, or the special tiramisu dessert. Veal and fresh pasta are outstanding. There's an excellent wine list. *2637 Peachtree Rd., tel. 404/231–1368. Jacket and tie required. Reservations required well in advance. AE, CB, DC, MC, V. Dinner only. Closed Sun. and Mon.*

Expensive **Pano's and Paul's.** An Atlanta classic, it's now in its 10th year of stylish pampering. Pano Karatassos and Paul Albrecht hit gold, thanks to their single-minded devotion to their customers' whims and needs, including dietary restriction. Lovely lights and rich fabrics fill the dining rooms designed by Penny Goldwasser. Many new ideas percolate through the kitchen; state-of-the-art dishes are introduced as specials and eventually included in the menu. Look for roasted Georgia quails with foie gras and trumpet mushrooms, smoked salmon crêpes with truffle horseradish sauce, and a combination of Maine lobster and capon breast with a mousseline of potato and celery. *1232 W. Paces Ferry Rd., tel. 404/261–3662. Jacket required. Reservations required (days, sometimes weeks ahead for a prime slot). AE, CB, DC, MC, V. Dinner only. Closed Mon.*

Moderate–Expensive **Buckhead Diner.** This million-dollar fantasy by the owners of
★ *Pano's and Paul's* is one of the hottest restaurants in town, a shimmering faux-diner wrapped in luscious hues of neon. Inlaid wood, Italian leather, hand-cut marble and mellow lights establish a langorous ambience reminiscent of the Orient Express. The cuisine is anything but diner: neo-Asian shrimp

wonton, buffalo milk mozzarella melted in fresh tomato coulis, veal meatloaf, and homemade banana walnut ice cream are some of the treats prepared by gifted young Gerry Klaskala. Interesting wines are available by the glass. *3073 Piedmont Rd., tel. 404/262-3336. Dress: informal. No reservations; expect a long wait. AE, CB, DC, MC, V. Closed Sun.*

Inexpensive **OK Café.** You'll go "back to the future" in this witty take-off on small town cafés. There's a great cast of cheeky waitresses, whimsical art, and very comfortable booths. Particularly good breakfasts (fried French toast, stout omelets) are served, but blue-plate-specials are not always reliable. The desserts are excellent. *3345 Lenox Rd., tel. 404/261-2888; also 1248 W. Paces Ferry Rd., tel. 404/233-2888. Dress: casual. No reservations. AE, MC, V. Open late.*

Wyolene's. Impudent and saucy, this amusing roadhouse winks an eye at the '50s. Free jukebox, big patio with dishevelled palm tree, and bags of white bread on the tables are part of its charm. Wyo's comfort food is the real thing, with no props: meatloaf, chicken-fried steak, macaroni and cheese, home-cooked vegetables, soft-serve ice cream. *2890 Peachtree Rd., tel. 404/365-0360. Dress: casual. No reservations. AE, DC, MC, V.*

Outside the **Aunt Fanny's Cabin.** This is a place where the real and the fake
Perimeter interlock. There are some overdone folksy touches, but the old
Moderate building and its many additions are always packed with people having a good time. Whole Greyhound busloads come to drink mint juleps (that taste like a blend of chemicals). They also eat fried chicken (not better or worse than many) and country ham (its usual leathery, salty self). *2155 Campbell Rd. in Smyrna, tel. 404/436-5218. Dress: informal. Reservations for 12 or more. AE, CB, DC, MC, V. Dinner only.*

Lodging

One of America's three most popular convention destinations, Atlanta offers a broad range of lodgings. More than 12,000 rooms are in the compact downtown area, close to the Georgia World Congress Center, Atlanta Civic Center, Atlanta Merchandise Mart and Apparel Mart, and Omni Coliseum. Other clusters are in the affluent Buckhead corporate and retail area, and around Hartsfield International Airport.

Category	Cost*
Very Expensive	over $100
Expensive	$75–$100
Moderate	$50–$75
Inexpensive	under $50

double room; add 11% for taxes

The following credit-card abbreviations are used: AE, American Express; CB, Carte Blanche; DC, Diners Club; MC, MasterCard; V, Visa.

Downtown and **Atlanta Hilton & Towers.** The Hilton provides for the needs of
Midtown the business traveler. The top three Tower floors are comprised
Very Expensive of suites in Early American, contemporary, French Provincial

and Oriental styles; the remaining floors were recently renovated along contemporary, modular lines. Nikolai's Roof, a Russian restaurant, and Trader Vic's are excellent and popular. *255 Courtland St., 30043, tel. 404/659–2000 or 800/ HILTONS. 1,250 rooms and suites. Facilities: jogging track, 4 tennis courts, pool, health club, lounges, 4 restaurants including Trader Vic's, a rooftop nightclub. AE, CB, DC, MC, V.*

Atlanta Marriott Marquis. Immense and coolly contemporary, the Marquis seems to go on forever as you stand under the lobby's huge fabric sculpture that appears to be floating down from the sky-lit roof 50 stories above. Each guest room opens onto this atrium. *265 Peachtree Center Ave., 30303, tel. 404/521 –0000 or 800/228–9290. 1,674 rooms and suites. Facilities: 5 restaurants, 4 bars and lounges, health club, indoor/outdoor pool. AE, CB, DC, MC, V.*

Colony Square Hotel. Theatricality and opulence are epitomized by the dimly lit lobby with overhanging balconies, piano music, and fresh flowers. The hotel is one block from MARTA's Art Center station, across from the Woodruff Arts Center and the High Museum of Art, and it anchors the Colony Square office/residential/retail complex. *Peachtree and 14th Sts. (1 block from MARTA's Art Center rail station), 30361, tel. 404/ 892–6000 or 800/422–7895. 434 rooms, 32 suites. Facilities: lobby lounge, 2 restaurants, access (for a fee) to the Colony Club health club, racquetball courts, outdoor pool. AE, CB, DC, MC, V.*

Hyatt Regency Atlanta. The Hyatt's 23-story atrium/lobby (built in 1965) launched the chain's "atrium look." The rooms were recently renovated in honor of the hotel's 20th anniversary. Most guests are conventioneers. *264 Peachtree St. (connected to MARTA's Peachtree Center Station), 30303, tel. 404/577–1234. 1,279 rooms and 56 suites. Facilities: 4 restaurants, outdoor pool, health club, sauna. 2 ballrooms. AE, CB, DC, MC, V.*

Omni Hotel at CNN Center. The hotel is adjacent to the CNN Center, home of Ted Turner's Cable News Network. The lobby combines Old World and modern accents, with marble floors, Oriental rugs, exotic floral and plant arrangements, and contemporary furnishings. *100 CNN Center, near MARTA's Omni station stop, 30335, tel. 404/659–0000. 470 rooms. Facilities: 2 restaurants, lounge, access to the Downtown Athletic Club. AE, CB, DC, MC, V.*

Ritz-Carlton Atlanta. The mood here is set by traditional afternoon tea served in the intimate, sunken lobby beneath an 18th-century chandelier. Guest rooms are luxuriously decorated with marble writing tables, sofas, four-poster beds, and marble bathrooms. *181 Peachtree St., 30303, tel. 404/659–0400 or 800/241–3333. 454 rooms. Facilities: 2 restaurants, bar with live jazz, access (for a nominal fee) to the adjacent Phoenix Athletic Club. AE, CB, DC, MC, V.*

The Westin Peachtree Plaza. Every photograph of Atlanta's skyline taken in the last 10 years features this cylindrical glass tower, the tallest hotel in North America. The five-story atrium lobby is classic John Portman—the Atlanta-based architect who set a modern hotel style for the world. The hotel was recently renovated top to bottom to the tune of $35 million. For the best views, ask for floor 45 or higher. *210 Peachtree St. at International Blvd., 30303, tel. 404/659–1400 or 800/228–3000. 1,074 rooms. Facilities: 3 restaurants, 3 bars, a rooftop indoor/*

outdoor pool, health club, sauna, shopping gallery, kosher kitchen. AE, CB, DC, MC, V.

Inexpensive **Barclay Hotel.** This is a quiet, older downtown hotel patronized by budget travelers. The hotel's Wild Wild West Nightclub and Soda Club is geared toward teenagers under the drinking age. *Directly behind the Peachtree Center at 89 Luckie St. NW, 30303, tel. 404/524–7991. 73 rooms. Facilities: rooftop swimming pool and sun deck, restaurant. AE, CB, DC, MC, V.*

Buckhead **French Quarter Suites.** A baby grand plays daily in the atrium
Very Expensive lobby. All one-bedroom suites are decorated with contemporary furnishings and have Jacuzzis. Some have refrigerators. *2780 Whitley Rd., 30339, tel. 404/980–1900 or 800/843–5858. 155 suites. Facilities: Café Orleans, bar, lounge with live entertainment, outdoor pool, and exercise and sauna rooms. AE, CB, DC, MC, V.*

The Ritz-Carlton, Buckhead. Not to be confused with the Ritz-Carlton in Atlanta, its classy downtown cousin, this suburban hotel caters more to social events and shopping lovers. *3434 Peachtree Rd., 30326, tel. 404/237–2700 or 800/241–3333. 553 rooms. Facilities: The Café, with live music and dance floor; The Dining Room, The Bar, with evening entertainment, indoor swimming pool and deck, health center. AE, CB, DC, MC, V.*

Westin Lenox. This elegant 25-story hotel opened in Lenox Square in December 1988. It is sumptuous, but in a subdued style emphasizing intimacy and comfort. Irregularly shaped rooms have spacious baths with separate shower stall and tub. Homey traditional decor and tasteful reproduction antique furniture add to its informal tone. *3300 Lenox Rd., 30326, tel. 404/ 262–3344. 371 rooms, including 3 club floors and suites. Facilities: indoor pool, health club, 2 lounges, Swan Room restaurant, ballroom and meeting rooms. AE, CB, DC, MC, V.*

Moderate **Beverly Hills Inn.** This three-story inn has hardwood floors and English antiques. Most rooms and suites have kitchen facilities and dinettes. Downstairs is the library/parlor and the garden room, where complimentary breakfasts are served. *65 Sheridan Dr., 30305, tel. 404/233–8520. 18 rooms, 4 suites. AE, MC, V.*

The Arts

Culture here now means more than church suppers, stock-car racing, and country music. The Atlanta Symphony Orchestra plays the great halls of Europe and New York, the Atlanta Ballet is rated one of the top companies in the country, and the Alliance Theatre sells more season tickets than any other regional theater in the country.

For the most complete schedule of cultural events, check the "Weekend" tabloid section of Saturday's *Atlanta Journal-Constitution.* Also check *Creative Loafing,* a lively community weekly distributed at restaurants, bars, and stores throughout the metro area.

SEATS, Inc. (tel. 404/577–2626) handles tickets for the Fox Theatre, Atlanta Civic Center, and other large houses. However, most companies sell tickets through their own box offices.

Theater Consistently one of the city's best, the **Alliance Theatre** performs everything from Shakespeare to the latest Broadway and off-Broadway shows in the Woodruff Arts Center *(see* Exploring).

Academy Theatre. The city's oldest theater troupe moved into a new theater complex in 1987. The mainstage theater seats 450; new plays are showcased in the 200-seat First Stage and 75-seat Lab Theatre. Also using the Academy complex is **Jomandi Productions,** the city's major African-American company. *173 14th St. NW, tel. 404/892-0880.*

Horizon Theatre Co. This experimental company produces new works by contemporary playwrights as well as mime shows. *1038 Austin Ave. in Little Five Points, tel. 404/584-7450.*

Touring Braodway musicals, pop music, and dance concerts are presented in **The Atlanta Civic Center** (395 Piedmont Ave., tel. 404/523-6275) and the **Fox Theatre** (660 Peachtree St., tel. 404/881-1977. See Exploring).

Concerts Modeled after the Viennese choir, the **Atlanta Boy's Choir** (tel. 404/378-0064) performs frequently at Atlanta locations and makes national and international tours.

The long-established **Atlanta Chamber Players** (tel. 404/872-3360) perform classical works at various Atlanta locations.

The city's **Atlanta Symphony Orchestra** (tel. 404/892-2414) performs its fall–spring subscription series in the 1,800-seat Symphony Hall at Woodruff Arts Center. During the summer, the orchestra accompanies big-name artists in Chastain Park and plays free Sunday evening concerts in Piedmont Park.

Opera **The Atlanta Opera Association** (tel. 404/872-1706), made up of local singers and musicians, is augmented by internationally known artists.

Dance **The Atlanta Ballet Company** (tel. 404/873-5811), founded in 1929, has received international recognition for its high-quality productions of classical and contemporary works. Performances are at the Fox Theatre and Atlanta Civic Center.

Nightlife

"We entertain at home," Atlantans proudly sniffed some 20 years ago. Today, the pursuit of entertainment—from midtown to Buckhead—is known as the "Peachtree Shuffle." Throughout the city you will find a vibrant nightlife, with everything from piano bars to high-energy dance clubs. Locals seem to take pride in the fact that Atlanta has always had more saloons than churches . . . and, in the south, that's saying something.

Most bars and clubs are open seven nights, until 2–4 AM. Those featuring live entertainment usually have a cover charge. For a listing of entertainment, consult both the "Weekend" section of Saturday's *Atlanta Journal-Constitution* and *Creative Loafing.*

Blues New Orleans–style blues send jam-packed crowds into a frenzy at **Blind Willie's** (818 N. Highland Ave., tel. 404/456-4433), a storefront club in trendy Virginia/Highland. Chicago-style blues and zydeco are on the musical menu at the popular **Blue's Harbor** (Underground Atlanta, tel. 404/261-6717).

Jazz   **The Bar** at the Ritz-Carlton Buckhead *(see* Lodging) has dark wood paneling, a small museum's worth of original art, a real fire crackling in the hearth throughout the winter, fashionably dressed patrons sipping drinks while a jazz combo plays. Atlanta doesn't get any more uptown than this.

Dante's Down the Hatch (3380 Peachtree Rd., tel. 404/266–1600) is one of the city's best-known showplaces, where The Paul Mitchell Trio conjures silky-smooth sounds in the "hold" of a make-believe sailing ship. Fondues and a large wine selection add to the experience.

Highland Brewing Co. (816 N. Highland Ave., tel 404/876–7115) presents jazz Thursday through Sunday starting at 9 in a snug Art-Deco style cellar cafe.

Rock   **The Cotton Club** (1021 Peachtree St., tel. 404/874–2523) is a loud, usually packed, midtown club that features both local and national performers in a variety of musical styles.

Club Rio (195 Luckie St., tel. 404/525–7467), a late-night downtown club, is the "in" place to be seen dancing to hot new music. The action begins about midnight and roars until 6.

Little Five Points Pub (1174 Euclid Ave., tel. 404/577–7767) is a scruffy club that often showcases top talent in folk, rock, and progressive music.

Bars and Lounges   **Atkins Park Bar & Grill** (794 N. Highland Ave., tel. 404/876–7249), one of Atlanta's oldest neighborhood bars, is packed nightly with a mostly young crowd. It's a fun place to meet-and-mingle in a nonmeat-market atmosphere.

Confetti (3909 Roswell Rd., tel. 404/237–4238) is the consummate singles bar, which attracts a young crowd perpetually on the make. Good drinks and loud music around a congenial bar and postage-stamp-size dance floor.

Sexy, well-dressed single professionals mingle, dine, and dance in **élan** (4505 Ashford-Dunwoody Rd., tel. 404/393–1333), a glossy suburban club that has held its magnetism for nearly 10 years.

The antithesis of hip-and-trendy, 30-year-old **Manuel's Tavern** (602 N. Highland Ave., tel. 404/525–3447)—ancient by Atlanta standards—is a neighborhood saloon in the truest sense. A blend of families, politicians, writers, students, professionals, and blue-collar workers enjoy good drinks, bar food (chili dogs, french fries, strip steaks), and conversations. A lively summertime Shakespeare festival is staged in an adjoining room.

Nonalcoholic   **Joyful Noise** (2669 Church St., tel. 404/768–5100), a Christian supper club on Atlanta's south side, has a buffet supper and live entertainment performed by gospel and other religious musical groups.

Savannah

by Honey Naylor   Savannah. The very sound of the word conjures up misty images of mint juleps, live oaks dripping with Spanish moss, handsome mansions, and a somewhat decadent city moving at a lazy Southern pace. Why, you can hardly say "Savannah" without drawling.

Well, brace yourself. The mint juleps are there all right, along with the moss and the mansions and the easygoing pace, but this Southern belle rings with surprises.

Take, for example, St. Patrick's Day: Why on earth does Savannah, of all places, have a St. Patrick's Day celebration second only to New York's? The greening of Savannah began more than 164 years ago and nobody seems to know why, although everybody in town talks a blue (green) streak about St. Patrick's Day. Everything turns green on March 17, including the faces of startled visitors when green scrambled eggs and green grits are put before them. One year, some well-oiled revelers even tried to dye the Savannah River green.

Savannah's beginning was February 12, 1733, when English General James Edward Oglethorpe and 120 colonists arrived at Yamacraw Bluff on the Savannah River to found the 13th and last colony in the New World. As the port city grew, Englishmen, Scottish Highlanders, French Huguenots, Germans, Austrian Salzburgers, Sephardic Jews from Spain and Portugal, Moravians, Italians, Swiss, Welsh, and Irishmen all arrived to create what could be called a rich gumbo.

In 1793, Eli Whitney of Connecticut, who was tutoring on a plantation near Savannah, invented a mechanized means of "ginning" seeds from cotton bolls. Cotton soon became king, and Savannah, already a busy seaport, flourished under its reign. Waterfront warehouses were filled with "white gold," and factors, or brokers, trading in the Savannah Cotton Exchange set world prices. The white gold brought in solid gold, and fine mansions were built in the prospering city.

It was a Yankee who ushered in Savannah's Golden Age, and it was Yankees who shattered it. In 1864, Savannahians, having seen what Sherman did to the rest of Georgia, surrendered their city to the Union general rather than see it torched. In December of that year, Sherman sent a now-famous telegram to Lincoln. It read, "I beg to present to you as a Christmas gift, the City of Savannah with 150 heavy guns and plenty of ammunition and also about 25,000 bales of cotton."

Following Reconstruction and the collapse of the cotton market, Savannah itself virtually collapsed. The city languished for more than 50 years. Elegant mansions were either razed or allowed to decay, and cobwebs replaced cotton in the decaying riverfront warehouses.

But in 1955, Savannah's spirits rose again. News that the exquisite Isaiah Davenport home (324 E. State St.) was to be destroyed prompted seven outraged ladies to raise enough money to buy the house. They saved it the very day before the wrecking ball was to swing.

Thus was born the Historic Savannah Foundation, the organization responsible for the restoration of downtown Savannah. More than 1,000 structures have been restored in the 2.5-square-mile Historic District, the nation's largest urban Historic Landmark district, and many of them are open to the public during the annual tour of homes (Mar. 24–28).

When visiting the city, you'll hear a lot about the "Savannah colors." As old buildings were scraped down in preparation for restoration, Savannah showed its true colors—rich mauves, blues, grays, and golds appearing beneath old layers of paint.

Those colors are in full view now, making Savannah one of the nation's most colorful cities.

Arriving and Departing

By Plane Savannah International Airport, eight miles west of downtown, is served by **American, Continental, Delta, Eastern, United,** and **USAir.** There is no international passenger service.

Between the Airport **Vans** operated by **McCalls Coastal Express** (tel. 912/966–5364)
and Center City leave the airport daily between 7 AM and 10 PM destined for downtown locations. The trip takes 20–30 minutes, and the one-way fare is $8.

Taxi fare from the airport to downtown hotels is $15 for one person, $3 for each additional person.

By car, drive south on Dean Forest Drive to I–16, then east on I–16 into downtown Savannah.

By Train **Amtrak** (800/USA–RAIL) has regular service along the Eastern Seaboard, with daily stops in Savannah. The Amtrak station (2611 Seaboard Coastline Dr., tel. 912/234–2611) is four miles southwest of downtown. Cab fare into the city is about $4.

By Bus The **Greyhound/Trailways** station (tel. 912/233–7723) is downtown at 610 W. Oglethorpe Avenue. You can travel nonstop between Atlanta and Savannah on minivans operated by **Peachtree Express** (tel. 912/355–0459; in GA 800/627–3900).

By Car I–95 slices north–south along the Eastern Seaboard, intersecting 10 miles west of town with east–west I–16, which dead-ends in downtown Savannah. U.S. 17, the Coastal Highway, also runs north–south through town. U.S. 80, which connects the Atlantic to the Pacific, is another east–west route through Savannah.

Getting Around

Despite its size, the downtown Historic District should be explored on foot. Its grid shape makes getting around a breeze, and you'll find any number of places to stop and rest.

By Bus Buses require 75¢ in exact change, and 5¢ extra for a transfer. **Chatham Area Transit (CAT)** (tel. 912/233–5767) operates buses in Savannah and Chatham County Monday–Saturday from 6 AM to 11:30 PM, Sunday 6 AM to 6:30 PM.

By Taxi Taxis start at 60¢ and cost $1.20 for each mile. **Adam Cab Co.** (tel. 912/927–7466) is a reliable, 24-hour taxi service.

Important Addresses and Numbers

Tourist For trip planning information, write to the **Savannah Area Con-**
Information **vention and Visitors Bureau** (222 W. Oglethorpe Ave., Savannah 31499, tel. 800/444–CHARM). The **Savannah Visitors Center** (301 W. Broad St., tel. 912/944–0455) has free maps and brochures, lots of friendly advice, and an audiovisual overview of the city. The center is also the starting point for a number of guided tours. *Open Mon.–Fri. 8:30–5, weekends and holidays 9–5.*

Emergencies Dial 911 for **police** and **ambulance** in an emergency.

Hospitals Area hospitals with 24-hour emergency rooms are **Candler General Hospital** (5353 Reynolds St., tel. 912/356–6037) and **Memorial Medical Center** (4700 Waters Ave., tel. 912/356–8390).

Pharmacies **Revco Discount Drug Center** (Medical Arts Shopping Center, 4800 Waters Ave., tel. 912/355–7111) and **Pharmor** (7400 Abercorn St., tel. 912/352–8127).

Guided Tours

Orientation Tours The **Historic Savannah Foundation Tours** (tel. 912/234–TOUR) are conducted by members of the nonprofit organization that began, and continues, restoration of the city's fine old buildings. Guides are both knowledgeable and enthusiastic, and you'll ride in sleek, 20-passenger, climate-controlled vans. Tours of the Historic District and of the Victorian District each take about two hours. **Colonial Historic Tours** (tel. 912/233–0083) will take you on a two-hour tool around town on minibuses or on an "Old Time Trolley."

Special-Interest Tours **Helen Bryant's Shoppers Walk** (tel. 912/355–7731) is a three-hour browse for hidden treasures with a native Savannahian. The **Garden Club of Savannah** (tel. 912/238–0248) takes you into private gardens tucked behind old-brick walls and wrought-iron gates. The **Negro Heritage Trail** (tel. 912/234–8000), tracing the city's 250-year black history, is a van tour with a knowledgeable guide who will tell you about the Gullah culture of the Georgia and Carolina sea islands. Tours commence at the Black Heritage Museum in the King-Tisdell Cottage (514 E. Huntingdon St.).

Cap'n Sam's Cruises (tel. 912/234–7248) churn along the Savannah River in small, colorful paddlewheelers. Cap'n Sam Stevens has been a fixture on the riverfront for more than 50 years. He and his guides offer a wealth of information and trivia about Savannah's historic ties to its river. There are two-hour narrated harbor tours, twilight cocktail cruises, and moonlight dinner cruises, with daily departures from the dock on Riverfront Plaza/River Street behind City Hall.

Carriage Tours of Savannah (tel. 912/236–6756) show you the Historic District by day or by night at a 19th-century clip-clop pace, with coachmen spinning tales and telling ghost stories along the way. A romantic evening champagne tour in a private carriage will set you back $50–$60, plus $16 per bottle of bubbly. Regular tours are a more modest $9.50 adults, $4.50 children 11 and under. Daily departures are from City Market and Madison Square; evening departures are behind the Hyatt Regency Hotel.

Low-Country Tours The **Historic Savannah Foundation Tours** (tel. 912/234–TOUR), **Colonial Historic Tours** (912/233–0083), and **Gray Line** (tel. 912/236–9604) all make four-hour excursions to the fishing village of Thunderbolt; the Isle of Hope, with stately mansions lining Bluff Drive; the much-photographed Bonaventure Cemetery on the banks of the Wilmington River, with 200-year-old oaks draping Spanish moss over the graves of many notable Savannahians; and Wormsloe Plantation, with its mile-long avenue of arching oaks.

Walking Tours The **Historic Savannah Foundation** (tel. 912/234–TOUR) offers two strolls through the Historic District, one of which includes breakfast at Mrs. Wilkes's Boarding House. Both of the personalized strolls focus on the city's architecture and gardens.

Cycle Carriage Company (346 Whitaker St., tel. 912/234–8277) is in a class by itself. Its canopied contraptions look a bit like old-time Tin Lizzies but are actually bicycles built for four. The four-wheel critters have baskets up front, where small children get a free ride, and two seats to the rear, where the big folks do the steering—and the pedaling. Regular bicycles are also available.

Exploring Savannah

Numbers in the margin correspond with points of interest on the Savannah Historical District map.

General Oglethorpe himself designed the original town of Savannah and laid it out in a perfect grid. The Historic District is neatly hemmed in by the Savannah River, Gaston Street, and East and West Broad streets. Streets are arrow-straight, public squares of varying sizes are tucked into the grid at precise intervals, and each block is sliced in half by an alley. Bull Street, anchored on the north by City Hall and the south by Forsyth Park, charges down the center of the grid and lunges around the five public squares that stand in its way. (Maneuvering a car around Savannah's squares is a minor art form.)

The Historic District There are two excellent reasons for making your first stop the **Savannah Visitors Center** *(see* Tourist Information in Important **❶** Addresses and Numbers), the most obvious being the maps and brochures you'll need for exploring. The other reason is the structure that houses the Center. The big red-brick building with its high ceilings and sweeping arches was the old Central of Georgia railway station, completed in 1860.

The Visitors Center lies just north of the **site of the Siege of Savannah.** During the American Revolution, the Redcoats seized Savannah in 1778, and the Colonial forces made several attempts to retake it. In 1779, the Colonials, led by Polish Count Casimir Pulaski, laid siege to the city. They were beaten back, and Pulaski was killed while leading a cavalry charge against the British.

On the battle site, adjacent to the Visitors Center in a restored **❷** shed of the railway station, the **Great Savannah Exposition** offers an excellent introduction to the city. Two theaters present special-effects depictions of Oglethorpe's landing and of the siege. There are various exhibits, ranging from old locomotives to a tribute to Savannah's own world-famous songwriter Johnny Mercer, as well as two restored dining cars that aren't going anywhere, but you can climb aboard for a bite to eat. *303 W. Broad St., tel. 912/238–1779. Admission: $3.75 adults; $2.50 children 4–12, under 4 free. Open daily 9–5.*

Turn left on Broad Street and walk two blocks to the **❸** **Scarbrough House** headquarters for the Historic Savannah Foundation. The exuberant Regency mansion was built during the 1819 cotton boom for Savannah merchant prince William Scarbrough and designed by English architect William Jay. A Doric portico is capped by one of Jay's characteristic half-moon windows. Four massive Greek Doric columns form a peristyle in the atrium entrance hall. Three stories overhead is an

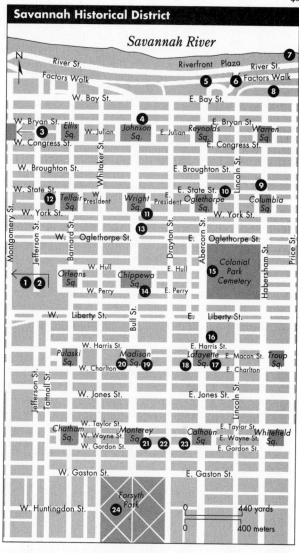

Savannah Historical District

arched, sky-blue ceiling with sunshine filtering through a sky-light. Exhibits of works by local artists are displayed throughout the house. *41 W. Broad St., tel. 912/233-7787. Admission: $1.50 adults, 75¢ children. Open Mon.–Sat. 10–4.*

Continue east across Franklin Square and stroll through City Market, with its sidewalk cafes, jazz joints, and shops. Now head east on St. Julian Street to **Johnson Square.** Laid out in 1733 and named for South Carolina Governor Robert Johnson, this was the earliest of Oglethorpe's original 24 squares. The square was once a popular gathering place, where Savannahians came to welcome President Monroe in 1819, to greet the Marquis de Lafayette in 1825, and to cheer for Georgia's secession in 1861. It was here that Lafayette laid the cornerstone for the monument that marks the grave of his friend and Revolutionary War hero, Major-General Nathaniel Greene. (It was on Greene's plantation after the war that Eli Whitney invented the cotton gin.)

Time Out Food carts are parked in Johnson Square; you can pick up an ice cream cone, a hot dog, or a cold drink and relax on one of the park benches.

That building to the north with the glittering gilt dome at the foot of Bull Street is **City Hall,** dating from 1905. (The dome was regilded in 1987.) The lower stories of City Hall face the spot from which the SS *Savannah* set sail in 1819, the first steamship to cross any ocean. Just to the west of City Hall, on Yamacraw Bluff, is a marble bench, appropriately called **Oglethorpe's Bench,** that marks the site of the general's field tent.

5 **6** Cobblestone ramps lead from Bay Street down to **Factors Walk** and, below it, to **River Street.** Cars can enter Factors Walk via the ramps, and so can pedestrians. (These are serious cobblestones, and you will suffer if you wear anything but the most comfortable shoes you own.) There is also a network of iron walkways connecting Bay Street with the multistoried buildings that rise up from the river level, and iron stairways plunge (word used advisedly) from Bay Street down to Factors Walk.

Foreign vessels still call at the Port of Savannah, the largest port between Baltimore and New Orleans. Paper and other products have replaced the cotton exports, and in 1977 a multimillion-dollar riverfront revitalization transformed the decayed warehouses into a nine-block marketplace with everything from sleek boutiques to musty taverns.

Learning about the port and the river is a breeze aboard one of **Cap'n Sam's Cruises,** so you may want to break up your walking tour at this point to board one of his paddlewheelers *(see Guided Tours).*

There are benches all along **Riverfront Plaza** where you can watch the parade of freighters and pug-nosed tugs, and the tugboat-shape sandboxes where youngsters can play. Each weekday, Dixieland music can be heard from the cabin of the **River Street Rambler,** a brightly-painted freight train that rumbles down River Street to the port. River Street is the main venue for many of the city's celebrations, including the First Saturday festivals when flea marketeers, artists, and craftsmen display their wares and musicians entertain the crowds.

7 Even landlubbers can appreciate the fine craftsmanship of the ship models in the **Ships of the Sea Museum.** The four floors of the museum contain models of steamships, nuclear subs, China clippers with their sails unfurled, Columbus's ships, a showcase filled with ships-in-bottles, and a collection of fine Royal Doulton porcelain seafarers. *503 E. River St. and 504 E. Bay St., tel. 912/232–1511. Admission: $2 adults, 75¢ children 7–12. Open daily 10–5. Closed major holidays.*

8 If you entered the museum at the River Street entrance and worked your way up all four floors, you'll be topside again on Bay Street. The tree-shaded park along Bay Street is **Emmet Park,** named for Robert Emmet, a late 18th-century Irish patriot and orator. Walk west along Bay Street and turn left onto

Abercorn Street. In **Reynolds Square** you'll see the statue of John Wesley, who preached in Savannah and wrote the first English hymnal here in 1736. The monument to the founder of the Methodist Church is shaded by greenery and surrounded by park benches. On the square is the **Olde Pink House** (23 Abercorn St.). Built in 1771, it is one of the oldest buildings in town. The porticoed pink stucco Georgian mansion has been a private home, a bank, and headquarters for a Yankee general during the war. It is now a restaurant (*see* Dining).

From Reynolds Square walk south on Abercorn Street, turn left onto Broughton Street, and two blocks down turn right onto Habersham Street. This will bring you to the **Isaiah Davenport House.** Semicircular stairs with wrought-iron trim lead to the recessed doorway of the red-brick Georgian mansion that master builder Isaiah Davenport built for himself in 1815. Three dormer windows poke through the sloping roof of the stately house, and inside there are polished hardwood floors, fine woodwork and plasterwork, and a soaring elliptical staircase. The furnishings are Hepplewhite, Chippendale, and Sheraton, and in the attic there is a collection of antique dolls and a dollhouse with tiny 19th-century furnishings. *324 E. State St., tel. 912/236–8097. Admission: $2.50 adults, $1.25 children. Open Mon.–Sat. 10–4:30, Sun. 1:30–4:30.*

Walk west on State Street two blocks to the **Owens-Thomas House.** This was William Jay's first Regency mansion in Savannah, built in 1817, and it is the city's finest example of that architectural style. The thoroughly English house was built largely with local materials, including tabby—a mixture of oyster shells, sand, and water that resembles concrete. The entry portico is of Doric design with curving stairs leading to a recessed door topped by a fanlight. Of particular note are the curving walls of the house, Greek-inspired ornamental molding, Jay's half-moon arches, stained-glass panels, and Duncan Phyfe furniture. You'll see hoopskirt chairs (whose short arms accommodated the circular skirts of many Southern belles), canopied beds, a pianoforte, and displays of ornate silver. From a wrought-iron balcony, in 1825, the Marquis de Lafayette bade a two-hour au revoir to the crowd below. *124 Abercorn St., tel. 912/233–9743. Admission: $3 adults; $2 students; $1 children 6–12, under 6 free.*

Stroll through **Oglethorpe Square,** across State Street, and continue two blocks west to **Wright Square.** The square was named for James Wright, Georgia's last Colonial governor. Centerpiece of the square is an elaborate monument erected in honor of William Washington Gordon, founder of the Central of Georgia Railroad. A slab of granite from Stone Mountain marks the grave of Tomo-Chi-Chi, the Yamacraw chief who befriended General Oglethorpe and the colonists.

Continue west on State Street, strolling, if you like, through **Telfair Square** to reach the **Telfair Mansion and Art Museum.** The South's oldest public art museum is housed in yet another of Jay's Regency creations, this one designed in 1819. Within its marbled halls there are American, French, and German Impressionist paintings; a large collection of works by Kahlil Gibran; plaster casts of the Elgin Marbles, the Venus de Milo, and the Laocoön, among other classical sculptures; and a room that contains some of the Telfair family furnishings, including a Duncan Phyfe sideboard and Savannah-made silver. The mansion is also notable for Jay's distinctive moldings, cornices, and mantlepieces. *121 Barnard St., tel. 912/232–1177. Admission: $2.50 adults, $1 students, 50¢ children 6–12; free on Sun. Open Tues.–Sat. 10–5, Sun. 2–5.*

⑬ At the next corner, turn left onto Oglethorpe Avenue and cross Bull Street to reach the **Juliette Gordon Low House.** This majestic Regency mansion is attributed to William Jay (and why not?) and in 1965 was designated Savannah's first National Historic Landmark. "Daisy" Low, founder of the Girl Scouts, was born here, and the house is now owned and operated by the Girl Scouts of America. Mrs. Low was also an artist, and her paintings and other artworks are on display in the house, along with original family furnishings of the 19th century. *142 Bull St., tel. 912/233–4501. Admission: $2.25 adults, $1.25 children, discounts for Girl Scouts. Open Mon.–Sat. 10–4, Sun. 12:30–4:30. Closed every Wed., and Sun. in Dec. and Jan.*

⑭ **Chippewa Square** is a straight shot south on Bull Street. There you can see the imposing bronze statue of the general himself, James Edward Oglethorpe.

⑮ From Chippewa Square, go east on McDonough Street to reach the **Colonial Park Cemetery.** Savannahians were buried here from 1750 to 1853. Shaded pathways lace through the park, and you may want to stroll through and read some of the old inscriptions. There are several historical plaques in the cemetery, one of which marks the grave of Button Gwinnett, a signer of the Declaration of Independence.

⑯ The **Cathedral of St. John the Baptist** soars like a hymn over the corner of Abercorn and Harris streets, two blocks south of the cemetery. The French Gothic cathedral, with the pointed arches and free-flowing traceries characteristic of the style, is the seat of the Diocese of Savannah. It is the oldest Roman Catholic church in Georgia, having been founded in the early 1700s. Fire destroyed the early structures, and the present cathedral dates from the late 19th century. Most of the cathedral's impressive stained-glass windows were made by Austrian glassmakers and imported around the turn of the century. The high altar is of Italian marble, and the Stations of the Cross were imported from Munich.

⑰ Across from the cathedral is **Lafayette Square,** named for the Marquis de Lafayette. The graceful three-tier fountain in the square was donated by the Georgia chapter of the Colonial Dames of America.

⑱ Across the square is the **Andrew Low House.** The house was built for Andrew Low in 1849, and later belonged to his son William, who married Juliette Gordon. After her husband's death, "Daisy" Low founded the Girl Scouts in this house on March 12, 1912. Robert E. Lee and William Thackeray were both entertained in this mansion. In addition to its historical significance, the house boasts some of the finest ornamental ironwork in Savannah. Members and friends of the Colonial Dames have donated fine 19th-century antiques and stunning silver to the house. *329 Abercorn St. Admission: $2 adults, $1 students, 75¢ children and Girl Scouts. Open daily 10:30–4:30. Closed Christmas, Thanksgiving, and New Years.*

⑲ Two blocks to the west is **Madison Square,** laid out in 1839 and named for James Madison. The statue depicts Sergeant William Jasper hoisting a flag and is a tribute to his bravery during the Siege of Savannah. Though mortally wounded, he rescued the colors of his regiment in the assault on the British lines.

20 On the west side of the square is the **Green-Meldrim House,** designed by New York architect John Norris and built about 1850 for cotton merchant Charles Green. The house was bought in 1892 by Judge Peter Meldrim, hence the hyphenated name. Meldrim's heirs sold the house to St. John's Episcopal Church, for which it is now the parish house. It was here that General Sherman established residence after taking the city in 1864. Here the general lived in a splendid Gothic Revival mansion, complete with crenelated roof and oriel windows. The gallery that sweeps around three sides of the house is awash with filigreed ironwork. The mantles are Carrara marble, the woodwork is carved black walnut, and the doorknobs and hinges are silver-plated. There is a magnificent skylight above a gracefully curved staircase. The house is furnished with 16th- and 17th-century antiques. *On Madison Sq. Admission: $2.50. Open Tues., Thurs., Fri., and Sat. 10–4. Closed during special church functions.*

Time Out Students from the Savannah College of Art and Design buy art supplies and books at **Design Works Bookstore.** There is also a soda fountain and tables in this old Victorian drugstore, where you can get short orders, burgers, and deli sandwiches. *Corner of Bull and Charlton Sts., tel. 912/238–2481. Open Mon.– Thurs. 8–8, Fri. and Sat. 9–4.*

The fifth and last of Bull Street's squares is **Monterey Square,** which commemorates the victory of General Zachary Taylor's forces in Monterey, Mexico, in 1846. The square's monument honors General Casimir Pulaski, the Polish nobleman and Revolutionary War hero who lost his life during the Siege of Savannah.

21 On the east side of the square stands **Temple Mickve Israel,** which was consecrated in 1878. Five months after the founding of Savannah, a group of Spanish and German Jews arrived, bringing with them the prized "Sephar Torah" that is in the present temple. The splendid Gothic Revival synagogue contains a collection of documents and letters pertaining to early Jewish life in Savannah and Georgia. *20 E. Gordon St. Admission free. Open weekdays 10–noon.*

22 A block east of the temple is a Gothic Revival church memorializing the founders of Methodism. The **Wesley Monumental Church,** patterned after Queen's Kirk in Amsterdam, celebrated a century of service in 1968. The church is noted for its magnificent stained-glass windows. In the Wesley Window there are busts of John and Charles Wesley.

23 At the **Massie Heritage Interpretation Center,** in addition to a scale model of the city, maps and plans, and architectural displays, is a "Heritage Classroom" that offers schoolchildren hands-on instruction about early Colonial life. *207 E. Gordon St., tel. 912/651–7380. Admission free, but a donation of $1.50 is appreciated. Open weekdays 9–4:30, weekends by appointment.*

24 The southern anchor of Bull Street is **Forsyth Park,** with 20 luxuriant acres. The glorious white fountain, dating from 1858, was restored in 1988. In addition to its Confederate and Spanish-American War memorials, the park contains the Fragrant Garden for the Blind, a project of Savannah garden clubs. There are also tennis courts and a tree-shaded jogging path. The park is often the scene of outdoor plays and picnic concerts.

The Victorian District
The **King-Tisdell Cottage,** perched behind a picket fence, is a museum dedicated to the preservation of black history and culture. The Negro Heritage Trail (*see* Special-Interest Tours) begins here, in this little Victorian house. Broad steps lead to a porch that's loaded with gewgaws, and dormer windows pop up through a steep roof. The interior is furnished to resemble a late 19th-century black coastal home. *514 E. Huntingdon St., tel. 912/234–8000. Admission: $1.50 adults, 50¢ children. Open weekdays noon–4.*

Other houses of interest in the Victorian district are at **118 E. Waldburg Street** and **111 W. Gwinnett Street.** A stroll along **Bolton Street** will be especially rewarding for fans of fanciful architecture. Of particular note is the entire 200 block, 114 W. Bolton Street, 109 W. Bolton Street, and 321 E. Bolton Street.

Day-tripping to Tybee Island

Tybee Island, which lies 18 miles east of Savannah right on the Atlantic Ocean, offers all manner of water and beach activities. The drive to Tybee takes about a half hour, and there are two historic forts to visit on the way.

To reach Tybee Island, drive east on Victory Drive (U.S. 80) all the way to the Atlantic. (The highway sometimes goes under the alias of Tybee Road.)

Fort Pulaski is 15 miles east of downtown Savannah. You'll see the entrance on your left just before Tybee Road reaches Tybee Island. A must for Civil War buffs, the fort was built on Cockspur Island between 1829 and 1847, and named for General Casimir Pulaski. Robert E. Lee's first assignment after graduating from West Point was as an engineer here. During the Civil War the fort fell on April 12, 1862, after a mere 30 hours of bombardment by newfangled rifled cannons. It was the first time such cannons had been used in warfare—and the last time a masonry fort was thought to be impregnable. The restored fortification, operated by the National Park Service, is complete with moats, drawbridges, massive ramparts, and towering walls. There is an interpretive center that offers historical demonstrations, self-guided trails, and ample picnic areas. *U.S. 80, tel. 912/786–5787. Admission: $2 adults, $1.50 students, senior citizens, and military. Open daily 8:30–5:15 in winter; 8:30–6:45 in summer. Closed Christmas and New Year's.*

Three miles farther along U.S. 80 is **Tybee Island.** "Tybee" is an Indian word meaning salt. The Yamacraw Indians came to the island to hunt and fish, and legend has it that pirates buried their treasure here.

The island is about five miles long and two miles wide, with a plethora of seafood restaurants, chain motels, condos, and shops. The entire expanse of white sand is divided into a number of public beaches, where visitors go shelling and crabbing, play on waterslides, charter fishing boats, swim, or just build sand castles.

The **Tybee Museum and Lighthouse** are at the very tip of the island. In the museum you'll see Indian artifacts, pirate pistols, powder flasks, old prints tracing the history of Savannah, even some sheet music of Johnny Mercer songs. The Civil War Room has old maps and newspaper articles pertaining to Sherman's occupation of the city. On the second floor there are model antique cars and ship models, and a collection of antique dolls. The lighthouse across the road is Georgia's oldest and tallest, dating from 1773, with an observation deck 145 feet above the sea. Bright red steps—178 of them—lead to the deck and the awesome Tybee Light. The view of the ocean will take away whatever breath you have left after the climb. *Meddin Dr. and the jumping off place, tel. 912/786-4077. Admission to both lighthouse and museum: $1 adults, 50¢ children 6–12. Museum open daily in summer 10–6; in winter weekdays 1–5, weekends 10–5. Lighthouse open daily in summer 1–5; in winter Thurs.–Mon. 1–5.*

Time Out **Spanky's Pizza Galley & Saloon,** overlooking the beach, has seafood platters, burgers, chicken dishes, and salads. *404 Butler Dr., tel. 912/786-5520. AE, MC, V. Open daily 11 AM–midnight.*

Heading west back to Savannah, take the Islands Expressway, which becomes the President Street Extension. About 3½ miles outside the city you'll see a sign for **Fort Jackson,** located on Salter's Island. The Colonial fort was purchased in 1808 by the federal government, and is the oldest standing fort in Georgia. It was garrisoned in 1812, and was the Confederate headquarters of the river batteries. The brick fort is surrounded by a tidal moat, and there are 13 exhibit areas. Battle reenactments, blacksmithing demonstrations, and programs of 19th-century music are among the fort's schedule of activities. The Trooping of the Colors and military tattoo take place at regular intervals during summer. *1 Ft. Jackson Rd., tel. 912/232-3945. Admission: $1.75 adults, $1.25 students, senior citizens, and military. Open Mar.–Nov., Tues.–Sun. 9–5; Dec.–Feb., weekends 9–5.*

Savannah for Free

Beach at Tybee Island (*see* Exploring).
There are many **celebrations** in Savannah, and most of them take place on River Street. Arts and crafts displays, music, and entertainment are always part of special events such as the February Georgia Day Festival, Oktoberfest, the Great American 4th of July, the Seafood-Fest, and First Saturday festivals every month. About 40,000 greenish folk flock to Riverfront Plaza after the St. Patrick's Day parade. Contact the Savannah Visitors Center (*see* Important Addresses and Numbers).
Free Concerts are given during summer months in Johnson Square (*see* Arts).
Oatland Island Education Center. Located only 15 minutes from downtown Savannah, this 175-acre maritime forest is not only a natural habitat for coastal wildlife (including timber wolves and panthers), it also offers environmental education for visitors. The center also houses the coastal offices of the

Georgia Conservancy. *711 Sandtown Rd., tel 912/897–3733. Open weekdays 8:30–5; Second Saturday events Oct.–May.*

Savannah Young People's Theater (*see* What to See and Do with Children).

Skidaway Island Marine Science Complex. On the grounds of the former Modena Plantation, the complex features a 12-panel, 12,000-gallon aquarium with marine and plant life of the Continental Shelf. Other exhibits highlight archaeological discoveries and undersea life of the Georgia coast. *McWhorter Dr., Skidaway Island, tel. 912/356–2496. Open weekdays 9–4, weekends noon–5.*

Telfair Mansion and Museum charges no admission on Sundays (*see* Exploring).

Watch the parade of ships on the Savannah River.

What to See and Do with Children

Community Children's Theater (tel. 912/233–9321, ext. 132) performs puppet shows, marionette shows, and live plays especially for children; performances are given at various locations.

Explore Savannah, Inc. (418 E. State St., tel. 912/354–4560 or 912/233–5238) designs individualized activity packages and tours for children ages 4–16. Professional guides conduct full- or half-day tours, and ticket prices, which start at $10, include transportation, meals, and snacks.

Fort Pulaski and Jackson (*see* Exploring).

Juliette Gordon Low Girl Scout National Center (*see* Exploring).

Oatland Island Education Center (*see* Savannah for Free).

Exhibits at the **Savannah Science Museum** include live and mounted reptiles and amphibians, a "walk-in" human heart and mouth, a solar energy unit, Indian artifacts, plans, and planetarium shows. *4405 Paulsen St., tel. 912/355–6705. Admission: $1 adults, 50¢ children. Open Tues.–Sat. 10–5, Sun. 2–5; planetarium shows weekends at 3 PM.*

Tybee Island Museum and Lighthouse (*see* Exploring).

Off the Beaten Track

If your tastebuds are fixin' for real down-home barbecue, head for **Wall's.** There's a counter where you place your order and a couple of orange plastic booths. Entertainment is provided by a small black-and-white TV set. You reach in the refrigerator case to get your canned beverage, and your food comes served in Styrofoam cartons. A sign taped up over the counter reads, "When I work, I works hard. When I sit, I sits loose—when I think, I falls asleep." Plain? Not really. There is richness in them thar barbecued spare ribs, barbecued sandwiches, and deviled crabs (the three items make up the entire menu. A large carton of ribs costs $7. *515 E. York Ln., between Oglethorpe Ave. and York St., tel. 912/232–9754. Dress: bibs. No credit cards. Open Thurs. 11–10, Fri. and Sat. 11–11.*

Shopping

Regional wares to look for are handcrafted items from the Low Country—handmade quilts and baskets; wreaths made from Chinese tallow trees and Spanish moss; preserves, jams, and jellies. The favorite Savannah snack, and a popular gift item, is the benne wafer. It's about the size of a quarter and comes in a variety of flavors.

Shopping Districts **Riverfront Plaza/River Street** is nine blocks of shops housed in the renovated waterfront warehouses, where you can find everything from popcorn to pottery. **City Market**, located on West St. Julian Street between Ellis and Franklin squares, has sidewalk cafes, jazz haunts, shops, and art galleries. If you're in need of anything from aspirin to anklets, head for **Broughton Street** and wander through its many variety and specialty stores.

Savannah's major suburban shopping mall is **Oglethorpe Mall** (7804 Abercorn St. Ext.). The enclosed center has four department stores (Sears, Penney's, Belk, and Maas Bros./Jordan Marsh) and over 100 specialty shops, fast-food, and full-service restaurants.

Specialty Shops **Arthur Smith** (1 W. Jones St., tel. 912/236–9701) houses four
Antiques floors of 18th- and 19th-century furniture. At **Nostalgia Station** (307 Stiles Ave., tel. 912/236–8176) you can get some of Savannah's architecture to go—beveled and stained glass, brackets, ornamental accent pieces. They'll crate and deliver it for you, too. The best in bronzes, silver, crystal, and antique jewelry can be found at **Coachlight Antiques** (423-B Bull St., tel. 912/ 234–4081).

Artwork **Exhibit A** (342 Bull St., tel. 912/238–2480), the gallery of the Savannah College of Art and Design, has hand-painted cards, handmade jewelry, and paintings by regional artists. **Gallery 209** (209 E. River St., tel. 912/236–4583) is a co-op gallery with paintings, watercolors, and sculptures by local artists.

Benne Wafers You can buy boxed bennes in most gift shops, but **The Cooky Shanty** (2233 Norwood Ave., tel. 912/355–1716) is where they originated. You can buy them and watch them being made here.

Books The nine rooms of **E. Shaver's** (326 Bull St., tel. 912/234–7257) bookstore, are stocked with books on architecture and regional history, as well as used and rare books. **The Book Lady** (17 W. York St., tel. 912/233–3628) specializes in used, rare, and out-of-print books; it also provides a search service.

Country Crafts **Callaway Gardens Country Store** (301 E. River St., tel. 912/236–4055) carries lots of gift-packaged preserves and jellies, sauces, bacon and hams, cookbooks, and gifts. At **Charlotte's Corner** (1 W. Liberty St., tel. 912/233–8061) there are handmade quilts and baskets made from quilts, regional cookbooks, aprons, and Savannah-made potpourris. **Mulberry Tree** (17 W. Charlton St., tel. 912/236–4656) is another crafty shop for handmade quilts and baskets, antique dolls, jams, jellies, preserves, and wreaths.

Participant Sports

Bicycling Pedaling is a breeze on these flatlands. The **Historic Savannah Foundations** (tel. 912/233–3597) provides rental bikes at the DeSoto Hilton Hotel (Bull and Liberty Sts.) and the Hyatt Regency Hotel (2 W. Bay St.).

Bird-watching, **Palmetto Coast Charters** takes small groups to the barrier is-
Crabbing, Shelling lands (Box 536, Tybee Island 31328, tel. 912/786–5403). **Coastal Island Cruises** takes in Tybee, Little Tybee, Cockspur, and

Wilmington islands (525 Quarterman Dr., on Wilmington Island, behind Palmer's Seafood Restaurant at Turner's Creek, tel. 912/897–1604).

Boating Boats can be rented at **Bellaire Woods Campground,** 2½ miles west of I-95 on GA 204 (15 mi from downtown Savannah, tel. 912/748–4000) and at **Water Way RV Park** on the Ogeechee River (U.S. 17, tel. 912/756–2296). Pedal boats can be rented for pedaling around **Lake Mayer** (Lake Mayer Park, Sallie Mood Dr. and Montgomery Crossroads Dr., tel. 912/352–1660). There are public boat ramps at **Bell's Landing** on the Forest River (Apache Rd. off Abercorn St.); **Islands Expressway** on the Wilmington River (Islands Expressway adjacent to Frank W. Spencer Park); and **Savannah Marina** on the Wilmington River in the town of Thunderbolt.

Golf There's a 27-hole course at **Bacon Park** (Skidaway Rd., tel. 912/354–2625), and a 9-hole course at **Mary Calder Park** (Bay St. Ext., tel. 912/238–7100).

Health Clubs The following private clubs are open to guests for a fee:

Savannah Downtown Athletic Club (7 E. Congress St., tel. 912/236–4874). Nautilus and free-weight equipment, whirlpool, sauna, aerobics, and karate classes.

Racquet Plus (4 Oglethorpe Professional Bldg., tel. 912/355–3070). Racquetball courts, Nautilus equipment, whirlpool, and sauna.

YMCA Family Center (6400 Habersham St., tel. 912/354–6223). Gymnasium, exercise classes, pool, and tennis—for men and women.

Jewish Educational Alliance (5111 Abercorn St., tel. 912/355–8111). Racquetball courts, gymnasium, weight room, sauna, steam, whirlpool, and aerobic dance classes.

Jogging Flat-as-a-pancake **Forsyth Park** is a favorite jogging path, with plenty of shade trees and benches. The beach at **Tybee Island** is another great favorite of joggers. Suburbanites favor the jogging trails in **Lake Mayer Park** (Montgomery Crossroads Rd. at Sallie Mood Dr.) and **Daffin Park** (1500 E. Victory Dr.).

Tennis There are 14 lighted courts in **Bacon Park** (Skidaway Rd., tel. 912/354–5925); four lighted courts in **Forsyth Park** (Drayton and Gaston Sts., tel. 912/352–1660); and eight lighted courts in **Lake Mayer Park** (Montgomery Crossroads Rd. and Sallie Mood Dr., tel. 912/352–9915).

Dining

Situated on a river, 18 miles inland from the Atlantic Ocean, Savannah naturally has excellent seafood restaurants. Barbecue is also a local favorite, and there are a number of Continental restaurants as well. The Historic District is loaded with eateries, especially along River Street. Savannahians also like to drive out to eat in Thunderbolt and on Skidaway, Tybee, and Wilmington Islands.

The most highly recommended restaurants in each price category are indicated by a star ★.

Category	Cost*
Very Expensive	over $30
Expensive	$25–$30
Moderate	$15–$25
Inexpensive	under $15

*per person without tax, service, or drinks

The following credit-card abbreviations are used: AE, American Express; CB, Carte Blanche; DC, Diners Club; MC, MasterCard; V, Visa.

American
Very Expensive

Olde Pink House. The brick Georgian mansion, built for James Habersham in 1771, is one of Savannah's oldest structures. The cozily elegant tavern has original Georgia pine floors and crystal chandeliers, and antique furniture that was shipped from England. Cocktails are served below in the romantic Planters Tavern, where black leather chairs are pulled up around an open fireplace in the wintertime. Veal Thomas Jefferson is a sautéed cutlet topped with fresh crabmeat and béarnaise sauce, and garnished with asparagus and shrimp. "Mr. and Mrs. Habersham's Dinner," purportedly the favorite dinner of the original occupants, begins with a shrimp appetizer and moves on to black-turtle bean soup, salad, "an intermission of sorbet," chateaubriand carved tableside, and a dessert. *23 Abercorn St., tel. 912/232–4286. Jacket and tie required for dinner. Reservations suggested for dinner. AE, DC, MC, V.*

Expensive
★

45 South. This was a popular southside eatery that moved in 1988 to the sprawling Pirates' House complex. 45 South is a small, stylish restaurant with contemporary decor in lush mauve and green Savannah colors. There is a changing menu that might include lunch entrees of grilled marinated swordfish steak served with a bean, asparagus, and radicchio salad; or medallions of pork tenderloin with grilled onions, peppers, and rosemary. Dinner entrees include peppered breast of duck with acorn squash and fresh spinach; and trout with a ragout of zucchini and basil. *20 E. Broad St., tel. 912/354–0444. Jacket and tie required. Reservations accepted. MC, V.*

Inexpensive
★

Crystal Beer Parlor. A comfortable family tavern famed for hamburgers, thick-cut french fries, onion rings, and frosted mugs of draft beer. The menu also offers fried oyster sandwiches, gumbo, and shrimp salad. *301 W. Jones St. at Jefferson St., tel. 912/232–1153. Dress: informal. No reservations. No credit cards.*

★

Mrs. Wilkes Boarding House. There's no sign out front, but you won't have any trouble finding this famed establishment. At breakfast time and noon (no dinner is served) there are long lines of folks waiting to get in for a culinary orgy. Charles Kuralt and David Brinkley are among the celebrities who have feasted on the fine Southern food, served at big family-style tables. For breakfast there are eggs, sausage, piping hot biscuits, and grits. At lunch, bowl after bowl is passed around the table. Fried or roast chicken, collard greens, okra, mashed potatoes, cornbread, biscuits—the dishes just keep coming. *107 W. Jones St., tel. 912/232–5997. Dress: informal. No reservations. No credit cards.*

Dining

Crystal Beer Parlor, **1**
45 South, **18**
LaToque, **20**
Mrs. Wilkes Boarding House, **5**
Olde Pink House, **15**
Pirates' House, **19**
River House, **4**
Shrimp Factory, **12**

Lodging

Ballastone Inn, **10**
Days Inn, **3**
DeSoto Hilton, **11**
Eliza Thompson House, **9**
Foley House, **8**
Forsyth Park Inn, **6**
The Gastonian, **16**
Hyatt, **7**
Jesse Mount House, **2**
The Mulberry, **17**
Olde Harbour Inn, **13**
River Street Inn, **14**

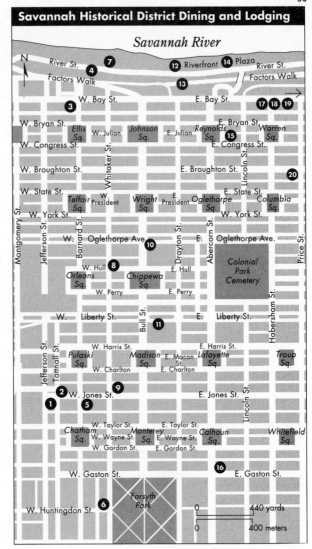

Savannah Historical District Dining and Lodging

Savannah River

Continental	**LaToque.** Swiss-born owner/chef Christian Bigler prepares

Continental
Moderate–Expensive
★

LaToque. Swiss-born owner/chef Christian Bigler prepares fish, shellfish, veal, duckling, and pork in traditional European style, with rich brandy, wine, and cream sauces. The dining room has an understated elegance, with starched white tablecloths and dark red decor. *420 E. Broughton St., tel. 912/ 238–0138. Jacket and tie required. Reservations accepted. AE, MC, V. Closed Sun.*

Seafood
Expensive
★

Elizabeth on 37th. Elizabeth and Michael Terry's restaurant is in an elegant turn-of-the-century mansion, with hardwood floors and spacious rooms. Elizabeth is the chef, called by *Town & Country* magazine, "One of America's great new women chefs." Among her specialties is flounder Elizabeth, a filet broiled in a crab, cream, and sherry sauce. While the emphasis is on sea creatures served in delicate sauces, there are other excellent offerings, including steak au poivre, quail, lamb, and chicken dishes. *105 E. 37th St., tel. 912/236–5547. Jacket and tie required. Reservations suggested for dinner. AE, MC, V. Closed Sun.*

Pirates' House. You'll probably start hearing about the Pirates' House about 10 minutes after you hit town. There are all sorts of legends about it involving shanghaied sailors and ghosts. It's a sprawling complex with nautical and piratical trappings, and 23 rooms with names like The Jolly Roger and The Black Hole; children love the place. The menu is almost as big as the building, with heavy emphasis on sea critters. For starters there are oysters, escargots, and soft-shell crabs. The large portions of gumbo and seafood bisque come in iron kettles. Flounder Belle Franklin is crabmeat, shrimp, and filet of flounder baked in butter with herbs and wines and a glaze of cheeses and toasted almonds. You can pick out your live Maine lobster from a big saltwater tank. There are 40 listings on the dessert menu; try the warm chocolate-chip pie topped with whipped cream. The large bar upstairs has a ceiling all a-twinkle with ersatz stars. *20 E. Broad St., tel. 912/233–5757. Dress: informal. Reservations accepted. AE, CB, DC, MC, V. Sun. jazz brunch.*

Moderate–Expensive **River House.** This stylish restaurant sits over the spot where the SS *Savannah* set sail for her maiden voyage across the ocean in 1819. For starters try the snails wrapped in puff pastry, baked and served with beurre blanc sauce; or oysters on the half shell. There are a number of mesquite-grilled entrees, including swordfish topped with raspberry butter sauce and grouper Florentine, served with creamed spinach and a fresh dill and lemon butter sauce. Entrees are served with hush puppies, and fish dishes come with freshly made angel-hair pasta. *125 W. River St., tel. 912/234–1900. Dress: informal for lunch; jacket and tie required for dinner. Reservations accepted. AE, DC, MC, V.*

Inexpensive–Moderate **Seashell House.** It may not look like much from the outside, but the steamed seafood inside is regarded by many to be the best in the city. It specializes in crab, shrimp and oysters, as well as a Low Country Boil that includes shrimp, sausage, corn, and whatever else comes to mind that day. It also features a seafood platter second to none. Be prepared to roll up your sleeves and dig in. *3111 Skidaway Rd., tel. 912/352–8116. Dress: casual. No reservations. AE, MC, V.*

★

Shrimp Factory. Like all riverfront restaurants, this was once an old warehouse. Now it's a light and airy place with exposed brick, wood paneling, beamed ceilings, and huge windows that let you watch the parade of ships on the water. A house specialty is pine bark stew—five native seafoods simmered with potatoes, onions, and herbs, and served with blueberry muffins. The extensive lunch and dinner menus have few offerings that don't come from the sea. Blackened dolphin filet is smothered with herbs and julienned sweet red peppers in butter sauce. Baked deviled crabs are served with chicken baked rice. Fish entrees are accompanied by angel-hair pasta, and there is a delicious whipped cheese spread for the warm French bread. *313 E. River St., tel. 912/236–4229. Dress: informal. Reservations accepted. AE, DC, MC, V.*

Lodging

While Savannah has plenty of chain hotels and motels, ranging from the simple to the sublime, the city's most distinctive lodgings are the historic inns. There are more than two dozen historic inns, guest houses, and bed-and-breakfasts in the Historic District.

If "historic inn" brings to your mind images of roughing it in picturesque but shabby genteel mansions with slightly antiquated plumbing, you're in for a surprise. Most of the inns are in mansions, most of them with high ceilings, spacious rooms, and ornate carved millwork. Most have canopied, four-poster, or Victorian brass beds and 19th-century antiques. Most of them *also* have enormous marble baths with whirlpools, hot tubs, or Jacuzzis (if not all of the above), and many of them have a film library for the in-room VCRs. Virtually all have turndown service with a chocolate or praline and, in some, a discreet brandy is placed on your nightstand. In most cases, Continental breakfast and afternoon aperitifs are included in the rate.

The most highly recommended properties in each price category are indicated by a star ★.

Category	Cost*
Very Expensive	over $100
Expensive	$75–$100
Moderate	$50–$75
Inexpensive	under $50

double room; add taxes or service

The following credit-card abbreviations are used: AE, American Express; CB, Carte Blanche; DC, Diners Club; MC, MasterCard; V, Visa.

Inns and Guest Houses
Very Expensive
★
Ballastone Inn. This sumptuous inn is located within a mansion, dating from 1835, that was once, so it is said, a bordello. The Ballastone is notable for the wildly dramatic designs of its Scalamandre wallpaper and fabrics, which show off the Savannah colors to full advantage. Each of the 19 rooms has a different theme, with distinctive colors, ambience, and 18th-or 19th-century antiques. In Scarborough Fair, a vivid red and yellow room, the fabric pattern was adapted from a Victorian china serving platter in the Davenport House. That exquisite third-floor room has two queen-size Victorian brass beds, a Queen Anne lowboy and writing desk, and a Victorian slipper chair. On the garden level (there are three stories in addition to the garden level), rooms are small and cozy, with exposed brick walls, beamed ceilings, and in some cases windows at eye level with the lush courtyard. One such room is the Sorghum Cane, trimmed in the bronze color of sugar cane molasses; it has two queen-size brass beds, wicker furniture, and wall fabric patterned after the etched glass window of a restored local house. Afternoon tea or wine served daily; bedtime turn-downs with chocolate and brandy. *14 E. Oglethorpe Ave., 31401, tel. 912/236–1484. 19 rooms with bath.   Facilities: con-*

cierge, courtyard, Jacuzzis, in-room VCR, film library. AE, MC, V.

Foley House. In the parlor of this four-story 1896 house, carved gargoyles flank the original fireplace and there is a graceful brass-and-crystal chandelier. On the newel post in the hall there is an elaborate lamp that worked as an extra in *Gone With the Wind*. There are four rooms in the carriage house and 16 spacious rooms (four with Jacuzzis) in the main house, all with canopied or four-poster beds, polished hardwood floors covered with Oriental rugs, and 19th-century antiques. There is a splendid tapestry in the Essex Room (an especially romantic room with a balcony on Chippewa Square), a king-size bed and day bed, and an extra large bath with whirlpool. When you call to reserve, ask about the special package deals. *14 W. Hull St., 31401, tel. 912/232-6622, in GA 800/822-4658, outside GA 800/647-3708. 20 rooms with bath. Facilities: concierge, courtyard with hot tub, VCRs, film library. AE, MC, V.*

★ **The Gastonian.** Hugh and Roberta Lineberger's inn will probably, to put it modestly, knock your socks off. The mansion was built in 1868, and each of its 13 sumptuous suites is distinguished with vivid Scalamandre colors. The Caracalla Suite is named for the marble bath with an eight-foot whirlpool tub. The huge bedroom has a king-size canopy bed, working fireplace, and a lounge with a mirrored wet bar. The French Room, resembling a 19th-century French boudoir, is done in blues and whites, with Oriental rugs and flocked wallpaper. All rooms have working fireplaces and antiques from the Georgian and Regency periods. In the morning, a full breakfast is served in the formal dining room—pancakes, eggs, waffles, country ham, grits, fresh fruit, biscuits, and juice—or you can opt for a Continental breakfast in your room. Each guest receives a fruit basket and split of wine upon arrival. *220 E. Gaston St., 31401, tel. 912/232-2869. 13 suites with bath. Facilities: concierge, VCRs, film library, whirlpools, courtyard, and sun deck with hot tub. AE, MC, V.*

Expensive–
Very Expensive **Olde Harbour Inn.** The building dates from 1892, when it was built on the riverfront as a warehouse and processing plant, but the old inn is actually a thoroughly modern facility that housed condos until 1987. Each suite has a fully equipped kitchen, including dishwasher and detergent. All suites overlook the river, and have wall-to-wall carpeting, exposed brick walls painted white, and a canopied or four-poster bed. There are studio suites; regular suites with living room, bedroom, kitchen, and bath; and loft suites. (The latter are lofty indeed, with 25-foot ceilings, balconies overlooking the water, huge skylights, and ample room to sleep six.) Each evening a dish of sherbet is brought to your room and placed in the freezer, and each morning croissants, blueberry muffins, juice, and coffee are served in a cozy breakfast room. *508 E. Factors Walk, 31401, tel. 912/234-4100 or 800/553-6533. 24 suites with bath. Facilities: concierge, room service, fully equipped kitchen, cable TV with remote control, VCR, film library, honor bar, valet laundry, and parking. AE, MC, V.*

Expensive **Eliza Thompson House.** This 25-room guest house, located on
★ one of the Historic District's prettiest tree-lined streets, was originally built in 1847 for "Miss Eliza." There are king- and queen-size four-poster and canopied beds; some rooms with wall-to-wall carpeting, others with Oriental rugs covering the

Georgia pine floors. The choice rooms overlook the large brick courtyard, which is a popular place for wedding receptions. In nice weather the complimentary breakfast is served at tables placed around a tiered fountain. *5 W. Jones St., 31401, tel. 912/ 236–3620 or 800/845–7638. 25 rooms with bath. Facilities: concierge. AE, MC, V.*

★ **Forsyth Park Inn.** As the name suggests, this Victorian mansion sits across the street from Forsyth Park. In the foyer is a grand piano, and afternoon wines and cheeses are taken to the accompaniment of Mercer and Gershwin music. Rooms are outfitted with 19th-century furnishings, including king- and queen-size four-poster beds, and have working fireplaces, large marble baths (some with whirlpools). The carriage house, just off the courtyard, has a suite with bath, complete kitchen, and a screened porch. *109 W. Hall St., 31401, tel. 912/ 233–6800. 9 rooms with private bath; 1 private guest cottage. AE, V, MC.*

Bed-and-Breakfast **Jesse Mount House.** The Georgian home of Lois and Howard
Expensive Crawford (the house is named for the original owner in 1854)
★ has two full floors for guests, one on the garden level and the other on the second floor. The three-bedroom suite on the upper level has a sunny sitting room with white-iron furniture, shower-bath, refrigerator and coffeemaker, wineglasses, and dishes; two of the bedrooms have fireplaces with gas logs. Breakfast (freshly squeezed orange juice, croissants, blueberry muffins, coffee) can be taken either in your own quarters or with the Crawfords in the formal dining room. *209 W. Jones St., 31401, tel. 912/236–1774. 2 3-bedroom suites with bath. Facilities: cable TV, private phones. No credit cards.*

R.S.V.P. Savannah (417 E. Charlton St., 31401, tel. 912/232–RSVP) is a bed-and-breakfast service that can reserve accommodations for you in Savannah, Tybee, and the surrounding area.

Hotels and Motels **DeSoto Hilton.** Three massive chandeliers glisten over the jar-
Expensive– dinieres, fresh flowers, and discreetly placed conversation
Very Expensive areas of the spacious lobby. The chandeliers are from the his-
★ toric DeSoto Hotel that stood on this site long ago. Guest rooms are on the cushy side, in Savannah peach and green, with wall-to-wall carpeting, traditional furniture, and king, queen, or two double beds. (Best view is from the corner kings, which have the added attraction of coffeemakers, refrigerators, and such). Suites have kitchens and custom-made contemporary furnishings in the bedroom, sitting room, and dining area. *15 E. Liberty St., 31401, tel. 912/232–9000 or 800/445–8667. 254 rooms; 9 suites with bath. Facilities: concierge, free parking, restaurant and lounge, outdoor pool with sundeck, golf and tennis privileges at area clubs. AE, CB, DC, MC.*

Hyatt. When this riverfront hotel was built in 1981, preservationists opposed a seven-story structure in the historic district. Its modern design has a towering atrium and a pleasant central lounge, as well as glass elevators. Its rooms have mauve furnishings and balconies overlooking the atrium, the Savannah River, or Bay St. MD's Lounge is the ideal spot to have a drink and watch the river traffic drift by. *2 W. Bay St., tel. 912/238–1234 or 800/228–9000. 346 rooms. Facilities: 2 restaurants, 2 lounges, indoor pool, gift shop, AE, CB, DC, MC, V.*

★ **The Mulberry.** There are so many objets d'art in the public rooms that the management has obligingly provided a walking

tour brochure. There are, to mention but a few, 18th-century oil paintings, an English grandfather clock dating from 1803, Chinese vases from the Ching Dynasty, an ornate Empire game table—and to think this was once a Coca-Cola bottling plant. The restaurant is a sophisticated affair with crystal chandeliers and mauve velvet Regency furniture. There is a spacious courtyard covered with a mosquito net, which keeps it about 10 degrees cooler in the summer. The guest rooms are in a traditional motif; suites have queen-size beds, wet bars, amenity packages, and river views. *601 E. Bay St., 31401, tel. 912/238–1200 or 800/554–5544 (in GA 800/282–9198). 100 rooms, 25 suites with bath. Facilities: concierge, bar, restaurant, outdoor pool, rooftop deck with Jacuzzi, accommodations for nonsmokers and the handicapped. AE, DC, MC, V.*
River Street Inn. This elegant Legacy Hotel offers panoramic views of the Savannah River. Rooms are furnished with antiques and reproductions from the era of King Cotton. Amenities include turn-down service. The interior is so lavish, it's difficult to believe it was only recently a vacant warehouse dating back to 1830. One floor includes charming shops, another a New Orleans-style restaurant and blues club. *115 E. River St., tel. 912/234–6400. 44 rooms. Facilities: restaurant, lounge, shops. AE, DC, MC, V.*

Moderate **Days Inn.** This downtown hotel is located in the Historic District near the City Market, only a block off River Street. Its compact rooms have modular furnishings and most amenities, including HBO/ESPN on the tube and valet service. Interior corridors and an adjacent parking garage minimize its motel qualities. *201 W. Bay St., tel. 912/236–4440 or 800/325–2525. 235 rooms. Facilities: restaurant, pool, gift shop. AE, DC, MC, V.*

Nightlife

Savannah's nightlife is a reflection of the city's laid-back, easy-going personality. Some clubs feature live reggae, hard rock, and other contemporary music, but most stay with traditional blues, jazz, and piano bar vocalists. After-dark merrymakers usually head for watering holes on Riverfront Plaza or the southside.

Jazz Clubs **Savannah Blues** (117 E. River St., tel. 912/234–6400, ext. 107) offers a variety of live music, including blues, on Tuesdays, Fridays and Saturdays in the brick basement of a cotton warehouse.

Bars and **Congress Street Station** (121 W. Congress St., tel. 912/236–
Nightclubs 7309) is a small dark club that formerly was called Nightflight. It's still the city's liveliest music hall, featuring a variety of name performers in rock, blues, jazz, reggae, folk, country and comedy. The age of the crowd on the tiny dance floor depends on who's on the bandstand.
Kevin Barry's Irish Pub (117 W. River St., tel. 912/233–9626), a cozy pub with a friendly bar and traditional Irish music, is *the* place to be on St. Patrick's Day. The rest of the year there's a mixed bag of tourists and locals, young and old. **Hollywood's** (9 W. Bay St., tel. 912/233–8347), across from the Hyatt Regency, is a very active singles bar, where young locals and out-of-towners mix it up to taped Top-40 music.

The Golden Isles and Okefenokee Swamp

The Golden Isles are a string of lush, subtropical barrier islands meandering lazily down Georgia's Atlantic coast from Savannah to the Florida border. Three of the islands—Jekyll Island, Sea Island, and St. Simons Island—are connected to the mainland by bridges in the vicinity of Brunswick; these are the only ones accessible by automobile. The Cumberland Island National Seashore is accessible by ferry from St. Mary's. Little St. Simons Island, a privately owned retreat with a guest lodge, is reached by a private launch from St. Simons.

The islands have a long history of human habitation; Indian relics have been found on them that date back to about 2500 BC. According to legend, the various Indian nations agreed that no wars would be fought there and that tribal members would visit only in a spirit of friendship.

Each Golden Isle has a distinctive personality, shaped by its history and ecology. About 50 miles inland is the Okefenokee Swamp National Wildlife Refuge, which has a character all its own.

Cumberland Island National Seashore

Numbers in the margin correspond with points of interest on the Golden Isles map.

❶ The largest, most southerly, and most primitive of Georgia's coastal islands is **Cumberland,** a 16-by-3-mile sanctuary of marshes, dunes, beaches, forests, lakes and ponds, estuaries and inlets. Waterways are home to gators, otters, snowy egrets, great blue herons, ibis, wood storks, and more than 300 other bird species. In the forests are armadillo, wild horses, deer, raccoons, and an assortment of reptiles.

After the ancient Guale Indians came 16th-century Spanish missionaries, 18th-century English soldiers, and 19th-century planters. During the 1880s, Thomas Carnegie of Pittsburgh built several lavish homes here, but the island remained largely as nature created it. In the early 1970s, the federal government established the Cumberland Island National Seashore and opened this natural treasure to the public.

Getting Around The only public access to the island is by *The Cumberland Queen*, a reservations-only, 150-passenger ferry based near the National Park Service Information Center at the docks at St. Mary's on the mainland. From mid-May through Labor Day, the *Queen* departs from St. Mary's daily at 9 and 11:45 AM and departs from Cumberland at 10:15 AM and 4:45 PM. The trip takes 45 minutes. For the remainder of the year there is no ferry on Tuesday and Wednesday.

Important Addresses and Numbers To make ferry reservations or obtain further information, contact the **National Park Service** (Cumberland Island National Seashore, Box 806, St. Mary's 31558, tel. 912/882–4335). Ferry bookings are very heavy during summer, but cancellations and no-shows often make last-minute space available.

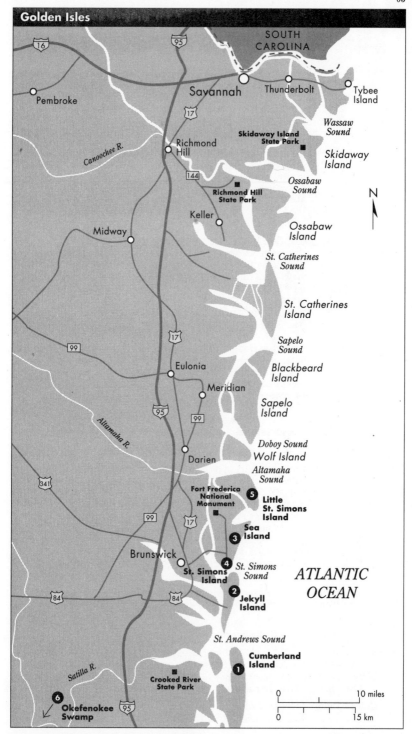

Golden Isles

SOUTH CAROLINA

Pembroke

Savannah   Thunderbolt   Tybee Island

Wassaw Sound

Canoochee R.

Richmond Hill

Skidaway Island State Park

Skidaway Island

Ossabaw Sound

Richmond Hill State Park

Keller

Ossabaw Island

N

Midway

St. Catherines Sound

St. Catherines Island

Sapelo Sound

Eulonia

Blackbeard Island

Meridian

Sapelo Island

Altamaha R.

Doboy Sound

Darien

Wolf Island

Altamaha Sound

Fort Frederica National Monument

5 Little St. Simons Island

3 Sea Island

Brunswick

4 St. Simons Sound

St. Simons Island

ATLANTIC OCEAN

2 Jekyll Island

St. Andrews Sound

Satilla R.

1 Cumberland Island

Crooked River State Park

6 Okefenokee Swamp

0   10 miles

0   15 km

Exploring From the Park Service docks at the island's southern end, you can follow wooded nature trails, swim and sun on 18 miles of undeveloped beaches, go fishing and bird-watching, and view the ruins of Carnegie's great estate, **Dungeness.** You can also join history and nature walks led by Park Service rangers. There is no transportation on the island, so the length of your explorations will be determined by your own interests and energy. Bear in mind that summers are hot and humid, and that you must bring your own food, soft drinks, sunscreen, and a reliable insect repellant. *Nothing can be purchased on the island.*

Lodging Novice campers usually prefer **Sea Camp,** a five-minute walk
Camping from the *Cumberland Queen* dock, with rest rooms and showers adjacent to campsites. The beach is just beyond the dunes. Experienced campers will want to hike 3–10 miles to several areas where cold-water spigots are the only amenities. Contact the National Park Service (*see* Important Addresses and Numbers).

Hotels **Greyfield Inn.** The island's only hotel lodgings are in a turn-of-the-century Carnegie family home. Greyfield's public areas are filled with family mementoes, furnishings, and portraits (you may feel as though you've stepped into one of Agatha Christie's mysterious Cornwall manors). Prices include all meals, sales tax, mandatory gratuity, and pickup and drop off by the inn's ferry at Fernandina Beach, Florida. *Drawer B, Fernandina Beach, FL 32034, tel. 904/261–6408. 9 rooms. MC, V. Very Expensive (over $100).*

Riverview Hotel. Rooms are spartan but air-conditioned in this hotel opposite the Park Service docks in St. Mary's. Seagle's Restaurant serves inexpensive breakfast, lunch, dinner, and cocktails. *105 Osborne St., St. Mary's 31558, tel. 912/882–3242. 18 rooms. Facilities: restaurant, lounge. AE, DC, MC, V. Moderate ($50–$75).*

Jekyll Island

For 56 winters, between 1886 and 1942, America's rich and famous faithfully came south to **Jekyll Island.** Through the Gilded Age, the Great War, the Roaring '20s, and the Great Depression, Vanderbilts and Rockefellers, Morgans and Astors, Macys, Pulitzers, and Goodyears shuttered their Fifth Avenue castles and retreated to the serenity of their wild Georgia island. There they built elegant "cottages," played golf and tennis, and socialized. Early in World War II, the millionaires departed for the last time. In 1947, the state of Georgia purchased the entire island for the bargain price of $650,000.

Getting Around Glynco Jetport, six miles north of Brunswick, is served by **At-**
By Plane **lantic Southeast Airlines** (tel. 404/765–2000) flights from Atlanta.

By Car From Brunswick by car, take the Jekyll Island Causeway ($1 per car).

Important **The Jekyll Island Convention and Visitors Bureau** (901 Jekyll Is-
Addresses and land Causeway, Jekyll Island 31520, tel. 912/635–3636), at the
Numbers end of the causeway, is open daily 9–5.

Guided Tours Tours of the **Jekyll Island Club Historic District** originate at the Museum Orientation Center on Stable Road. Ninety-minute

tours are given in open-air trolleys. Sites include several restored homes and buildings in the 240-acre historic district:
Indian Mound; William Rockefeller's shingled cottage; and
Faith Chapel, illuminated by stained-glass windows signed by
Louis Comfort Tiffany. Audiovisual orientations are presented
a half-hour before each tour departs. *Exit 35, tel. 912/635-
2236. Admission: $6 adults, $4 children 6–18. Tours operate
daily Labor Day–Memorial Day 10 AM, noon, 2 PM; Memorial
Day–Labor Day, tours at 10 AM, noon, 2 and 4 PM.*

Exploring   Jekyll Island is still a vast playground, but no longer restricted
to the rich and famous. For recreation, there is golf (63 holes),
tennis, fishing, biking, and jogging. There is also a new water
park, picnic grounds, and tours of the historic homes.

One side of the island is flanked by nearly 10 miles of hard-
packed Atlantic beaches; the other, by the Intracoastal Waterway and picturesque salt marshes. Deer and wild turkeys
inhabit interior forests of pine, magnolia, and moss-veiled live
oaks. Egrets, pelicans, herons, and sandpipers skim the gentle
surf.

Jekyll's clean, mostly uncommercialized beaches are free and
open to the public year-round. Bathhouses with rest rooms,
changing areas, and showers are open at regular intervals
along the beach. Beachwear, suntan lotion, rafts, snacks, and
drinks are available at the **Jekyll Shopping Center,** facing the
beach at Beachview Drive.

Participant Sports   Jekyll's 63 holes of golf include three 18-hole courses (tel. 912/
Golf   635–2368) with a main clubhouse on Capt. Wylly Rd. and a 9-
hole course (tel. 912/635–2170) on Beachview Dr.

Tennis   Nine courts include J.P. Morgan's indoor court (tel. 912/635–
2860).

Water Park   **Summer Waves,** an 11-acre water park, opened in June 1988
with an 18,000-square-foot wave pool; two 330-foot water
slides; a children's activity pool; and a 1,000-foot river for tub-
ing and rafting. *210 Riverview Dr., tel. 912/635–2074. Admission: $7.95 adults, $5.95 children 4–8. Open daily 10–6.*

Dining   **The Grand Dining Room.** In the Jekyll Island Club Hotel the
dining room sparkles with silver and crystal. What sets the
meals apart from the ordinary are the sauces that flavor the
dishes of fresh seafood, beef, veal, and chicken. *371 Riverview
Dr., tel. 912/635–2600, ext. 1002. Jacket required for dinner.
Reservations recommended. AE, CB, DC, MC, V. Expensive
($30–$40).*
Saint Andrews Landing. This locally popular restaurant specializes in seafood. Recommended is the pecan shrimp and the
Friday night seafood buffet (seasonal). The candle-lit dining room has sweeping ocean views. The Hunt Club Lounge
upstairs has live entertainment Tuesday–Saturday, and
drinks are served poolside at the Barefoot Bar. *975 N. Beachview Dr., tel. 912/635–2531. Dress: informal. Reservations for
large parties. AE, CB, DC, MC, V. Moderate–Expensive
($20–$40).*

Lodging   **Jekyll Island Club Hotel.** Built in 1887, the four-story clubhouse, with wraparound verandas, towers, and turrets, once
served as dining area, social center, and guest accommodations
for some of the wealthiest families in the United States. In
1985, a group of Georgia businessmen spent $17 million restor-

ing it to a splendor that would astonish even the Astors and Vanderbilts. The guest rooms and suites are custom-decorated with mahogany beds, armoires, and plush sofas and chairs. All have flowery views of the Intracoastal Waterway. All suites have Jacuzzis. The adjacent Sans Souci Apartments, former "bachelor quarters" built in 1886 by J.P. Morgan and William Rockefeller, have been converted into guest rooms. The hotel is operated as a Radisson Hotels resort. *371 Riverview Dr., Jekyll Island 31520, tel. 800/822–1886 or 800/843–5355 in GA. 60 rooms. Facilities: restaurant, outdoor pool, free shuttle to nearby beaches, tennis courts. AE, CB, DC, MC, V. Very Expensive (over $100).*

Holiday Inn Beach Resort. Nestled amid natural dunes and oaks in a secluded oceanfront setting, this hotel has a private beach, but its rooms with balconies still don't have an ocean view. Its recreational activities include outdoor pool and playground, tennis courts and 63 holes of golf. *200 S. Beachview Dr., Jekyll Island 31520, tel. 912/635–3311 or 800-HOLIDAY. 205 rooms. Facilities: restaurant, lounge with live entertainment, satellite cinema, some in-room saunas and whirlpools, bike rentals. AE, CB, DC, MC, V. Expensive ($75-$100).*

Jekyll Inn. The largest facility on the island, once a Hilton Inn, changed its affiliation to Best Western in 1989. Located on a landscaped 15-acre site, these oceanfront units, including some villas with kitchenettes, also underwent a $2.5 million renovation. Rooms were redecorated with new lighting and carpeting and saunas and Jacuzzis in some bathrooms. Island decor was added to the second-floor Ocean View lounge. *975 Beachview Dr., Jekyll Island 31520, tel. 912/635–2531 or 800/528–1234. 264 rooms. Facilities: restaurant, large pool, playground. AE, CB, DC, MC, V. Moderate-Very Expensive ($75-over $100).*

Sea Island

❸ **Sea Island** has been the domain of the **Cloister Hotel** since 1928. Attached to St. Simons Island by a bridge over a narrow waterway, and a good many steps up the social ladder, the resort lives up to its celebrity status. Guests lodge in spacious, comfortably appointed rooms and suites in the Spanish Mediterranean main hotel and in beachside cottages and villas.

For recreation, there's a choice of golf, tennis, swimming in pools or at the beach, skeet shooting, horseback riding, sailing, biking, lawn games, surf and deep-sea fishing. After dinner, a big-band orchestra plays for dancing in the lounge.

Like a person of some years, the Cloister has its eccentricities. Guest rooms were only recently equipped with TVs. Credit cards are not honored, but personal checks are accepted. Gentlemen must cover their arms in the dining rooms, even at breakfast. And for the most part, nouvelle cuisine, new American cuisine, and other culinary trends trends of the '80s have yet to breach the hotel's traditional menus.

There is no admission gate, and nonguests are free to admire the beautifully planted grounds and to drive past the mansions lining Sea Island Drive. Space permitting, they may also play at the Sea Island Golf Course and on the tennis courts and dine in the main dining room. *The Cloister, Sea Island 31561, tel. 912/638–3611, reservations 800/SEA–ISLAND. 264 rooms, 450 cottages, 44 condos. Full American Plan. No credit cards, but personal checks are accepted. Very Expensive (over $100).*

St. Simons Island

4 As large as Manhattan, with over 10,000 year-round residents, **St. Simons** is the Golden Isles' most complete and commercial resort destination. Fortunately, the accelerated development of condos, shopping districts, and other amenities in recent years has failed to spoil the natural beauty of the island's regal live oaks, beaches, and wavering salt marshes. Visits are highlighted by swimming and sunning on hard-packed beaches, biking, hiking, fishing, horseback riding, touring historic sites, and feasting on fresh local seafood at a growing number of restaurants. All of Georgia's beaches are in the public domain.

Getting Around
By Plane Glynco Jetport, six miles north of Brunswick, is served by **Atlantic Southeast Airlines** (tel. 404/765–2000) flights from Atlanta.

By Car Reach St. Simons by crossing the Torras Causeway from Brunswick. The island's accommodations and sights are widespread, so you'll need a car.

Important Addresses and Numbers **St. Simons Island Chamber of Commerce** (Neptune Park, St. Simons Island 31522, tel. 912/638–9014) can provide helpful information about the area.

Exploring Many sights and activities are in **the village** area along Mallery Street at the south end of the island. Shops sell groceries, beachwear, and gifts. There are also several restaurants, pubs, and a popular public pier.

Also on the island's southern end is **Neptune Park,** which includes picnic tables, miniature golf, and beach access. In the summer, a freshwater swimming pool, with showers and rest rooms, is open in the **Neptune Park Casino** (tel. 912/638–2393), in addition to a roller-skating rink, bowling lanes, and snack bars. Also in the park is **St. Simons Lighthouse,** a beacon since 1872. The **Museum of Coastal History** in the lightkeeper's cottage has permanent and changing exhibits of coastal history. *Tel. 912/638–4666. Admission (including the lighthouse): $1.50 adults, $1 children 6–12. Open Tues.–Sat. 1–4, Sun. 1:30–4.*

Ft. Frederica National Monument, at the north end of the island, includes the tabby ruins of a fort built by English troops in the mid-1730s as a bulwark against a Spanish invasion from Florida. Around the fort are the foundations of homes and shops built by soldiers and civilians. Start your tour at the **National Park Service Visitors Center,** which has a film and displays. *Tel. 912/638–3639. Admission: $1 adults, 50¢ children. Open daily 9–5.*

On your way to Frederica, pause at **Christ Episcopal Church** on Frederica Road. Consecrated in 1886 following an earlier structure's desecration by Union troops, the white frame Gothic structure is surrounded by live oaks, dogwoods, and azaleas.

The interior is highlighted by beautiful stained-glass windows. Donations welcome.

Dining **Alfonza's Olde Plantation Supper Club.** Seafood, superb steaks, and plantation fried chicken are served in a gracious and relaxed environment. The club also has a cocktail lounge. *Harrington Ln., tel. 912/638–9883. Dress: informal. Reservations recommended. MC, V. Moderate ($20–$30).*

Blanche's Courtyard. Located in the village, this lively restaurant/nightclub is gussied up in "Bayou Victorian" dress, with lots of antiques and nostalgic memorabilia. True to its bayou decor, the menu features Cajun-style seafood as well as your basic steak and chicken. A ragtime band plays for dancers on the weekends. *440 Kings Way, tel. 912/638–3030. Dress: informal. Reservations accepted. AE, DC, MC, V. Moderate ($20–$30).*

Emmeline & Hessie. A large dining room and bar offer patrons a spectacular view of the marina and marshes. Specialties are seafood, steak, and lobster. There's also a bakery, a deli, and a seafood market on the premises. There's usually a line here, but it's well worth the wait to watch the sun set over the marshes as you dine. During the summer months, live bands play on the outdoor terrace. *Golden Isles Marina, tel. 912/638–9084. Dress: informal. No reservations. AE, MC, V. Inexpensive–Moderate ($15–$30).*

The Crab Trap. One of the island's most popular spots, the Crab Trap offers a variety of fried and broiled fresh seafood, oysters on the half shell, clam chowder, heaps of batter fries, and hush puppies. The atmosphere is rustic-casual—there's a hole in the middle of every table to deposit corn cobs and shrimp shells. *1209 Ocean Blvd., tel. 912/638–3552. Dress: informal. No reservations. MC, V. Inexpensive (under $20).*

Spanky's. This trendy restaurant and bar in the Golden Isles Marina is popular for hamburgers, pizza, salads, sandwiches, seafood, beer, and cocktails. The panoramic view is also a drawing point. *225 Marina Dr., tel. 912/638–0918. Dress: informal. No reservations. AE, MC, V. Inexpensive (under $20).*

Lodging **The King and Prince Hotel and Villas.** This hotel facing the beach stepped into the deluxe resort category with a recently completed, multimillion-dollar modernization and expansion. Guest rooms are spacious, and villas offer from two to three bedrooms. *Box 798, 201 Arnold Rd., St. Simons Island 31522, tel. 912/638–3631. 124 rooms, 44 villas. Facilities: restaurant, indoor/outdoor pool, tennis, golf, bike rentals. AE, CB, DC, MC, V. Very Expensive (over $100).*

Sea Palms Golf and Tennis Resort. A contemporary resort complex with fully furnished, ultramodern villas nestled on an 800-acre site. *5445 Frederica Rd., St. Simons Island 31522, tel. 912/638–3351. 263 rooms. Facilities: restaurant, 2 pools, health club, 27-hole golf course, tennis, waterskiing, children's recreation programs. AE, CB, DC, MC, V. Very Expensive (over $100).*

Queen's Court. This family-oriented complex in the village has clean, modest rooms, some with kitchenettes. The grounds are beautiful. *437 Kings Way, St. Simons Island 31522, tel. 912/638–8459. 23 rooms. Facilities: color cable TV, shower baths, pool. MC, V. Inexpensive (under $50).*

Little St. Simons Island

Six miles long, two to three miles wide, skirted by Atlantic ⑤ beaches and salt marshes teeming with birds and wildlife, **Little St. Simons** is custom-made for Robinson Crusoe–style getaways. The island has been owned by one family since the early 1900s, and the only development is a rustic but comfortable guest compound. The island's forests and marshes are inhabited by deer, armadillos, horses, raccoons, gators, otters, and over 200 species of birds.

Guests are free to walk the six miles of undisturbed beaches, swim in the mild surf, fish from the dock, and seine for shrimp and crabs in the marshes. There are also horses to ride, nature walks with experts, and other island explorations that can be made by boat or in the back of a pickup truck.

Dining and Lodging
River Lodge and Cedar House. Up to 24 guests can be accommodated in the lodge and house. Each has four bedrooms with twin or king-size beds, private baths, sitting rooms, and screened porches. Older hunting lodges have some private and some shared baths. None of the rooms are air-conditioned, but ceiling fans make sleeping comfortable. The rates include all meals and dinner wines (cocktails available at additional cost). Meals, often featuring fresh fish, pecan pie, and home-baked breads, are served family-style in the lodge dining room. *Box 1078, Little St. Simons Island 31522, tel. 912/638–7472. Facilities: stables, pool, beach, transportation from St. Simons Island, transportation on the island, fishing boats, interpretive guides. Minimum two-night reservations. MC, V. Very Expensive (over $100).*

Okefenokee Swamp National Wildlife Refuge

Covering more than 700 square miles of southeast Georgia, spilling over into northeast Florida, the mysterious rivers and ⑥ lakes of the **Okefenokee Swamp** bristle with seen and unseen life. Scientists agree that Okefenokee is not duplicated anywhere else on Earth. The swamp is actually a vast peat bog, remarkable in geologic origin and history. Once part of the ocean floor, it now rises more than 100 feet above sea level.

As you travel by canoe or speedboat among the water-lily islands and the great stands of live oaks and cypress, be on the lookout for otters, egrets, muskrats, herons, cranes, and gators cruising the dark channels like iron-clad subs. The Okefenokee Swamp Park, eight miles south of Waycross, is a major visitor gateway to the refuge. The Swamp Park is a nonprofit development operating under a long-term lease. There are two other gateways to the swamp: an eastern entrance in the Suwanee Canal Recreation Area, near Folkston; and a western entrance at Stephen C. Foster State Park, outside the town of Fargo.

Seminole Indians, in their migrations south toward Florida's Everglades, once took refuge in the Great Okefenokee. Noting the many floating islands, they provided its name—"Land of the Trembling Earth."

Exploring
Okefenokee Swamp Park. South of Waycross, via U.S. 1, the park offers orientation programs, exhibits, observation areas,

wilderness walkways, an outdoor museum of pioneer life, and boat tours into the swamp that reveal its ecological uniqueness. A boardwalk and 90-foot tower are excellent places to glimpse cruising gators and a variety of birds. Gate admission includes a guided boat tour and all exhibits and shows. You may also arrange for lengthier explorations with a guide and a boat. *Waycross 31501, tel. 912/283–0583. Admission: $6 adults, $4 children 6–11. Open daily spring and summer, 9–6:30; fall and winter, 9–5:30.*

Suwanee Canal Recreation Area. This area, eight miles south of Folkston, via GA 121/23, is administered by the U.S. Fish and Wildlife Service. Stop first at the Visitor Information Center, which has an orientation film and exhibits on the Okefenokee's flora and fauna. A boardwalk takes you over the water to a 40-foot observation tower. At the concession building you may purchase snacks and sign up for guided boat tours into an 11-mile waterway, which resulted from efforts to drain the swamp a century ago. Hikers, bicyclists, and private motor vehicles are welcome on the Swamp Island Drive; several interpretive walking trails may be taken along the way. Picnicking is allowed. *Park Supt., Box 336, Folkston 31537, tel. 912/496–7156. Admission to the park is free. 1-hr tours: $4.25 adults, $2 children 5–11; 2-hr tours: $8.50 adults, $4 children 5–11. Refuge open Mar.–Sept., 10, 7 AM–7:30 PM; Sept. 11–Feb., 8–6. Closed major holidays.*

Stephen C. Foster State Park. Eighteen miles from Fargo, via GA 11, is an 80-acre island park entirely within the Okefenokee Swamp National Wildlife Refuge. The park encompasses a large cypress and black gum forest, a majestic backdrop for one of the thickest growths of vegetation in the southeastern United States. The lush terrain and the mirrorlike black waters of the swamp provide at least a part-time home for more than 225 species of birds, 41 species of mammals, 54 species of reptiles, 32 species of amphibians, and 37 species of fish. Park naturalists leading boat tours will spill out a wealth of swamp lore as riders observe gators, many bird species, and native trees and plants. You may also take a self-guided excursion in rental canoes and fishing boats. Camping is also available here (*see* Lodging). *Fargo 31631, tel. 912/637–5274. Admission free. Open Mar.–Sept. 14, 6:30 AM–8:30 PM; Sept. 15–Feb., 7 AM–7 PM.*

Lodging
Camping

Laura S. Walker State Park. Near Okefenokee Swamp Park, but not in the swamp, are campsites ($8 a night) with electrical and water hookups. Be sure to pick up food and supplies on the way to the park. *Park Supt., Waycross 31501, tel. 912/283–4424. Facilities: playground, fishing docks, pool, picnic areas. Inexpensive (under $20).*

Stephen C. Foster State Park. The park has furnished two-bedroom cottages ($45 a night Sun.–Thurs.; $55 weekends) and campsites with water, electricity, rest rooms, and showers ($8 a night). Because of roaming wildlife and poachers, the park's gates close between sunset and sunrise. If you're staying overnight, stop for groceries in Fargo beforehand. *Park Supt., Fargo 31631, tel. 912/637–5274. Inexpensive–Moderate ($8–$75).*

3 North Carolina

Introduction

by Carol Timblin

The author won first place in the Lowell Thomas Travel Journalism Competition and the Discover America Award in 1988, was a contributor to Rand McNally's Guide to Shenandoah National Park, Great Smoky Mountains National Park, and Blue Ridge Parkway *(1984), and is the coauthor of* Insiders' Guide to Charlotte.

Bluish purple mountains covered with mist. Clear streams and large expanses of freshwater lakes. Growing cities surrounded by industrial plants and patches of red clay. Pine barrens and golf courses scattered in the Sandhills that were once the beaches of the Atlantic. Great flat fields of soybeans, corn, and tobacco in the east. Fleets of boats and ships anchored at marinas on the Intracoastal Waterway. Tall dunes, sprinkled with sea oats, and long stretches of sandy beaches. A string of lighthouses along a chain of barrier islands, over a hundred miles long.

This is North Carolina. Though its profile is currently changing to high-tech, with a concentration of activities at the Research Triangle Park near Raleigh and the University Research Park at Charlotte, there are no huge megalopolises, and the largest city, Charlotte, has a population of only 390,000. What goes on in the small towns and medium-size cities still sets the tone for much of the state—with great emphasis on civic and church functions, festivals and celebrations, friendliness and hospitality.

In Colonial days, North Carolina produced mostly tar, pitch, and turpentine. During the Civil War, Confederate Army General Robert E. Lee gave the state its nickname—the Tar Heel State. He borrowed the tar heel image from compatriot Jefferson Davis, who alleged he would coat the heels of his soldiers with tar to help them stand their ground.

Geography has dramatically carved out three distinct regions in North Carolina. The Appalachian Mountains give way to the rolling hills of the Piedmont Plateau, which in turn evolve into the Coastal Plain—a stretch of more than 500 miles from the Tennessee border to the Atlantic Ocean. Each region has its own unique place in the state's rich history, spanning four centuries. Charlotte and the capital city of Raleigh lead the state in growth and development, with Greensboro, Winston-Salem, and High Point (the Triad) following. Wilmington is a bustling port city, in marked contrast to the tranquil villages along the Outer Banks. Golf is the recreational focus of the Sandhills, while snow skiing has taken hold in The High Country (Boone, Blowing Rock, Banner Elk). Asheville has maintained its status as a resort city for over 100 years and continues to grow in popularity as a travel destination.

North Carolina has courted visitors since the first English settlers arrived here in 1584. During the Depression of the 1930s, state officials began to realize anew the importance of tourism and put up a hospitality sign. Since then, a good highway system and excellent airport facilities have been developed. Eight welcome centers now serve visitors throughout the state. Tourism is growing here, and industry officials predict it will overtake tobacco and textiles by the year 2000. The welcome mat is out in North Carolina, so make the most of it while exploring and enjoying the treasures of the Tar Heel State.

North Carolina

KENTUCKY

TENNESSEE

VIRGINIA

SOUTH CAROLINA

GEORGIA

ATLANTIC OCEAN

Chesapeake Bay

N

Elizabeth City

Kitty Hawk

Cape Hatteras National Seashore

Albemarle Sound

Pamlico Sound

Cape Lookout National Seashore

Murfreesboro

17

64

264

New Bern

Morehead City

17

Croatan National Forest

Hoffman National Forest

Onslow Bay

Jacksonville

41

Wilmington

Rocky Mount

Roanoke Rapids

85

95

70

701

421

117

Durham

Raleigh

Fayetteville

95

Bladen Lakes State Forest

86

Chapel Hill

421

Southern Pines

11

29

Greensboro

Asheboro

220

Aberdeen

Pinehurst

Reidsville

40

Uwharrie National Forest

52

High Point

Winston-Salem

77

85

Charlotte

121

40

Gastonia

74

Pisgah National Forest

26

Asheville

40

Nantahala National Forest

APPALACHIAN MTS.

0   50 miles

0   50 km

Charlotte

Charlotte, once a sleepy Southern crossroads, is growing up to be one of the nation's most sophisticated cities—with luxury hotels, world-class restaurants, sporting events, and varied cultural activities. Even stock car racing at the Charlotte Motor Speedway has become trendy with the opening of an adjacent $20 million office building and an exclusive Speedway Club overlooking the track. Charlotte is the banking capital of the Southeast and home to national and international corporations that have played a vital role in shaping the city's history. Charlotte-Douglas International Airport is one of the fastest-growing in the country.

Though Charlotte dates to Revolutionary times (it is named for King George III's wife, Queen Charlotte), its Uptown is sparkling new with an ever-changing skyline. In recent years, urban revival has brought people back to the city to enjoy entertainment and cultural events. Cityfair, a complex of shops and restaurants, has recently added new vitality to the city, and further plans call for a new performing arts center to be built at The Square (Trade and Tryons Sts.). The new National Basketball Association team—the Charlotte Hornets—has led the league in attendance during its first season in the new 23,000-seat Coliseum. Hornet mania has gripped the city, with fans wearing teal and purple team colors and sporting various likenesses of Hugo the hornet on their cars.

In spite of all the new glitz and glamour, Charlotte has not outgrown its down-home flavor, and people still love the traditional pleasures of spreading a picnic in Freedom Park as they listen to the Charlotte Pops, politicking and munching barbecue at Mallard Creek Church, or watching the fireworks at Memorial Stadium on the Fourth of July.

Arriving and Departing

By Plane
Airports and Airlines
Charlotte-Douglas International Airport (tel. 704/359–4000), located on the west side of the city off I–85, serves the metropolitan area. Carriers include **American, Delta, Eastern, Pan American, TWA, United,** and **USAir. Henson Aviation** and **USAir Express** provide service to nearby cities and towns.

Between the Airport and Center City
By Bus. You can take a bus into the city during peak business hours (6–9 AM and 3–5 PM). The fare is 70¢ per person. **By Taxi.** To get to the central city, take a taxi or limousine. Taxis cost around $11 per person ($2 each additional person); limousines are approximately $4 per person.

By Car. Follow the road leading from the airport to the Billy Graham Parkway and then go north. Take I–85 north to the Brookshire Freeway (NC 16E) exit. Follow that route to the Tryon Street exit, which leads to the Uptown area.

By Train
Amtrak (1914 N. Tryon St., tel. 704/376–4416 or 800/872–7245) offers daily service to Washington, DC, to Atlanta, GA, and points beyond. Both trains depart in the wee hours of the morning.

By Bus
Greyhound/Trailways (601 W. Trade St., tel. 704/527–9393) serves the Charlotte area.

By Car Charlotte is a transportation hub of the Southeast. I–85 and I–77, north–south routes, run through the city, and I–40, an east–west route, is 40 miles to the north. U.S. 74, a major east-west route, also serves the city. I–277 and Charlotte 4 are inner–city loops. An outer beltway is planned, but at this time NC 51 is something of a perimeter route around part of the city, connecting Pineville, Matthews, and Mint Hill. Harris Boulevard connects I–77 to the University City area.

Getting Around

By Bus **Charlotte Transit** (tel. 704/336–3366) provides public transportation throughout the city. The Transit Mall has bus shelters on Trade and Tryon streets in Uptown. Fares are 70¢ for local rides and $1 for express service; senior citizens with ID cards pay 25¢ between 9 and 3, after 6, and on weekends. Free bus service is available between Mint and Kings Drive on Trade and between Stonewall and 11th on Tryon weekdays 9–3.

By Taxi Visitors may choose from a half dozen different taxi companies. **Yellow Cab** (tel. 704/332–6161) has a shiny fleet of cars, and **Crown Cab** (tel. 704/334–6666), distinguished by its white cars with a crown on top, gets high marks. Passengers pay a set flat rate.

Important Addresses and Numbers

Tourist Information The **Visitor Information Center** is operated by the Charlotte Convention and Visitors Bureau (229 N. Church St., tel. 704/371–8700. Open weekdays 8:30–5. Parking is limited). The **N.C. Welcome Center** (on I–77 north at the North Carolina-South Carolina line, tel. 704/588–2660. Open daily 8–5 except Christmas, New Year's Day, and a half day on Thanksgiving) provides information on Charlotte and the entire state. The **Charlotte-Douglas International Airport** has unmanned information kiosks (open at all times).

Emergencies Dial 911 for **police** and **ambulance** in an emergency. Hospital emergency rooms are open 24 hours a day. **Care Connection,** operated by Presbyterian Hospital, will give physician referrals and make appointments (tel. 704/371–4111, open weekdays 8:30–4:30). **Healthfinder,** run by Mercy Hospital, is a similar operation (tel. 704/379–6100, open weekdays 8:30–5). Another option is the Mecklenburg County Medical Society, which also gives physician referrals (tel. 704/376–3688, open weekdays 9–noon).

Pharmacy **Eckerd Drugs** (Park Road Shopping Center, tel. 704/523–3031; and 3740 Independence Blvd., tel. 704/536–1010).

Guided Tours

Five balloon companies give aerial tours, which end with champagne: **Air Fair Balloons** (tel. 704/522–0965), **Balloons Over Charlotte** (tel. 704/541–7058), **Big Oh Balloons** (tel. 704/563–0818), **Fantasy Flights** (tel. 704/552–0469), and **Windborne Adventures** (tel. 704/376–8955).

Exploring Charlotte

Numbers in the margin correspond with points of interest on the Charlotte map.

Uptown Charlotte is ideal for walking, but some form of transportation is needed for visiting surrounding sites. Buses are adequate for getting around within the city limits; otherwise, you will need a car. Discovery Place provides free parking for its visitors; the Convention Center and Cityfair offer parking at a reasonable rate. The original city was laid out into four wards from The Square, at Trade and Tryon streets. The Visitor Information Center, on Church Street, can provide information on a self-guided walking tour of Fourth Ward and a historic tour of Uptown, as well as maps and brochures covering other areas.

Uptown Charlotte Walking Tour   A walking tour of Charlotte may take a half hour or a full day, depending on whether you're interested in shopping, architecture, or history. Take time to stroll down **Tryon Street** and enjoy the ambience of this revitalized area. Take note of the outdoor sculptures and the creative architecture of some of the newer buildings, particularly the **First Union Tower,** currently Charlotte's signature building. During the warm months there will probably be some lunchtime entertainment going on at various plazas. Be sure to wander through the **Overstreet Mall,** a labyrinthian maze of shops and restaurants between the major office buildings.

❶ Begin your tour at **Discovery Place,** across the street from the **Visitor Information Center** on Church Street. You'll want to make the hands-on **Science Museum** a priority, so plan to set aside at least two hours for this experience. The museum is for children of all ages. Enjoy the aquariums, the rain forest, and science theater, and check the schedule for special exhibits. The museum has begun an $18-million renovation, which will include an Omnimax theatre to be completed in early 1991. *301 N. Tryon St., tel. 704/372–6261. Admission: $4 adults, $3 senior citizens, $2 children 3–5. Vistascope films $1. Open daily except Thanksgiving and Christmas, weekdays 9–5 (9–6 during June, July, and Aug.), Sat. 9–6, and Sun. 1–6.*

❷ **Fourth Ward,** Charlotte's new "old" city, which lies just west of Discovery Place, offers a refreshing change from the newly developed parts of town. A self-guided tour, available from the Visitor Information Center, points to 18 historic sites in the area, including the **Old North Carolina Medical College Building** (229 N. Church St.), where the center itself is located. Be sure to stop by **Old Settlers Cemetery,** just a few paces from the center. Some of the stones date to the 1700s, including the grave of Thomas Polk, a founding father. **First Presbyterian Church,** which takes up a city block and faces W. Trade Street, reflects the prosperity of the early settlers and their descendants. By the turn of the last century, they had built this Gothic Revival complex with stained glass to replace a much simpler meeting house. **Fourth Ward Park** is an oasis in the middle of the city. It is filled with thousands of people during the annual SpringFest. You can't miss the flamingo pink **Overcarsh House** (1879), perched above the park. It is one of two bed-and-breakfast houses in Fourth Ward. **Alexander Michael's**

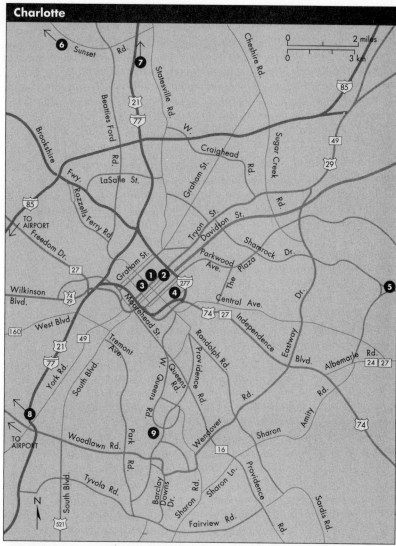

Charlotte

The Afro-American
Cultural Center, **4**

Discovery Place, **1**

The Energy
Explorium, **7**

Fourth Ward, **2**

Hezekiah Alexander
Homesite, **5**

The James K. Polk
Memorial, **8**

Latta Plantation
Park, **6**

The Overstreet Mall, **3**

Wing Haven Gardens
and Bird Sanctuary, **9**

(401 W. Ninth St.), is a favorite eatery. **Poplar Street Books** is housed in the Victorian Young-Morrison House (226 W. Tenth St.). U.S. President Taft spent the night in the **Liddell-McNinch House** (51 N. Church St.) when he visited Charlotte in 1909.

Spirit Square (110 E. Seventh St.), Charlotte's arts center, is under renovation and is expected to reopen in 1990. The Public Library, which includes a mural of a Romare Bearden painting, reopened on North Tryon Street in mid–1989. Open weekdays 9–9, Sat. 9–6, and Sun. 2–6. Cityfair is a shopping-restaurant cluster on College Street.

❸ The **Overstreet Mall** is a good place to wind up a walking tour. You'll find some expensive specialty shops and several informal restaurants here.

Other Charlotte Area Attractions Driving Tour
Other attractions are spread out across the city, so you may want to concentrate on one or two. You can reach the Afro-American Cultural Center, Hezekiah Alexander Homesite, Mint Museum, and Charlotte Nature Museum by city bus; for visits elsewhere, a car is needed.

❹ From Uptown Charlotte, follow Seventh Street east until you get to N. Myers Street. The **Afro-American Cultural Center**, a black arts center, including galleries, a theater, and bookstore, is housed in the restored building that formerly served as the Little Rock AME Zion Church. *Open Tues.–Sat. 10–6, Sun. 1–6.*

❺ From Seventh Street, take Central Avenue east to Eastway Drive. Turn left on Eastway and follow it for several blocks until you turn right on Shamrock Drive, where the **Hezekiah Alexander Homesite and History Museum** is preserved as a memorial to one of the Mecklenburg County's earliest settlers. The stone house, built in 1774, is the oldest dwelling in the county. Here, Alexander and his wife Mary reared 10 children and farmed the land. Costumed docents give guided tours of the homesite, including the reconstructed spring house and log kitchen. Special seasonal events, held during the spring, summer, and at Christmastime, commemorate the early days. *3500 Shamrock Dr., tel. 704/568–1774. Admission: $1 adults, 50¢ children 6–16. Open Tues.–Fri. 10–5, weekends 2–5. Closed holidays.*

❻ **Latta Plantation Park,** located northwest of town (off I–77, near Huntersville), centers around a Catawba River plantation house, built by merchant James Latta in the early 1800s. Costumed guides give tours of the house, which is on the National Register of Historic Places. In addition to the house, visitors enjoy the farm animals, an equestrian center, Audubon center, and the Carolina Raptor Center, where injured wildlife is cared for. *5225 Sample Rd., Huntersville, tel. 704/875–1391. Admission: $1 adults, 50¢ for students in grades K–12. Park open daily 7 AM to dark. House tours are offered Wed.–Sun. at 2, 3, and 4 PM.*

❼ Continue on I–77N to **The Energy Explorium,** operated by Duke Power Company on Lake Norman. Hands-on exhibits allow you to experience the excitement of creating nuclear power and other kinds of energy. A wildflower garden and picnic area offer diversion of a different kind. *McGuire Nuclear Plant, off I–77 and NC 73, Cornelius, tel. 704/875–5600. Admission free.*

Open Mon.–Sat. 9–5, Sun. noon–5 (June–Aug., Sun. noon–6). Closed major holidays.

What to See and Do with Children

Carowinds, an 83-acre theme amusement park, straddles the North Carolina-South Carolina line. Young children love the Kids Karnival and teenagers seek thrills on the White Water Falls water coaster. For grown-ups, there are serene rides and Broadway-style shows. The Paladium offers musical concerts with star entertainers. *Carowinds Blvd., tel. 704/588–2600. Open daily 10–8; closed Fri. June–Aug.; closed weekends Mar.–Apr., Sept.–early Oct. Call 800/822–4428 for ticket prices.*

The Nature Museum, a sister to Discovery Place, is a delight to young children. It features some live animals and exhibits, plus a small planetarium. *1658 Sterling Rd., tel. 704/332–4140. Admission: $1. Open weekdays 9–5, Sat. 9–6, Sun. 1–5. Closed Thanksgiving and Christmas.*

Freedom Park, across the footbridge from the Nature Museum, offers acres of space and a shimmering lake where you can feed the ducks. Children love climbing on the train engine, fire trucks, and airplanes, as well as using the playground equipment. *2435 Cumberland Ave., tel. 704/336–2663. Admission free.*

❽ The **James K. Polk Memorial,** now a state historic site, marks the humble 1795 birthplace of the 11th president. Guided tours of the log cabins are available, and the buildings are decorated with fresh pine boughs and candles at Christmastime. Exhibits in the center depict early life in Mecklenburg County. *U.S. 521, Pineville, tel. 704/889–7145. Admission free. Open Apr.–Oct., Mon.–Sat. 9–5, Sun. 1–5; Nov.–Mar., Tues.–Sat. 10–4 and Sun. 1–4.*

Reed Gold Mine, east of Charlotte in Cabarrus County, is where America's first gold rush began following Conrad Reed's discovery of a 17-pound nugget in 1799. Visitors may explore the underground mine shaft and gold holes, pan for gold during the summer months, learn about the history of gold mining, or enjoy a picnic. *Off NC 27 between Midland and Stanfield, tel. 704/786–8337. Gold panning is $3 (group rate $1 per person), but admission is free. Open Mon.–Sat. 9–5, Sun. 1–5 Apr.–Oct.; Tues.–Sat. 10–4, Sun. 1–4 Nov.–Mar.*

The recently renovated **Schiele Museum of Natural History and Planetarium** in Gastonia offers some outstanding exhibits, including one on the natural history of the state and another on land mammals of North America. Visitors also enjoy the living history demonstrations at the pioneer site, as well as the nature trail. *Garrison Blvd., Gastonia, tel. 704/866–6902. Admission free. Open Tues.–Fri. 9–5, weekends 2–5. Closed on Thanksgiving Day and Christmas week.*

The **Spencer Shops–N.C. Transportation Museum,** north of Salisbury, was once Southern Railway's largest repair facility between Washington, DC, and Atlanta, GA. A restored train takes passengers on a short ride over the 57-acre complex, with a stop at the round house. The museum, a state historic site, traces the development of transportation in North Carolina from Indian times to the present. There are some unique train memorabilia in the gift shop. *Off I–85 at Spencer, tel. 704/ 636–2889. Admission free. Train rides $1–$3. Open Mon.– Sat. 9–5, Sun. 1–5 Apr.–Oct. Tues.–Sat. 10–4, Sun. 1–4, Nov.–Mar.*

Off the Beaten Track

❾ A visit to **Wing Haven Gardens and Bird Sanctuary** will take you into Myers Park, one of Charlotte's loveliest neighborhoods. The three-acre garden, developed by the Clarkson family, is home to more than 135 species of birds. *248 Ridgewood Rd., tel. 704/331–0664. Admission free. Open Sun. 2–5, Tues.–Wed. 3–5 or by appointment.*

Davidson is a delightful college town several miles north of Charlotte, via I–77. Throughout the year, Davidson College, a small Presbyterian liberal arts college with a national reputation for excellence, offers a number of cultural activities— including plays, concerts, art exhibits, and lectures. The shopping district has received a face lift in recent years. Stop in at the M & M Soda Shop to find out what really goes on in this quaint village. *For more information, contact the Town of Davidson, tel. 704/892–7591.*

Shopping

Charlotte is the largest retail center in the Carolinas. Uptown Charlotte, as well as suburban malls, cater to shoppers' needs. Villages and towns in outlying areas offer some regional specialties. Uptown shops are open 10–5:30 daily except Sunday. Malls are open Monday–Saturday 10–9 and Sunday 1–6. Sales tax is 5%.

Shopping Districts **Uptown Charlotte** is fun and exciting, especially with the addition of *Cityfair*, a 120,000-square-foot retail and entertainment center.

Midtown Square, located in the old Charlottetown Mall (the city's first indoor mall), has maintained a fresh look since it was renovated a few years ago. Here you can find savings at such outlets as the Dress Barn and Burlington Coat Factory.

Park Road Shopping Center is one of the city's first modern shopping developments. It features an old-fashioned Woolworth's store, J.C. Penney's, Bush Stationers, and other shops. *Villa Square*, in Myers Park, houses a number of upscale trendy shops in what was once a private estate built to look like an Italian villa. *SouthPark*, located in the most affluent section of the city, caters to upscale customers. *Belk, Ivey's, Thalheimers, Montaldo's,* and *Sears* are here. *Specialty Shops on the Park*, across from Southpark, is another cluster of expensive shops. *Eastland Mall*, on the east side of town, features an ice skating rink, plus Ivey's, Belk, J.C. Penney's, Sears, and other retail stores. *Windsor Square* is a large complex of outlet stores.

Department Stores *Belk, Ivey's, Montaldo's, Thalheimers,* and *Upton's* all offer quality merchandise.

Specialty Stores The towns of Waxhaw, Pineville, and Matthews are the best
Antiques places to find antiques. Each has a number of shops, and Waxhaw sponsors an annual antiques fair each February. If you want to combine shopping with lunch, Matthews offers a choice

of restaurants. Shops are usually open Monday through Saturday in Pineville and Matthews. In Waxhaw, some shops are open on Sunday but closed on Monday. You can also find a good selection of antiques at the Metroliner Expo, which is the first and third weekends of the month.

Books There are some excellent bookshops in Charlotte. Sure-bets are the **Intimate** at Eastland and South Park, the **Little Professor Book Shop** in the Park Road Shopping Center and **Matthews Festival, Poplar Street Books** in Fourth Ward, and **Brandywine Books** on Selwyn Avenue.

Crafts The best buys are in the **Metroliner Expo.** The **Carolina Christmas Craft Show** in October, the **Southern Christmas Show** in November, the **Southern Spring Show** in February, and the **Carolina Spring Craft Show** in late March offer shoppers the opportunity to see a variety of crafts in one setting.

Participant Sports

Bicycling There is a 10-mile designated route between Southpark and Uptown Charlotte. North Carolina has designated tours stretching from the coast to the mountains. Route maps are available from the NC Department of Transportation (Box 25201, Raleigh 27611).

Camping Near Charlotte, try McDowell Park and Nature Reserve, Carowinds and Duke Power State Park. In neighboring South Carolina, try Heritage USA or Kings Mountain State Park.

Canoeing Inlets on Lake Norman and Lake Wylie are ideal for canoeing, as are some spots of the Catawba River. The Pee Dee River east of Charlotte and the New River offer other options.

Fishing Enthusiasts enjoy fishing in Charlotte's neighboring lakes and streams, as well as farther away on the coast and in mountain streams. A state license is required and may be purchased at local bait and tackle shops. For details, contact the Division of Boating and Inland Fishing (tel. 919/733–3633).

Golf Charlotte has several good public golf courses, among them Crystal Springs, Renaissance, and Pebble Creek. The Visitor Information Center (tel. 704/371–8700) can provide a complete list. The renowned Pinehurst-Southern Pines golf area is only a two-hour drive from Charlotte.

Hiking Crowder's Mountain and Kings Mountain near Gastonia and the Uwharrie Mountains east of Charlotte offer plenty of varied terrain and challenge for hikers.

Jogging Jogging trails and tracks can be found in most city and county parks and at many local schools. Contact the Mecklenburg County Parks and Recreation Department (tel. 704/336–3854). or Charlotte Parks and Recreation (tel. 704/336–2884).

Physical Fitness The Charlotte YWCAs and YMCAs will permit guests who have a Y membership in another location to use their facilities for a $5 fee. Many hotels in town also offer fitness centers.

Tennis Courts are available in several city parks, including Freedom, Hornet's Nest, Park Road, and Veterans. A growing number of hotels and motels provide courts as well. For details on city-county courts call the Charlotte Parks and Recreation Department (tel. 704/336–2884).

Spectator Sports

Baseball The Charlotte Knights play April–August at Knight Stadium, I–77 and Gold Hill Road (tel. 704/332–3746).

Basketball The Charlotte Hornets have taken the city by storm. Some tickets are available through the ticket office (tel. 704/357–4738) or Rigby's restaurants (tel. 704/525–5752).

Racing NASCAR races, such as the Coca-Cola 600 and the Oakwood Homes 500, draw huge crowds at the Charlotte Motor Speedway near Concord (tel. 704/455–2121).

Dining

by Peg Robarchek The choice of good places to eat in Charlotte is extremely varied, including many restaurants specializing in international cuisine. Local specialties include barbecued pork and chicken, fresh seafood, fried chicken, and country ham. Hush puppies, made from cornmeal batter and fried in deep fat, almost always accompany fish and barbecue here. Grits is another Southern specialty widely served in North Carolina, usually with breakfast. There is also a wide selection of places that feature steaks and roast prime ribs of beef.

The most highly recommended restaurants in each price category are indicated by a star ★.

Category	Cost*
Very Expensive	over $20
Expensive	$15–$20
Moderate	$10–$15
Inexpensive	under $10

per person without tax (5% in Charlotte), service, or drinks

The following credit-card abbreviations are used: AE, American Express; CB, Carte Blanche; DC, Diners Club; MC, MasterCard; V, Visa.

American **Jonathan's Uptown.** Next door to Spirit Square performing arts
Very Expensive center, Jonathan's is an easy walk from most Uptown hotels.
★ And it is as noted for the lively entertainment in its Jazz Cellar as it is for its food, which changes weekly to highlight the distinctive cuisines of different regions of the U.S. Dinner specialties include sautéed venison loin, grilled or blackened mahi mahi, a variety of steaks, and roast duck with regional sauces and stuffings. Fresh food is flown in every day from Chesapeake Bay, Bayou Lafourche, and elsewhere. Coolly dark and elegantly appointed, Jonathan's has a comfortable bar as well as a roomy dining area. *330 N. Tryon St., tel. 704/332–3663. Jacket and tie suggested. Reservations recommended for lunch and dinner. AE, DC, MC, V. Very Expensive.*

Moderate– **Longhorn Restaurant and Saloon.** Longneck beers, buckets of
Expensive roasted peanuts, and Margaritas that live up to the Texas tradi-
★ tion of being the biggest and the strongest will help you make it through the wait, which stretches to an hour on weekends at

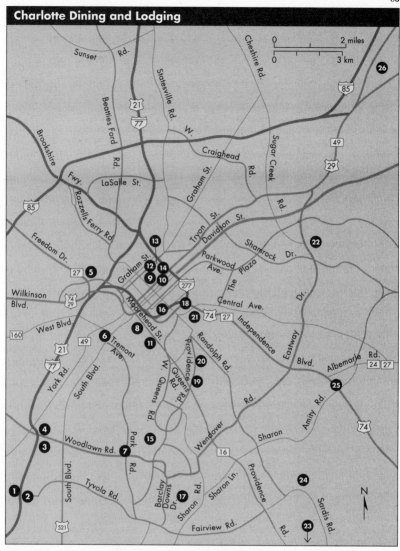

Charlotte Dining and Lodging

0 — 2 miles
0 — 3 km

Dining

Alexander Michael's, **12**

Anntony's Caribbean Cafe, **21**

Bavarian Haus, **7**

Cafe Society, **15**

Catherine's on Providence, **19**

Dickadee's Front Porch, **25**

Hog Heaven, **22**

Jonathan's Uptown, **14**

La Paz, **20**

Lizzie's, **3**

Longhorn, **8**

The Open Kitchen, **5**

Pewter Rose Bistro, **6**

Lodging

Adam's Mark, **16**

The Dunhill, **13**

511 Queens Road, **18**

Hilton at University Place, **26**

Holiday Inn at Woodlawn, **4**

The Homeplace, **24**

Inn on Providence, **23**

Marriott City Center, **10**

Marriott Executive Park, **1**

The Morehead, **11**

The Park Hotel, **17**

Radisson Plaza Hotel, **9**

The Royce, **2**

this popular watering hole. The atmosphere is loose but not raucous. The menu concentrates on steaks, including a filet mignon as thick and tender as any you'll ever order. *700 E. Morehead St., tel. 704/332–2300. Dress: informal. Reservations not accepted. AE, MC, V.*

Inexpensive– **Catherine's on Providence.** Elegant food is seldom served under
Moderate the same roof with low prices, but Catherine's has cornered the
★ market on this unlikely pairing. Vegetables get an image boost at Catherine's, where the menu changes daily. Smothered cabbage, marinated cucumbers, and Greek tomato salad are good examples of the way ordinary produce is transformed into gourmet food. Tender rib roast and roast pork loin with mustard sauce are menu regulars. Breakfast also ventures away from the usual, with homemade corned beef hash, oven-browned potatoes, and Catherine's own blend of granola topped with fresh fruit. Soft candlelight and warm woods create a cozy feeling, but the noise level is a bit high for intimacy. *829 Providence Rd., tel. 704/372–8199. Dress: informal. Reservations not accepted. AE, MC, V.*

Caribbean **Anntony's Caribbean Cafe.** This recently expanded diner is al-
Inexpensive most hidden at the far end of a nondescript shopping center on the fringes of the Elizabeth neighborhood. But crowds quickly discovered its low, low prices and extraordinary food. Tender, tangy Caribbean barbecued chicken and Trinidad spareribs are weekday specialties, with the added weekend bonus of four-alarm curry sauce with either beef, chicken, lamb, or beef. Come early: Anntony's is notorious for selling out. *Pecan Point Shopping Center, 2001 E. 7th St., tel. 704/342–0749. Dress: casual. Reservations not accepted. No credit cards.*

Continental **Cafe Society.** This elegant restaurant in a neighborhood half-
Very Expensive way between Uptown and SouthPark is small, quiet, and softly
★ lit. The unobtrusive, strictly professional service is almost as pleasurable as the superbly prepared food. Fine wines by the glass and elegant appetizers—smoked salmon or baked brie—prepare you for a leisurely meal. Pasta for the sophisticated palate and tender veal prepared a half-dozen surprisingly different ways put this establishment at the top of the list for fine dining in Charlotte. *2839 Selwyn Ave., tel. 704/332–1166. Jacket and tie suggested. Reservations recommended on weekends. AE, MC, V.*

Lizzie's. The biggest draw at Lizzie's is the entertainment. The piano bar is packed most nights with people who love to dance to the '30s and '40s standards sung by owner Liz King and other talented vocalists. Sunday evening jam sessions often draw some of the best musicians in town. While food here is average, the prices are not. Highlights are steak tartar, black bean soup, veal Oscar, coconut shrimp, roast duckling flambéed with Grand Marnier, and fresh rainbow trout stuffed with crabmeat. The menu suggests a wine to go with each entree, and also offers to fill any special request if you give the kitchen 48 hours notice. Reservations for dinner in a booth near the dance floor are sometimes your best bet for hearing the show. *4809 S. Tryon St., tel. 704/527–3064. Jacket and tie suggested. Reservations recommended. AE, MC, V.*

Expensive **Alexander Michael's.** This is one of the city's most popular restaurants and watering holes. The biggest attraction is the location, in the heart of restored Fourth Ward, a few blocks from uptown. You'll want to roam the historic neighborhood to walk off your crabmeat quesadillas, shrimp primavera, or chicken in Sauvignon and garlic cream sauce. Alexander Michael's also has a wide selection of unusual beers and fine wines. *401 W. 9th St., tel. 704/332-6789. Dress: informal. Reservations not accepted. AE, MC, V.*

★ **Dikadee's Front Porch.** Owner Nick Colias named his restaurant from childhood memories of his grandmother's front porch. Although nowadays you'll find no front porch on which to enjoy your meal, you will enjoy the homey atmosphere. Desserts are a specialty, including Nick's famous white chocolate Basket of Sin and Sex in a Pan. The Louisiana filet mignon, prepared Creole-style, is one of the best variations on a filet you'll find. All the food is lightly prepared, with the emphasis on delicate seasonings. Intimate dining areas and candlelit tables make this a perfect romantic getaway. *4329 E. Independence Blvd., tel. 704/537-3873. Dress: informal. Reservations accepted Mon.-Thurs. AE, DC, MC, V. Closed Sun.*

French **Pewter Rose Bistro.** Housed in the second-floor loft of a reno-
Moderate vated textile mill in historic Dilworth, just a five-minute drive from Uptown, the Pewter Rose Bistro is a favorite hangout for Charlotte's young professionals. Subtly offbeat in decor, the Pewter Rose specializes in fresh seasonal foods. Highlights of the menu are marinated grilled tuna steaks with a butter seasoned with ground horseradish root; fettuccine with cognac dill cream sauce and optional smoked salmon and caviar; and a decadent chocolate cranberry torte. The bar is pleasant and roomy, filled with comfy sofas and chairs to make the wait enjoyable. *1820 South Blvd., tel. 704/332-8149. Dress: informal. Reservations not accepted. AE, MC, V. Closed Sun., Mon.*

German **Bavarian Haus.** If your schedule is tight, make another choice.
Moderate But if you have time and if a cold, dark beer, sauerkraut that bites back, and—on weekends—conversation to accordion accompaniment have appeal, search out Bavarian Haus. A five-minute drive from the SouthPark area, it offers authentic *wiener schnitzel, schweinebraten,* and plump potato dumplings, along with bratwurst and fresh apple strudel. *Park Road Shopping Center, 4151-A Park Rd., tel. 704/523-2406. Dress: informal. Reservations recommended. AE, DC, MC, V.*

Italian **The Open Kitchen.** The overabundance of kitsch—everything
Moderate from college pennants to Chianti bottles strung across an archway—is part of the fun at The Open Kitchen, which has been packing in Charlotteans since 1952. The food is standard Italian fare: spaghetti with practically any kind of sauce you want, lasagna, chicken or shrimp cacciatore, fettuccine alfredo that's a bit too heavy on the sauce, and pizza. But the noisy, boisterous atmosphere and the quickly delivered food give the feeling that you've been dropped into the middle of an Italian family dinner. *1318 W. Morehead St., tel. 704/375-7449. Dress: casual. Reservations accepted. AE.*

Mexican **La Paz.** The food is worth the wait at La Paz. Crowd into the
Moderate tiny upstairs bar, grab a Dos Equis or a Margarita and a basket
★ of chips and hot sauce and be prepared to wait—easily an hour during peak dinner hours. Outstanding Mexican cuisine re-

wards your patience—*chiles rellenos*, king crab and gulf shrimp *burritos* and *fajitas*. The setting is intimate, if a bit crowded. Located near Uptown, off Providence Road (an extension of East Third Street from Uptown). *523 Fenton Pl., tel. 704/372–4169. Dress: informal. Reservations not accepted. AE, DC, MC, V.*

Southern
Inexpensive

Hog Heaven. North Carolinians are as serious about their barbecue as they are about basketball. So don't ask where to go for the best barbecue, just head for Hog Heaven, a tiny restaurant decorated in Early Auto Racing—complete with checkered flags and laminated photos of racetrack legends. In addition to barbecued chicken or ribs, the beef or pork sandwiches here are generous and filled with the undeniable flavor of long, slow, hickory-smoked cooking. Sandwiches are made with barbecued slaw, so unless you're ready for the full North Carolina experience, ask for your slaw on the side. Homemade pies for dessert. *1600 Purser Dr., tel. 704/535–0154. Dress: casual. Reservations not accepted. No credit cards.*

Lodging

At the rate Charlotte keeps adding hotel rooms, visitors should have no trouble locating rooms: approximately 15,000 are available. You can choose from economy motels, convention hotels, or bed-and-breakfast houses. Most of the major chains are represented, including Hilton, Marriott, Sheraton, and Royce, as are less expensive options—EconoLodge, Comfort Inn, Days Inn, La Quinta, Motel 6, Hampton, Sterling Inn, and Red Roof Inn. Mid-priced motel chains include Holiday Inn, Howard Johnson, Ramada Inn, and Quality Inn. Some hotels offer great weekend packages. New to Charlotte in the past year are The Dunhill Hotel, Compri, Embassy Suites, Days Hotel, and other hotels. A 3% accommodations tax and 5% sales tax are added to every room charge. The Charlotte Convention and Visitors Bureau publishes a comprehensive accommodations brochure on the area (tel. 704/371–8700).

Category	Cost*
Very Expensive	over $100
Expensive	$60–$100
Moderate	$30–$60
Inexpensive	under $30

double room; add 8% for taxes

The following credit-card abbreviations are used: AE, American Express; CB, Carte Blanche; DC, Diners Club; MC, MasterCard; V, Visa.

Hotels
Moderate–
Very Expensive

511 Queens Road. This all-suite hotel is in the heart of Myers Park, the city's classiest neighborhood. The suites—which have living rooms, dining rooms, kitchens, and bedrooms—are ideal for families. Guests receive complimentary breakfast. *511 Queens Rd., 28207, tel. 704/336–6700. AE, DC, MC, V.*

Expensive

The Dunhill. This upscale small hotel in the heart of Uptown caters to those in search of service and special amenities. Guests are picked up in a Rolls Royce at the airport. High tea, evening cocktails, and a full breakfast are complimentary. Thistles Restaurant serves three meals a day. *237 N. Tryon St., 28202, tel. 704/332–4141 or 800/252–4666. 60 rooms, small meeting rooms, terry robes, guest privileges at YMCA. AE, MC, V, DC.*

Marriott City Center. This high-rise hotel sits in the middle of The Square in Uptown Charlotte. An atrium links the hotel with shops and offices. The lobby is dazzling but not imposing. Guests have the choice of dining in the elegant Chardonnay's or the more casual atmosphere of Sweetbay, which serves great hamburgers. Nightlife is centered in Chatfield's and the Lobby Bar, featuring piano music and complimentary hors d'oeuvres. *100 W. Trade St., 28202, tel. 704/333–9000. 431 rooms and suites. Facilities: indoor pool, whirlpool, sauna, health club, meeting rooms, airport shuttle. AE, CB, DC, MC, V.*

The Park Hotel. The ultimate in class, the Park offers both elegance and intimacy. The decor is 18th century, accented with original artwork commissioned by the hotel. Guests enjoy Morrocrofts Restaurant and Bar and Beau's Lounge. Special amenities include telephones with two incoming lines, and complimentary newspapers. *2200 Rexford Rd., 28211, tel. 704/364–8220. 196 rooms and suites. Facilities: swimming pool, health club, airport limousine service. AE, CB, DC, MC, V.*

Radisson Plaza Hotel. The Radisson set the stage for the redevelopment of Uptown Charlotte a few years ago and has remained a pacesetter. The 15-story hotel is a first-class property offering convenience and contemporary elegance. It is connected to major buildings and department stores by the Overstreet Mall. Guests may choose the casualness of Cafe Promenade or the sophistication of Reflections for dining. There's even a comedy club in the bar. If you join the Radisson Hospitality Club, you get a complimentary breakfast, happy hour drinks, unlimited local calls, and reduced car rental. All guests enjoy complimentary newspapers and free parking. *2 NCNB Plaza, 28280, tel. 704/377–0400. 381 rooms and suites. Facilities: outdoor pool, meeting rooms, airport transportation. AE, CB, DC, MC, V.*

Royce Hotel. This is one of Charlotte's most glitzy hotels. The lobby is all marble and glass. Dining is offered in The Veranda and entertainment in a trendy nightclub called Chelsea's. *5624 Westpark Dr. at I–77, 28217, tel. 704/527–8000. 184 rooms and suites. Facilities: outdoor pool, health club, complimentary airport transportation. AE, DC, MC, V.*

Moderate–
Expensive
Adam's Mark. This is one of the best places in town to have a meeting. The public rooms in this high-rise hotel are large and attractively decorated in rust tones. Rooms on the west side, overlooking McDowell Park, afford great views of the Charlotte skyline. There's a one-mile fitness trail in the park nearby. Guests enjoy dining in the Marker restaurant and relaxing in the adjoining lounge. Appleby's offers more casual meals. The high-energy disco atmosphere of Players Lounge attracts a large following. *555 S. McDowell St., 28204, tel. 704/372–4100. 588 rooms and suites. Facilities: indoor and outdoor pools, Nautilus-equipped health club, whirlpool, sauna, racquetball courts, meeting rooms, airport transportation. AE, CB, DC, MC, V.*

Charlotte Marriott Executive Park. This high-rise property commands a large presence in the I–77 cluster of hotels and motels. The public rooms are attractively decorated in rust colors, and the flooring is made of sand-colored tiles. Guests have a choice of gourmet dining at Ashley's or the more casual atmosphere of The Market. Cahoots is one of Charlotte's hot spots. The hotel also has a raw bar and the only wine bar in the city. *I–77 and Tyvola Rd., 28217, tel. 704/527–9650. 300 rooms and suites. Facilities: indoor and outdoor pools, tennis courts, exercise room, outdoor fitness center, concierge, game room, meeting rooms, airport shuttle. AE, CB, DC, MC, V.*

Hilton at University Place. The hotel dominates the European-style shopping and entertainment village near the University of North Carolina at Charlotte. Movies, restaurants, shops, a bank, and even a hospital are just a few steps from the hotel door. The interior of this high-rise features a three-story atrium. Dining is offered in Justin's, overlooking the adjacent lake. There is a happy hour buffet at the Lakeside Lounge. The 11th and 12th floors offer a number of special amenities, including concierge services, complimentary breakfast, evening hors d'oeuvres, and cocktails. *U.S. 29 and Harris Blvd., 28213, tel. 704/547–7444. 250 rooms and suites. Facilities: fitness center, outdoor lap pool, meeting rooms, airport transportation. AE, CB, DC, MC, V.*

Sheraton Airport Plaza. The atrium lobby is decorated with contemporary furnishings. Golf privileges are available at a nearby club. Amenities include newspapers, fresh fruit, and complimentary cocktail hour on Tuesday and Wednesday. *3315 I–85 at Billy Graham Parkway, 28208, tel. 704/392–1200. 226 rooms and suites. Facilities: indoor/outdoor pool, sauna, whirlpool, exercise room, meeting rooms, airport shuttle, car rental office. AE, CB, DC, MC, V.*

Woodlawn Holiday Inn is the largest of six properties in this chain in the Charlotte area. The contemporary lobby has a marble floor, and the Atrium restaurant resembles a large indoor garden with fountains. Guests have privileges at the American Fitness and Athletic Club on South Blvd. *Woodlawn and I–77, 28213, tel. 704/525–8350. 432 rooms and suites. Facilities: outdoor pool, hydra-spa, health club, meeting rooms, airport transportation, airline ticket office. AE, CB, DC, MC, V.*

Inns
Moderate–
Expensive

The Morehead Inn. The historic inn is an attractive alternative to hotel living without sacrificing city convenience. The former private residence is located in the Dilworth neighborhood. Public rooms are spacious and inviting and can be used for corporate meetings. Guests have the option of 12 distinct rooms, each with a private bath. A Continental breakfast is included. *1122 E. Morehead St., 28204, tel. 376–3357. 12 rooms. AE, CB, DC, MC.*

Bed-and-Breakfast
Moderate–
Expensive

The Inn on Providence. Another attractive bed and breakfast option for overnight stays. Darlene and Dan MacNeill offer five luxurious bedrooms, each with private bath, plus a home-cooked breakfast. Guests enjoy the spacious grounds and swimming pool in this quiet southeast Charlotte neighborhood. *6700 Providence Rd., 28226, tel. 704/366–6700. 5 rooms. MC, V.*

Moderate

The Homeplace. This spotless turn-of-the-century Victorian gem is now a bed-and-breakfast inn filled with antiques and memorabilia from yesteryear. The inn offers four guest rooms, each with a private bath, and breakfast prepared by owners

Peggy and Frank Darien. The Homeplace is located in a country/suburban neighborhood. *5901 Sardis Rd., 28226, tel. 704/365–1936. 4 rooms. AE, MC.*

Nightlife

Nightlife—if by that you mean good music, dancing, comedy, or drinking—has become more sophisticated in recent years with the coming of the larger hotel chains, though the honky-tonk bars are still prevalent.

Cahoots (5700 Westpark Dr. at I–77, tel. 704/527–9650). The walls of the Marriott vibrate from the loud music coming from this hotel bar, a popular spot for young singles.

Comedy Zone (2 NCNB Plaza, tel. 704/377–0400). Get your laughs for the evening at this spiffy club in the Radisson Plaza Hotel.

Grady's Goodtimes (5546 Albemarle Rd., tel. 704/537–4663). There's no live music at this eastside pub-restaurant, but the hospitality will compensate for it. The bartender will know your name after a drink or two.

Jazz Cellar at Jonathan's (330 N. Tryon St., tel. 704/332–3663). This is the place to hear jazz in Charlotte. Maria Howell and the 7th Street Band play here regularly, as well as regional and national groups.

Raleigh

North Carolina's capital city appears to be another Atlanta about to happen—from the hustle-bustle on the Beltline to the business deals being made at the 42nd Street Oyster Bar to the new glitzy convention hotels. American Airlines, which operates a major hub at the Raleigh-Durham Airport, offers service to Paris, Cancun, Bermuda, and Puerto Rico.

There's a vibrance in this overgrown college town and capital city that's unique in the state. The Duke, NC State, and UNC (Carolina) basketball teams have all become Atlantic Coast Conference (ACC) champions in recent seasons. Scientific breakthroughs are commonplace at Research Triangle Park, as is important medical research at local universities. People, however, still get as excited over barbecue as they do about politics. The City of Oaks, so called because of its profusion of oak trees, is small town and big town, Old South and New South, down-home and urbane, all in one.

Arriving and Departing

By Plane
Airports and Airlines
Raleigh is served by the Raleigh–Durham Airport (RDU, tel. 919/840–2123), located between the two cities near the Research Triangle Park, off I–40. **American, Delta, Eastern, Pan Am, TWA, United,** and **USAir** together offer over 250 daily flights. **American Eagle, USAir Express,** and **Wheeler** provide regional commuter service.

Between the Airport Since airport bus service is not available, the best way to get
and Center City downtown is by taxi or limousine. Taxis cost $15–$20; limousine
service is about half that price.

By Car. From the airport, take I–40 east to Exit 285. Then follow Wade Avenue east and turn right on Downtown Boulevard,
which leads into the heart of the city. The drive takes about
twenty minutes.

By Train **Amtrak** (320 W. Cabarrus St., tel. 919/833–7594 or 800/872–
7245) connects Raleigh with Washington, DC and New York to
the north and with Florida to the south. There are two daily
trains, one northbound and one southbound.

By Bus **Carolina Trailways** and **Greyhound/Trailways** (321 W. Jones St.,
tel. 919/828–2567).

By Car I–40 connects Raleigh to Durham, and Chapel Hill with U.S.
401, forming something of a perimeter route around the city.
U.S. 70 is also a major artery connecting to I–85 west of the city
and to the coast and I–95 on the east side. U.S. 1, which runs
north and south, also links to I–85 going northeast. U.S. 64
runs east and west through Raleigh.

Getting Around

By Bus **Capital Area Transit** (919/833–5701) is Raleigh's public trans-
port system. Fares are 75¢ for adults, 30¢ for senior citizens,
and 60¢ for adults between 9 AM and 3:30 PM. Children under 4
ride free.

By Taxi Approximately 16 taxi companies serve the Raleigh area. Fares
are calculated by the mile.

Important Addresses and Numbers

Tourist The **Raleigh Visitor Information Center** is operated by the
Information Greater Raleigh Chamber of Commerce, *800 S. Salisbury St.,
tel. 919/833–3005. Open weekdays 8:30–5. Free parking.*

The Raleigh Convention and Visitors Bureau offers information
on the area. *225 Hillsborough St., Suite 400, tel. 919/834–5900
in Raleigh; 800/552–8666; in NC, 800/868–6666.*

Capital Area Visitor Center offers information about tours
through state government buildings. *301 N. Blount St., tel.
919/733–3456. Open weekdays 8–5, Sat. 9–5, Sun. 1–5.*

Emergencies Dial 911 for **police** or **ambulance** in an emergency.

Doctor Hospital emergency rooms are open 24 hours a day. For minor
emergencies, the city has 10 urgent-care centers. If you are in
need of a local doctor, call the **Wake County Medical Society**
(tel. 919/821–2227) for a referral.

Pharmacy **Eckerd Drugs** (3427 Hillsborough Rd., Durham, tel. 919/383–
5591).

Guided Tours

Capital Area Visitor Center provides free tours of the executive
mansion, state capitol, legislative building, and other government buildings. *Tel. 919/733–3456. Open weekdays 8–5, Sat.
9–5, Sun. 1–5.*

Tours and Functions (tel. 919/782–8145) offers customized tours for groups in Raleigh and the surrounding area.

Exploring Raleigh

Raleigh is spread out, so a car is almost a necessity unless you limit your sightseeing to downtown. Downtown Raleigh offers plenty of parking, including public lots at the corner of Edenton and Wilmington streets and in the 400 block of N. Salisbury Street (50¢ cents per hour or $4 per day). There's also a big parking garage at the Raleigh Civic and Convention Center, but be prepared to pay hefty fees. Watch for one-way streets when driving. With the city growing so rapidly and confusion over roads mounting, getting around Raleigh without a map is often difficult. The streets in the downtown area, however, are laid out in an orderly grid fashion with the State Capitol as the hub (a good landmark).

Most of the attractions in the downtown Raleigh walking tour are state government buildings and are free to the public. You'll need several hours just to hit the high spots, even more time if you tend to get hooked on museums.

State Capitol Walking Tour After stopping in at the **Capital Area Visitor Center** to pick up maps and brochures, begin your tour at the **State Capitol,** which occupies the block facing Fayetteville Street Mall in the center of downtown between Wilmington and Salisbury streets. Finished in 1840 and restored during the 1976 Bicentennial, it exudes a special warmth not found in the more contemporary 1960s State Legislative Building. The old building that once housed all the functions of state government could tell many tales if its walls could talk. *Capitol Sq., tel. 919/733–4994. Open Mon.–Sat. 9–5, Sun. 1–5. Closed certain holidays.*

The **State Legislative Building,** on the corner of Halifax and Jones streets, sits one block north of the capitol. When the legislature is in session, the building hums with lawmakers and lobbyists. *Legislative Building, Jones St., tel. 919/733–7928. Open Mon.–Sat. 9–5, Sun. 1–5.*

A half block away is the **North Carolina Museum of Natural Sciences,** a favorite hang-out for children, who love its resident snakes and animal exhibits. The gift shop offers some unusual souvenirs. *1 W. Edenton St., tel. 919/733–7450. Open Tues.–Sat. 9–5, Sun. 1–5.*

Now step back in time at the **North Carolina Museum of History.** Here you'll see exhibits on period costumes, guns, and on many other subjects that chronicle the state's 400-year history. The gift shop is worth a look. *109 E. Jones St., tel. 919/733–3894. Open Mon.–Sat. 9–5, Sun. 1–6.*

The **Executive Mansion** (200 N. Blount St., tel. 919/733–3456), a brick turn-of-the-century Queen Anne cottage-style structure with gingerbread trim, is home to the governor. Tour hours vary; check with the Capital Area Visitor Center. A stroll through the nearby **Oakwood Historic District** will introduce you to more fine examples of Victorian architecture.

Time Out The **Side Street Cafe** has some of the best sandwiches, soups, and salads in town. *225 N. Bloodworth St., tel. 919/828–4927.*

The City Market (Martin St. and Moore Sq.) is coming alive again, after extensive renovations, as new shops and restaurants take up residence. *Open daily 10 AM–late evening.*

Fayetteville Street Mall extends from the State Capitol to the Raleigh Civic and Convention Center. Open to pedestrians only, it offers a chance to get in touch with the city at an easy pace. In the middle of the mall is a bronze statue of Sir Walter Raleigh, who started the first colony in North Carolina and for whom the city is named.

What to See and Do with Children

Pullen Park (500 Ashe Ave., near NCSU, tel. 919/755–6468) attracts large crowds during the summer to its 1911 Dentzel carousel and train ride. You can swim here, too, and enjoy an arts and crafts center and the Theater in the Park.

At the **North Carolina Museum of Life and Science** (433 Murray Ave., off I–85 in Durham, tel. 919/477–0431) visitors encounter life-size models of dinosaurs on the nature trail and get to ride a train through the 40-acre wildlife sanctuary. New at the hands-on museum is an animal habitat featuring native North Carolina animals. The aerospace exhibit is also outstanding.

Off the Beaten Track

Patterson's Mill Country Store. Step back into yesteryear when you visit the store at Leigh Farm just outside Chapel Hill. Browse through the pharmacy or see what a doctor's office was like a century ago. Shop for wooden toys, quilts, antiques, whirlygigs—all part of a fine collection of mercantile Americana. *Exit 173 to Chapel Hill off I–40. Farrington Rd., tel. 919/ 493–8149. Open Mon.–Sat. 10–5:30, Sun. 2–5:30. Closed Easter and Christmas Day.*

Historic Hillsborough. Wander through the streets of this colonial town (Exit 164 from I–85, west of Durham). Give yourself time to read the historical markers, visit the Orange County Historical Museum, or dine at the Colonial Inn, which dates to 1759. *Museum is open Tues.–Sun., 1:30–4:30.*

Shopping

Shopping Districts Because so many stores have moved to the suburbs, downtown shopping isn't what it used to be, and the stores that remain now close by 5 or 6 in the evening. The best of the surburban malls:

Cameron Village Shopping Center (Oberlin Rd. and Clark Ave.), Raleigh's oldest shopping center and one of the first in the Southeast, is anchored by JC Penney and Thalhimers.

Crabtree Valley Mall (Glenwood Ave.; U.S. 70) is the city's largest enclosed mall, with over a million square feet of retail space. Stores include Belk, Sears, Thalhimers, Miller and Rhodes.

North Hills Fashion Mall (Six Forks Rd. and Beltline) offers the latest in high fashion. Stores include Montaldo's, Tyler House, and Ivey's.

Brightleaf Square (905 W. Main St., Durham) is an upscale shopping-entertainment complex housed in old tobacco warehouses in the heart of downtown. Shoppers enjoy relaxing at the Duke of York restaurant and pub.

Specialty Stores
Books **DJ's College Textbooks** (2416 Hillsborough St., tel. 919/832–4125) is the place to buy not only used college texts but out-of-town papers and unusual magazines.

Flea Markets **Fairgrounds Flea Market.** You can find anything and everything here—from fine antiques to "early attic" furniture. *Hillsborough St. and Blue Ridge Rd., tel. 919/832–0361. Open weekends 9–5.*

Another option is the **Flea Market Mall.** *1924 North Blvd., tel. 919/839–0038. Open weekends 9–6.*

Food **Farmer's Market.** You can't go wrong on fresh produce at this Raleigh institution, which reflects the agrarian nature of the surrounding area. There's even a restaurant on site. *1491 Hodges St., tel. 919/733–7417 (market) or 919/833–7973 (restaurant). Open 24 hrs, June–September; 5 AM–6 PM, Mon.–Sat., Oct.–May.*

Participant Sports

Bicycling The city has designated 20 miles of greenways for biking, and maps are available at City Hall (tel. 919/890–3125).

Camping Try the North Carolina State Fairgrounds, William B. Umstead State Park, Clemmons State Park near Clayton, or Jordan Lake between Apex and Pittsboro. Other options are Lake Gaston and Kerr Lake near the Virginia line. *For details, call the Raleigh Convention and Visitors Bureau, tel. 919/834–5900, or the North Carolina Division of Travel and Tourism, tel. 919/733–4171.*

Canoeing Lake Wheeler and Shelley Lake are the best places for canoeing. The Eno River State Park near Durham is another option. The Haw River is popular as well, but can be treacherous after a heavy rain.

Fishing Fishing licenses may be purchased at local bait-and-tackle shops. Call the North Carolina Division of Boating and Inland Fishing (tel. 919/733–3633) for more information.

Golf The Raleigh area has more than 12 golf courses open to the public, including **Wildwood Green Golf Club** and **Wake Forest Country Club.** A complete list of courses is available from the Raleigh Convention and Visitors Bureau (tel. 919/834–5900). Pinehurst–Southern Pines, the Golf Capital of the World, offering more than 35 courses, is only a short drive away.

Hiking Jordan Lake, Lake Wheeler, William B. Umstead State Park, and Duke Forest in Durham offer thousands of acres for hiking. For trail information, call the North Carolina Division of Travel and Tourism, (tel. 919/733–4171).

Jogging Runners enjoy Shelley Lake, the track at NCSU, and the Capitol Area Greenway system, which is partially completed.

Physical Fitness The YMCA (1601 Hillsborough St., tel. 919/832–6601) will permit visitors to use their facilities for $3–$10, provided they have a YMCA membership elsewhere. The Y also accepts guests staying at certain local hotels. Hotels with fitness centers are noted in the accommodations listings.

River Rafting The Haw River is the closest place for shooting the rapids.

Skiing *(See* the North Carolina High Country and Asheville—Land of the Sky sections.)

Tennis More than 80 courts in city parks are available for use. Millbrook Exchange Park, (1905 Spring Forest Rd.) holds city tournaments. Call *Raleigh Parks and Recreation (tel. 919/876–2616) for information. Courts are also available at some hotels.*

Spectator Sports

Basketball The Raleigh area is basketball heaven with teams such as UNC–Chapel Hill, Duke, NC State, and NC Central University to cheer to victory. For information on Raleigh's favorite team—NCSU—contact the university ticket office (tel. 919/737–2106).

Dining

Dining is approaching a new sophistication in the Raleigh area, with many upscale restaurants opening around the city in addition to those found in hotels. You can also find informal places where barbecue, Brunswick stew, fried chicken, and lots of country vegetables are served in great quantities for very low prices.

Category	Cost*
Very Expensive	over $25
Expensive	$15–$25
Moderate	$8–$15
Inexpensive	under $8

**per person without tax (5%), service, or drinks*

The following credit-card abbreviations are used: AE, American Express; CB, Carte Blanche; DC, Diners Club; MC, MasterCard; V, Visa.

Expensive **The Angus Barn, Ltd.** This Raleigh tradition is housed in a huge rustic barn. Gingham- and denim-clad waiters and waitresses add authenticity to the farmlike scene. The astonishing wine and beer list covers 35 pages of the menu. The restaurant serves the best steaks, baby back ribs, and prime rib for miles around. Desserts are heavenly. Take-home products are sold in the Country Store. *U.S. 70W at Airport Rd., tel. 919/781–2444. Dress: informal. Reservations recommended. Sat.—first come, first served. AE, DC, MC, V.*
42nd St. Oyster Bar. This much talked-about restaurant is the place to see and be seen in Raleigh. Politicians, businessmen, and laborers sit side by side downing succulent oysters and other seafood dishes. *West and Jones Sts., tel. 919/831–2811. Dress: casual. Reservations limited. AE, DC, MC, V.*

Moderate **Est Est Est Trattoria.** The best place in town for authentic northern Italian pasta. *19 W. Hargett St., tel. 919/832–8899. Dress: informal. Reservations not required. MC, V.*
Neptune's Galley. In business for many years, this restaurant is known for its fresh seafood. Neptune's is also open for breakfast. *5111 Western Blvd., tel. 919/851–4993. Dress: casual.*

Reservations not required. Closed Sun. AE, CB, DC, MC, V.

Bullock's Bar-B-Cue (Durham). If you want to experience local cuisine, try the Brunswick stew, barbecue, southern fried chicken, and hush puppies at this casual eatery that offers eat-in or carry-out service. *3330 Wortham St., tel. 919/383-3211. First-come, first-served (come early). No credit cards. Closed Sun.*

Inexpensive   **Fat Daddy's Market & Grill.** A trendy establishment known for its hamburgers. *7112 Sandy Forks Rd., tel. 919/847-3738; 6201 Glenwood Ave., tel. 919/787-3773. Dress: casual. Reservations not required. AE, MC, V.*

Irregardless Cafe. This eatery is a delight to vegetarians and weight-conscious eaters. *901 W. Morgan St., tel. 919/833-8898. Dress: casual. Reservations not required. Sat. dinner only. Sun. brunch. MC, V.*

Joe's Place "Featuring Joe's Mom's Food." If you've got a farm-sized hunger, come here for a heaping plate of home-grown country food. *301 W. Martin St., tel. 919/832-5260. Dress: casual. Reservations not required. Closed Sat. and Sun.*

Lodging

Raleigh offers lodgings in all price ranges—from convention hotels to bed-and-breakfast houses to economy chains. Major hotel chains represented here are Holiday Inn, Hilton, Radisson, Marriott, and Sheraton. Inexpensive lodging is offered by Comfort Inn, Econo Lodge, Crickett Inn, and Days Inn. New on the hotel scene are Embassy Suites Hotel, Fairfield Inn, Hampton Inn, Hospitality Inn–Stony Brook, Quality Suites Hotel, Red Roof Inn, Sundown Inn–North, and others. Most lodgings also offer suites. Since Raleigh is a business town, many hotels and motels advertise special weekend rates.

Category	Cost*
Very Expensive	over $100
Expensive	$60–$100
Moderate	$30–$60
Inexpensive	under $30

*double room; add 8% for taxes

Expensive   **Holiday Inn State Capitol.** Built in the chain's familiar circular tower design, the hotel is easy to pick out in downtown Raleigh and affords the only panoramic view of the city. Sunday brunches, Friday buffets, and complimentary hors d'oeuvres on weekday afternoons in the Top of the Tower Restaurant and Lounge attract large crowds. The 20-story hotel has a contemporary look. It is ideally situated for people who have to conduct business downtown. Guests enjoy privileges at the nearby YMCA. *320 Hillsborough St., 27603, tel. 919/832-0501. 203 rooms and suites. Facilities: outdoor pool, exercise room, free parking, complimentary shuttle to airport and local sites, newspaper and complimentary Continental breakfast in lobby. AE, DC, V.*

The **North Raleigh Hilton Convention Center.** This is a favorite capital city spot for corporate meetings. The Tower Suites offer a complimentary Continental breakfast, free hors d'oeuvres, concierge, newspapers, and light secretarial service. Guests enjoy dining in Lofton's restaurant and listening to the piano afterwards in the lobby bar. Bowties is one of the city's hottest nightspots. *3415 Wake Forest Rd., 27609, tel. 919/872-2323. 341 rooms and suites. Facilities: indoor pool and spa, complimentary airport shuttle, meeting rooms. AE, DC, MC, V.*

The Oakwood Inn. Located in Historic Oakwood, one of the city's oldest downtown neighborhoods, this is an alternative to hotel/motel living. Built in 1871 and now on the National Register of Historic Places, the inn is furnished with Victorian period pieces. The proprietress serves a sumptous breakfast and gladly assists with dinner reservations and evening entertainment plans. *411 N. Bloodworth St., 27604, tel. 919/832-9712. 6 rooms with bath. AE, MC, V.*

Quality Inn Mission Valley is located on the site of an old Catholic mission near the NC State University campus. Over the years the motel has become a favorite gathering spot for parents and friends attending graduations and ball games. Maybe that's why each room has a card table! The lobby is as inviting as a Southern front porch. Joel Lane's Restaurant attracts a large crowd to its Sunday Brunch. *2110 Avent Ferry Rd., 27605, tel. 919/828-3173. 367 rooms and suites; efficiency apartments by the day, week, or month. Facilities: indoor pool, sauna, exercise room, meeting rooms, mini-conference center in Magnolia Cottage, complimentary airport shuttle. AE, CB, DC, MC, V.*

Radisson Plaza Raleigh. This is an architecturally exciting hotel in the heart of downtown, with brick walls and arches, cascading fountains, and an expansive atrium. The hotel is connected to the civic center via a plaza. The hotel offers the Provence Restaurant, Cafe Promenade, and the Goodies-To-Go deli. *420 Fayetteville St. Mall, 27601, tel. 919/834-9900. 362 rooms and suites. Facilities: indoor pool, whirlpool, free parking, meeting rooms, airport shuttle. AE, CB, DC, MC, V.*

Raleigh Marriott Crabtree Valley. This is one of the city's most luxurious hotels. Fresh floral arrangements adorn the elegantly decorated public rooms. Guests enjoy the intimacy of the Scotch Bonnets restaurant, the family atmosphere of Allie's, and Champions Sports Bar. The concierge floor offers complimentary Continental breakfast and hors d'oeuvres. *4500 Marriott Dr. (U.S. 70W near Crabtree Valley Mall) 27612, tel. 919/781-7000. 375 rooms and suites. Facilities: indoor/outdoor pool, whirlpool, exercise room, game room, golf and racquetball nearby, complimentary airport shuttle. AE, CB, DC, MC, V.*

The Residence Inn by Marriott. This all-suite, apartmentlike property in North Raleigh is ideal if you want to stay for a while or are traveling with your family. Each suite features a sitting area with a wood-burning fireplace and a fully equipped kitchen. The inn will even do all the cleaning and deliver your groceries and wood free of charge. Guests enjoy getting acquainted around the fireplace in the hotel's sunken lobby. *1000 Navaho Dr., 27609, tel. 919/878-6100. 144 suites. Facilities: outdoor pool, Jacuzzi, sport court, guest privileges at nearby racquet club, complimentary newspaper and breakfast buffet. AE, CB, DC, MC, V.*

The Velvet Cloak Inn. Sister to The Breakers in West Palm Beach, this hotel is in a class of its own. Curtis, the doorman who dresses to the nines in a tux and top hat, has been greeting guests here for years. Local brides have wedding receptions around the enclosed pool, and politicians frequent the bar. The Charter Room, an elegant restaurant, often features a harpist. Afternoon tea and cookies are served in the lobby. Rooms in the brick structure, decorated with delicate wrought iron, are frequently refurbished. *1505 Hillsborough St., 27605, tel. 919/828 –0333. 172 rooms and suites. Facilities: enclosed pool and tropical garden, complimentary coffee and newspaper in the lobby, guest privileges at the YMCA next door, airport shuttle, meeting rooms. AE, DC, MC, V.*

Fearrington House (Chapel Hill). This bed-and-breakfast inn is a member of Relais & Chateaux. It features a restaurant that serves regional food prepared in a classic manner. *8 mi south of Chapel Hill on US 15–501, (postal address: Fearrington Village Center, Pittsboro 27312), tel. 919/542–2121 or 800/334–5475. 14 rooms. MC, V.*

Moderate **The Arrowhead Inn.** This bed-and-breakfast inn, located a few miles outside Durham, offers alternative lodging in a homelike setting. The innkeepers have refurbished several rooms in this 1774 inn and are in the process of redoing others. Guests are served a hearty breakfast. *106 Mason Rd., Durham, 27712, tel. 919/477–8430. 6 rooms, some with private baths. Closed Christmas week. AE, MC, V.*

Best Western Crabtree. The Crabtree. An upscale version of this usually ho-hum motel chain. It is tastefully decorated in soft colors. Executive and Jacuzzi suites feature wet bars, king-size beds, and private balconies. Rates include Continental breakfast. The six-story motel is near restaurants and shopping. *6209 Glenwood Ave. (U.S. 70), 27612, tel. 919/782–1112. 142 rooms and suites. Facilities: outdoor pool, health spa, meeting rooms. AE, DC, MC, V.*

Brownestone Hotel. This high-rise property adjacent to Pullen Park and North Carolina State University is a favorite haunt of state government leaders. Guests who stay on the executive level receive complimentary wine and breakfast. *1707 Hillsborough St., 27605, tel. 919/828–0811. 210 rooms and suites. Facilities: outdoor pool, privileges at adjacent YMCA, jogging trails in Pullen Park, restaurant. AE, CB, DC, MC, V.*

Plaza Hotel. A full complimentary breakfast is served to guests on weekdays. The concierge level also offers hors d'oeuvres and the use of a computer. This high rise is decorated in bold colors —purple, aqua, burgundy—a refreshing change from standard hotel beige. *2101 Century Dr. (U.S. 70 at Beltline), 27612, tel. 919/782–8600. 176 rooms and suites. Facilities: indoor pool, sauna, complimentary airport shuttle. AE, CB, DC, MC, V.*

Ramada Inn Crabtree. This hotel gets the award for being the friendliest motel in town. It's also where football and basketball teams like to stay when they're here for a game, as evidenced by the helmet collection and other sports memorabilia in the Brass Bell Lounge. The Colonnade Restaurant is known for its Sunday buffets. Rooms have been refurbished recently, and the grounds are spacious and attractively landscaped. *3920 Arrow Dr. (U.S. 70 and Beltline), 27612, tel. 919/782–7525. 177 rooms and suites. Facilities: outdoor pool, jogging trail, meeting rooms, airport shuttle. AE, DC, MC, V.*

Nightlife

Much of the nightlife is centered in the larger hotels, such as the Hilton or the Marriott. **Cat's Cradle** (320 W. Franklin St., Chapel Hill, tel. 919/967–9053) is the place for rock 'n' roll, reggae, and New Wave sounds. **Charlie Goodnight's Comedy Club** (861 W. Morgan St., tel. 919/833–8356) combines dinner with a night of laughs. Mexican dishes are featured in the restaurant downstairs, steak and seafood upstairs.

Winston-Salem

The manufacture of cigarettes, textiles, furniture, and other products has built a solid economic base in the Winston-Salem area. There's also a healthy respect for the arts here. The North Carolina School of the Arts commands international attention. The Crosby golf tournament, formerly played at Pebble Beach, California, attracts the rich and famous. Old Salem, an 18th-century Moravian town within the city of Winston-Salem, has been drawing tourists since the late 1940s.

Arriving and Departing

By Plane   Six major airlines serve the Piedmont Triad International Airport: **American, Delta, Eastern, Continental, United,** and **USAir.**

By Bus   Contact **Greyhound/Trailways** (tel. 919/725–5692).

By Train   One daily northbound and one southbound **Amtrak** train serve Greensboro (tel. 919/855–3382), about 25 miles away.

Important Addresses and Numbers

Tourist   **Winston-Salem Convention and Visitors Bureau** (Box 1408,
Information   Winston-Salem 27102, tel. 919/725–2361 or 800/331–7018).

Emergencies   Dial 911 for **police** and **ambulance** in an emergency.

Guided Tours

Contact **Piedmont Guides** (Box 10254, Greensboro 27404, tel. 919/282–8687) for group tours to Triad attractions.

Exploring Winston-Salem

Old Salem is just a few blocks from downtown Winston-Salem and only a stone's throw from I–40 (take the Old Salem/Salem College exit). The 1700s live again in this village of 60 original brick and wooden structures. The aromas of freshly baked bread, sugar cakes, and ginger snaps mix with those of beeswax candles and newly dyed flax. Tradesmen work in their shops making pewterware, cooking utensils, and other items, while the womenfolk embroider and weave cloth. The Moravians, a Protestant sect, fled to Georgia to find religious freedom. From there they went to Bethlehem, Pennsylvania, but finally found the peace they sought in the Piedmont region of North Carolina. In 1753, they built Bethabara, located on Bethabara Road., off University Parkway, and then in 1766 they built Salem. Tour tickets will get you into several restored buildings at

Old Salem, but you may wander through the streets free of charge. *600 S. Main St., tel. 919/721–7300. Admission: $12 adults, $6 children ages 6–14; families $25; check into combination ticket to MESDA. Open Mon.–Sat. 9:30–4:30, Sun. 1:30–4:30.*

Time Out | **Winkler Bakery** will satisfy your craving for hot, freshly baked Moravian sugar cake. The bakery is included on tours and is also open to the public. *S. Main St., tel. 919/721–7302. Open Mon.–Sat. 9:30–4:30.*

Another way to step back into time is to enter the **Museum of Early Southern Decorative Arts (MESDA)**. Twenty rooms are decorated with period furnishings. *924 S. Main St., tel. 919/721–7360. Admission: full tour $6 adults, $3 children, ages 6–14; sampler tour $4 adults, $2 children ages 6–14. Open Mon.–Sat. 10:30–5, Sun. 1:30–4:30.*

Stroh Brewery, approximately 5 miles south of downtown via U.S. 52, rolls out 5.5 million barrels of beer a year as the second-largest brewery in the country. A single machine can fill and seal up to 1,500 12-ounce cans of beer per minute. You can see it made and enjoy a complimentary drink. *Schlitz Ave., U.S. 52S at S. Main St., tel. 919/788–6710. Admission free. Open weekdays 11–4:30.*

Historic **Bethabara Park** is another vision from the 1700s. You can explore the foundations of the town, as well as the three remaining historic structures. Kids love the reconstructed Indian fort. *2147 Bethabara Rd., tel. 919/924–8191. Admission free. Open weekdays 9:30–4:30, weekends 1:30–4:30. Guided tours Apr.–Dec. 15 or by appointment.*

Reynolda House is the lavish 60-room home of the late R. J. Reynolds, the tobacco king, that today houses an outstanding collection of American art. While you're on the estate, take time also to see the gardens and the stables, dairy barn, and other outbuildings now serving as a shopping complex. The house will close for renovations in September and reopen in late 1991. *Reynolda Rd., tel. 919/725–5325. Admission: $5 adults, $3 children and senior citizens. Open Tues.–Sat. 9:30–4:30, Sun. 1:30–4:30. Closed Mon.*

SECCA (the Southeastern Center for Contemporary Art) is near Reynolda House. This unique museum is the place to see the latest in Southern painting, sculpture, and printmaking. The Tudor-style facility, the former home of the late James G. Hanes, a textile industrialist, is as interesting as the exhibits. *750 Marguerite Dr., tel. 919/725–1904. Admission free. Open Tues.–Sat. 10–5, Sun. 2–5.*

Tanglewood Park (Hwy. 158, Clemmons, tel. 919/766–0591), a 10-minute drive west from the city via I–40, is the former home of the late William and Kate Reynolds and today serves as a public park. Visitors enjoy horseback riding, golf, tennis, boating, miniature golf, swimming, and an array of other activities, including PGA golf events and polo games. Overnight accommodations range from camping to rooms in the manor house.

What to See and Do with Children

Nature Science Center of Winston Salem. Look at the stars, handle live starfish in the tidal pool, pet the lambs and goats. *Museum Dr., Winston-Salem, tel. 919/767–6730. Admission: $3 adults, children $2. Open Mon.–Sat. 10–5, Sun. 1–5.*

Shopping

Crafts   The *New York Times* called the **Piedmont Craftsmen's Shop and Gallery** a "showcase for Southern crafts." *411 N. Cherry St., 919/725–8243. Open weekdays 10–6, Sat. 10–5, Sun. 1–5.*

Outlets   This is a textile center, so there are many clothing outlets clustered along the interstates. **Marketplace Mall** (2101 Peters Creek Pkwy., tel. 919/722–7779) is one option. The 100 stores in **Burlington Manufacturers Outlet Center** (tel. 919/227–2872) and **Waccamaw Pottery and the Burlington Outlet Mall** (tel. 919/229–0418) make the area off I–85 near Burlington truly the outlet capital of the South. *Most stores are open Mon.–Sat. 10–9, Sun. 1–6.*

Spectator Sports

Polo   On Sunday afternoons (Apr.–June and Sept.–Nov.) polo players entertain the crowds at Tanglewood Park. Contact the Forsyth County Park Authority, Inc. (Box 1040, Clemmons 27012, tel. 919/766–0591).

Dining

Traditional dining in these parts is Southern—fried chicken, ham, vegetables, biscuits, fruit cobblers, and the like. Chopped or sliced pork barbecue is also a big item. With the area becoming so sophisticated, though, there's a growing number of gourmet restaurants.

Category	Cost*
Very Expensive	over $25
Expensive	$15–$25
Moderate	$8–$15
Inexpensive	under $8

per person without tax (4.5%), service, or drinks

The following credit-card abbreviations are used: AE, American Express; CB, Carte Blanche; DC, Diners Club; MC, MasterCard; V, Visa.

Expensive   **La Chadiere.** Elegantly prepared French country dishes of pheasant, rabbit, veal, and other delicacies are served here in a country French atmosphere. Soft white walls, original paintings, and fresh flowers set off this restaurant in Reynolda Village. *120 Reynolda Rd., tel. 919/748–0269. Reservations strongly recommended. Closed Mon. AE, DC, MC, V.*

Moderate–Expensive   **Old Salem Tavern Dining Room.** Eat Moravian food in a Moravian setting served by waiters in Moravian costumes, all in the heart of Old Salem. Standard menu items are chicken pie, ragout of beef, and rack of lamb. From April through October you can dine outside under the arbor. *736 S. Main St., tel. 919/748-8585. Sun. brunch. Closed Thanksgiving, Christmas Eve, and Christmas Day. AE, MC, V.*

Moderate **Leon's Cafe.** This casual eatery near Old Salem serves some of the best gourmet food in town—fresh seafood, chicken breasts with raspberry sauce, lamb, and other specialties. *825 S. Marshall, tel. 919/725-9593. Reservations not accepted. No lunch. Closed Sun.–Tues., New Year's Day, Thanksgiving, Christmas, and the last two weeks in August. MC, V.*

Zevely House. Dine on chicken or game bird in a restored 19th-century house or in the adjoining garden. A children's menu is available. *Tel. 919/725-6666. Reservations advised. Closed for lunch on Mon. and Sat., New Year's Day and Christmas Day. AE, MC, V.*

Stars at Stevens Center. Have preview cocktails and dinner, then enjoy a play or concert, and come back for coffee and dessert afterwards—all in a restored Art Deco performing arts center in the heart of downtown Winston-Salem. *401 W. 4th St., tel. 919/761-0476. Reservations advised. No lunch. Closed New Year's Day, Thanksgiving, Christmas Eve, and Christmas Day. AE, CB, MC, V.*

Lodging

Category	Cost*
Very Expensive	over $100
Expensive	$60–$100
Moderate	$30–$60
Inexpensive	under $30

*double room; add 7.5% for taxes

The following credit-card abbreviations are used: AE, American Express; CB, Carte Blanche; DC, Diners Club; MC, MasterCard; V, Visa.

Very Expensive **Hyatt Winston-Salem.** This downtown property features an atrium and garden terrace. Redecorated in pastel colors, its large guest rooms have a soft contemporary look. *300 W. 5th St., 27101, tel. 919/725-1234 or 800/228-9000. 288 rooms. Facilities: indoor pool, Jacuzzi, exercise room; garage parking and airport transportation extra. AE, CB, DC, MC, V.*

Stouffer Winston Plaza. This hotel is centrally located, off I-40. The hotel has almost 10,000 square feet of meeting space that can be augmented by facilities at the Convention Center across the street. *425 N. Cherry St., 27101, tel. 919/725-3500. 318 rooms. Facilities: 2 restaurants, bar, indoor/outdoor pool, steam room, sauna, game room, and gift shop. AE, DC, MC, V.*

Moderate–Expensive **Brookstown Inn.** Sleep under a comfy handmade quilt in front of the fireplace or enjoy wine and cheese in the spacious lobby of this unusual bed-and-breakfast hotel, built in 1837 as one of the first textile mills in the South. Breakfast is included. *200 Brookstown Ave., 27102, tel. 919/725-1120. 52 rooms. Facilities: some rooms with whirlpools, airport transportation. AE, MC, V.*

Moderate **Ramada Hotel.** This hotel caters to convention and business clientele, with a spacious lobby decorated in beige and green. *420 High St., 27103, tel. 919/723–7911 or 800/2–RAMADA. 173 rooms. Facilities: John Casper's Lounge featuring comedy shows Fri. and Sat., restaurant, 7 meeting rooms, ballroom, outdoor pool, and van service to the airport. AE, DC, MC, V.*

Outer Banks and Historic Albemarle

North Carolina's Outer Banks are made up of a series of barrier islands stretching from the Virginia state line southward to Cedar Island. Throughout history they have posed a threat to ships, and hence the area became known as the Graveyard of the Atlantic. A network of lighthouses and lifesaving stations was built to make the Outer Banks safer for navigators. English settlers attempted to colonize the region more than 400 years ago, but the first colony disappeared mysteriously, without a trace. Their plight is retold in an annual outdoor drama, "The Lost Colony." The islands offered seclusion and privacy to pirates who hid out in the coves and inlets. The notorious pirate Blackbeard lived and died here. For many years the Outer Banks remained isolated, home only to a few families who made their living by fishing. Today the islands, linked by bridges and ferries, are popular among summer tourists. Much of the area is included in the Cape Hatteras National Seashore. The largest towns on the islands are Manteo and Nags Head.

On the inland side of the Outer Banks is the Historic Albemarle Region, a remote area of small villages and towns surrounding Albemarle Sound. Edenton served as the Colonial capital for a while, and today many of its early structures are preserved for posterity.

Getting Around

By Plane The closest commercial airports are the Raleigh-Durham Airport and Norfolk International, both of which are served by major carriers, including **American, Continental, Delta, Eastern, Pan Am,** and **USAir.**

By Train **Amtrak** service (tel. 800/872–7245) is available to Norfolk, VA, about 75 miles to the north.

By Car U.S. 158 links Manteo with Norfolk and other places north. U.S. 64 and 264 are western routes. NC 12 goes south toward Ocracoke Island and north toward Corolla. Toll ferries connect Ocracoke to Cedar Island and Swan Quarter. There is a free ferry across Hatteras Inlet.

By Taxi **Roy's Taxi Service** (tel. 919/441–6459 or nights 473–2726) serves the Outer Banks.

By Boat Seagoing visitors travel the Intracoastal Waterway through the Outer Banks and Historic Albemarle region. Boats may dock at Elizabeth City Manteo (the Salty Dawg Marina), and other ports.

Guided Tours

Historic Albemarle Tour, Inc., (Box 759, Edenton 27932, tel. 919/482–7325), offers guided tours of Edenton and publishes a brochure on a self-guided tour of the Albemarle Region.

Kitty Hawk Aerotours (tel. 919/441–4460) leave from the First Flight Airstrip for Kitty Hawk, Corolla, Cape Hatteras, Ocracoke, Portsmouth Island, and other areas along the Outer Banks. *Mar.–Labor Day.*

Ocracoke Trolley Tours (of Ocracoke Island) depart from Trolley Stop One. NC 12, Ocracoke. Tel. 919/928–4041. *June–Labor Day, Mon.–Sat.*

Important Addresses and Numbers

Tourist Information **Dare County Tourist Bureau,** (Box 399, Manteo, tel. 919/473–2138). Historic Albemarle Tour, Inc. (Box 759, Edenton 27932, tel. 919/482–7325). Outer Banks Chamber of Commerce (Box 1757, Kill Devil Hills 27948, tel. 919/441–8144).

Emergencies Dial 911 if you are north of Oregon Inlet and Roanoke Island; 919/986–2144 for Hattaras Island; 919/928–4631 for Ocracoke. The Outer Banks Medical Center at Nags Head is open 24 hours a day, tel. 919/441–7111.

Coast Guard Tel. 919/995–5881.

Exploring the Outer Banks

Numbers in the margin correspond with points of interest on the Outer Banks map.

You can begin your tour of the Outer Banks from either the southern end of the barrier islands at Cedar Island or the northern end at Nags Head. Unless you're camping, overnight stays will probably be in Ocracoke or in the Nags Head-Manteo area, where motels and hotels are concentrated. (There's also a motel at Cedar Island on the mainland where you catch the ferry to Ocracoke.) You can drive the 70-mile stretch of barrier islands in a day, but be sure to allow plenty of time during the summer season in case you have to wait for the next ferry to the mainland. A complete schedule is included on the state map. For reservations, call 919/225–3551 for departures from Cedar Island, 919/928–3841 from Ocracoke, or 919/926–1111 from Swan Quarter. Be wary of getting stranded on the islands during major storms and hurricanes when the roads and bridges become clogged with traffic.

① **Kill Devil Hills,** on U.S. 158 Bypass, midway between Kitty Hawk and Nags Head, is such an unimpressive location, it's hard to believe its historical significance as the site of man's first flight. The **Wright Brothers National Memorial,** a granite monument that resembles the tail of an airplane, stands as a tribute to Wilbur and Orville Wright, two bicycle mechanics from Ohio who took to the air on December 17, 1903. You can see a replica of *The Flyer* and stand on the exact spot where it made four take-offs and landings, the longest being a distance of 852 feet. Exhibits and an informative talk by a National Park Service ranger make the thrilling event come to life again. The Wrights' accomplishment was no easy task in this remote area

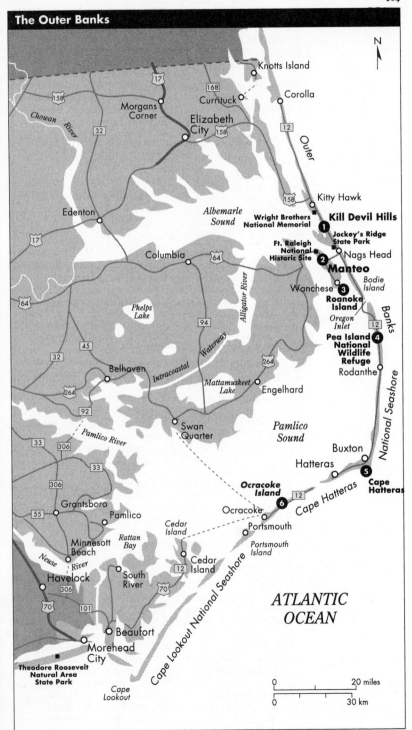

The Outer Banks

N

Knotts Island

Currituck

Corolla

17

168

158

Morgans Corner

Elizabeth City

Chowan River

32

158

Outer

12

Kitty Hawk

Edenton

17

Albemarle Sound

Wright Brothers National Memorial

Kill Devil Hills

①

Jockey's Ridge State Park

Ft. Raleigh National Historic Site

②

Nags Head

Columbia

64

Manteo

Wanchese

③

Bodie Island

Roanoke Island

64

Phelps Lake

94

Alligator River

Oregon Inlet

Banks

12

Pea Island National Wildlife Refuge ④

45

32

Belhaven

Intracoastal Waterway

264

Mattamuskeet Lake

Engelhard

Rodanthe

National Seashore

92

264

Pamlico River

Swan Quarter

Pamlico Sound

33

306

33

Buxton

Hatteras

306

Grantsboro

Pamlico

Cedar Island

Ocracoke Island

12

Cape Hatteras ⑤

55

Minnesott Beach

Neuse River

Rattan Bay

Ocracoke ⑥

Portsmouth

Cape Hatteras

Havelock

South River

Portsmouth Island

70

306

101

Cedar Island

12

ATLANTIC OCEAN

Beaufort

70

Morehead City

Theodore Roosevelt Natural Area State Park

Cape Lookout National Seashore

Cape Lookout

0   20 miles

0   30 km

of the world in those days. Without roads or bridges, they had to bring in the airplane unassembled. They also had to bring in all their food and supplies and build a camp (the Wrights at first used tents and later built a wooden storage shed, as well as living quarters). Wilbur and Orville made four trips to the site, beginning in 1900, each time conducting experiments to determine how to achieve their goal. The annual Wilbur Wright Fly-In, held at the Dare County Regional Airport every spring, attracts vintage aircraft from all over the country. Contact the *Superintendent, National Park Service, U.S. Department of the Interior, Rte. 1, Box 675, Manteo 27954, tel. 919/441-7430. Admission $3 per car, $1 per person, Golden Passport holders and those under 16 and over 65 free. Open daily 9-5 with extended hours in the summertime.*

A few miles south of Kill Devil Hills, via U.S. 158 Bypass, is **Jockey's Ridge State Park,** the tallest sand dune in the East and a popular spot for hang gliding and kite flying. You can join in the activities and have a picnic here. *Rte. 158 Bypass, Milepost 12, tel. 919/441-7132. Admission free. Open daily sunrise to sunset.*

②③ Take U.S. 64-264 from U.S. 158 Bypass to reach **Manteo** and **Roanoke Island,** the site of several attractions, including the Elizabethan Gardens, "The Lost Colony" Waterside Amphitheatre, and Fort Raleigh. The lush gardens were established as a memorial to the first English colonists. *U.S. 64, Manteo, tel.919/473-3234. Admission: $2 adults, children under 12 free when accompanied by an adult. Open Mar.–Nov., daily 9–5; Dec.–Jan., weekdays 9–5.*

Fort Raleigh is a reconstruction of what is thought to be the original fort of the first Carolinian colonists. Be sure to see the orientation film and then take a guided tour of the fort. A nature trail leads to an outlook over Roanoke Sound. On special occasions, musicians play 16th-century music in the visitor center. *Tel. 919/473-2111. Admission free. Open Sept.–May 9–5; June–Aug., Mon.–Sat. 9–8; and Sun. 9–6.*

"The Lost Colony" outdoor drama reenacts the story of the first colonists who settled here in 1584 and then disappeared during the time that some of their party returned to England for supplies. The drama celebrated its own 50th anniversary in 1987. *Tel. 919/473-3414. Admission: $10 adults, $4 children under 12. Reservations suggested. Performances are given from mid-June until late Aug., Mon.–Sat. at 8:30 PM. Backstage tours are offered afternoons, mid-June–Aug. (see the play first). Admission: $3 adults, $1.50 children under 12.*

A short distance from Waterside Amphitheatre is the **Elizabeth II State Historic Site,** a 16th-century sailing vessel that was recreated to commemorate the 400th anniversary of the landing of the first colonists on Roanoke Island. *Downtown Manteo, tel. 919/473-1144. Admission: $3 adults, $2 senior citizens, $1.50 children.Open Nov.–Mar., Tues.–Sun. 10–4; Apr.– Oct. 10–6.*

Resume your journey southward on the Outer Banks via NC 12, a road that will take you all the way to Ocracoke Island. On the way you will pass over **Oregon Inlet Bridge,** which arches for three miles over the treacherous channel of water between the ocean and Pamlico Sound. Since the bridge was built, fishing conditions have declined. The bridge connects Bodie Island to Hatteras Island, most of which belongs to the Cape Hatteras National Seashore.

❹ Pea Island National Wildlife Refuge, on NC 12 between Oregon Inlet and Rodanthe, is made up of more than 5,000 acres of marsh that serves as wildlife refuge. In this vicinity was the Pea Island Life Saving Station, whose courageous crew, led by Richard Etheridge, made daring rescues during the late 1800s and early 1900s. *Pea Island Refuge Headquarters, tel. 919/987–2394. Open Apr.–Nov. weekdays 8–4.*

❺ Cape Hatteras Lighthouse, about 30 miles south of Rodanthe, sits as a beacon to ships offshore. Threatened by erosion from the sea, the 208-foot lighthouse has been rescued numerous times by sandbagging and other methods, and its fate is still under debate. Offshore lie the remains of the *Monitor,* a Confederate ironclad ship that sank in 1862. The visitor center offers information on the national seashore. *Hatteras Island Visitor Center, tel. 919/995–4474. Open Sept.–May 9–5, June–Aug. 9–6.*

At Hatteras, board the free ferry to Ocracoke Island. Boats leave every 40 minutes, and the journey takes about half an hour.

❻ Ocracoke Island was cut off from the world for so long that native residents still speak in quasi-Elizabethan accents; today, however, the island is a refuge for tourists. There is a village of shops, motels, and restaurants around the harbor where the infamous pirate Blackbeard met his death in 1718. The Ocracoke Lighthouse is a photographer's dream. *For information, contact the Ocracoke Visitor Center on Cedar Island, tel. 919/928–4531.*

Beaches

More than 70 miles of unspoiled beaches stretch from Nags Head to Ocracoke Island. Preserved as Cape Hatteras National Seashore, this coastal area is ideal for swimming, surfing, windsurfing, diving, boating, and any number of water activities. If you want to swim, stay in areas where there are lifeguard stations—Coquina Beach, Salvo, Cape Hatteras, Frisco, and Ocracoke. Nags Head (so named because Bankers would tie lanterns around the heads of their horses to lure merchant ships), is the most commercial beach area, with lifeguards stationed near motels and hotels. You can explore the *Laura Barnes* shipwreck site at Coquina Beach, considered the best swimming hole on the Outer Banks. Facilities here include picnic shelters, restrooms, showers, and bath houses. Divers and surfers enjoy practicing their antics around Cape Hatteras.

Participant Sports

Camping   Camping is permitted in designated areas all along the Cape Hatteras National Seashore. All campgrounds in the park have cold showers, drinking water, tables, grills, and restrooms (except Ocracoke, which has pit toilets). Sanitary stations for recreational vehicles are located at Oregon Inlet, Cape Point at Cape Hatteras, and Ocracoke. Oregon Inlet, Cape Point, and Ocracoke are open from mid-April through mid-October; Salvo and Frisco, mid-June to late August. Be sure to take along extra-long tent stakes for sand, and don't forget the insect repellent. During the summer it's wise to make reservations through Ticketron offices, either in person or by writing the Ticketron headquarters at Box 2715, San Francisco, CA 94126. In addition to campsites in the National Seashore, there are many private campgrounds scattered along the Outer Banks. For information contact the North Carolina Travel and Tourism Division. tel. 919/733–4171 or 800/847–4862; ask for the *NC Camping and Outdoor Directory.*

Fishing This area is a paradise for fisherman who enjoy surf casting or deep sea fishing. You can board a charter boat or head your own craft out of Oregon Inlet. (Call 919/441–6301 for information on chartered trips.) North Carolina fishing licenses are available from local bait-and-tackle shops and marinas or from the N.C. Division of Boating and Inland Fishing (tel. 919/ 733–3633).

Hang Gliding Only a few miles from where Wilbur and Orville Wright first took flight, you can try your hand at hang gliding. There's probably not a safer place to attempt this aerial feat than from the giant sand dune at Jockey's Ridge State Park. Lessons are given by the **Kitty Hawk Kites,** purported to be the world's largest hang gliding school. Their shop is located on U.S. 158 at Milepost 13, tel. 919/441–4124.

Scuba Diving With over 600 known shipwrecks off the coast of the Outer Banks, diving opportunities are virtually unlimited. The *Monitor* is off-limits, however. Three dive shops along the Banks can help you organize an adventure: **Atlantic Divers** (tel. 919/441– 1111), **Hatteras Divers** (tel. 919/986–2557), and **Nags Head Pro Dive Shop** (tel. 919/441–7594).

Surfing and Windsurfing The Outer Banks offer ideal conditions for these sports. Contact **Kitty Hawk Sports** (U.S. 158 at Milepost 13, tel. 919/441– 4124).

Dining

Plan to get your fill of seafood during your visit to the Outer Banks; it's in abundant supply here, and a number of restaurants prepare it quite well. A complete list of restaurants is included in the *Outer Banks Vacation Guide,* published by the Dare County Tourist Bureau and the Outer Banks Chamber of Commerce.

Category	Cost*
Very Expensive	over $25
Expensive	$15–$25
Moderate	$8–$15
Inexpensive	under $8

per person without tax (5%), service, or drinks

The following credit-card abbreviations are used: AE, American Express; CB, Carte Blanche; DC, Diners Club; MC, Mastercard; V, Visa.

Kill Devil Hills
Moderate–
Expensive

Evan's Crabhouse. This casual restaurant is known for its crab soups, hot and spicy steamed crabs, crab cakes, crab cocktails, crab salads, and crabs in the shell. Meals are served on oilcloth covered tables. Take-out service available. *U.S. 158 Bypass at Milepost 10, tel. 919/441–5994. Lunch only Dec.–Mar. Reservations not required. MC, V.*

Manteo
Expensive

The Elizabethan Inn. Enjoy "Pastime with Goode Companie," a show with an authentic 16th-century Elizabethan feast at this inn. *US 64, tel. 919/473–2101. Reservations required. Wed.– Fri., mid-June–late Aug. AE, CB, DC, MC, V.*

Moderate

The Weeping Radish. This Bavarian-style restaurant is named for the radishes sprinkled with salt and served with Hoplen beer, brewed right on the premises. Waiters dressed in Bavarian costumes serve German dishes while German music plays in the background. Tours of the brewery are given upon request. *US 64, tel. 919/473–1157. Reservations required for parties of six.*

Nags Head
Expensive

Owens' Restaurant. Housed in an old Nags Head–style clapboard cottage, Owens' has been in the same family for over 40 years. Seafood is featured here—particularly the coconut shrimp and lobster bisque. Nightly entertainment is offered in the brass and glass Station Keeper's Lounge. *U.S. 158, Milepost 17, tel. 919/441–7309. Reservations accepted for large parties only. No lunch. Closed Dec.–Mar. AE, CB, DC, MC, V.*

A Restaurant by George. Located in the onion-domed Galleon Esplanade shopping center, the restaurant is as well-known for its exotic, tropical atmosphere as for its food. Diners may choose among several intimate rooms and then mix with the lounge crowd afterward. The Continental menu features steak, seafood, and fancy desserts. *US 158 at Milepost 11, tel. 919/441–4821. Reservations advised. AE, CB, MC, V.*

Moderate

Kelly's Outer Banks Restaurant & Tavern. This is a favorite gathering place on the Outer Banks. The menu is varied, with selections of seafood (including steamed or raw shellfish), beef, and chicken, but the restaurant is famous for its pasta and homemade desserts and breads. *U.S. 158 Bypass, Milepost 10½, tel. 919/441–4116. Reservations not required. No lunch. AE, MC, V.*

Lodging

The majority of motels and hotels are clustered in the Nags Head–Manteo area, but a small number of rooms are available in the Cape Hatteras area. There are 60 cottages for rent on Ocracoke Island, plus a dozen or so motels and tourist homes. Condos and beach cottages may be rented by the week or month through area realty companies. Consult the *Outer Banks Vacation Guide* for a complete listing of accommodations. The Outer Banks Chamber of Commerce (tel. 919/441–8144) can steer you in the direction of rental agencies.

Category	Cost*
Very Expensive	over $100
Expensive	$60–$100

Moderate	$30–$60
Inexpensive	under $30

double room; add 7.5% for taxes

The following credit card abbreviations are used AE, American Express; CB, Carte Blanche; DC, Diners Club; MC, MasterCard; V, Visa.

Duck
Very Expensive

Sanderling Inn and Restaurant. If you enjoy being pampered, come to this inn, located in a remote beach area north of Duck. Guests are treated to lounging robes, fruit and wine, and complimentary hors d'oeuvres. For recreation you can play tennis, go swimming, or take a nature walk through the Pine Island Sanctuary and then curl up with a good book from the inn's library—or enjoy a videotape. Though it was built in 1985 and has all the contemporary conveniences, the inn has the stately, mellow look of old Nags Head. The restaurant serves three meals a day, and reservations are required for dinner. Entrees include crab cakes, roast Carolina duckling with black cherry sauce, and fricassee of shrimp. *Rte. 1200, Box 319Y, 27949, tel. 919/261–4111. 60 rooms and efficiencies. Facilities: pool, tennis, Jacuzzi, hot tub, health club, bicycles, meeting rooms. AE, MC, V.*

Kill Devil Hills
Moderate–Expensive

Ramada Inn. Rooms in this convention-style hotel have ocean views and come with refrigerators and microwave ovens. Peppercorns Restaurant, overlooking the ocean, serves breakfast and dinner, and lunch is available on the sun deck next to the pool. *US 158, Milepost 9½, Box 2716, 27948, tel. 919/441–2151. 173 rooms. Facilities: pool, Jacuzzi, meeting rooms. AE, CB, MC, V.*

Ocracoke
Moderate–Expensive

The Berkeley Center Country Inn. Once a corporate retreat, this rustic property, which resembles a life-saving station, is now a bed-and-breakfast inn. Located next to the state ferry dock, it is within easy walking distance of everything in the village. The owners, Col. and Mrs. Wesley Egan, serve a scrumptious breakfast of fresh breads, preserves, and coffee. *NC 12, Box 220, 27960, tel. 919/928–5911. Open mid-Mar.– mid-Dec. Personal and traveler's checks only, no credit cards accepted.*

Moderate

The **Island Inn and Dining Room.** The inn has been in operation since 1940, though it was built as a private lodge back in 1901. Guests have a choice of new or traditional rooms, including the Crow's Nest on the third floor. The dining room is known for its oyster omelet, crab cakes, and hush puppies. Reservations are advised, particularly for dinner. *NC 12, Box 9, 27960, tel. 919/ 928–4351 (inn) or 919/928–7821 (dining room). Open Mar.– Nov. 35 rooms. Facilities: outdoor pool. MC, V.*

Asheville

In recent years this mountain city has been rated, among cities of its size, as American's number one place to live. It has scenic beauty, low levels of pollution, a good airport and road system, a moderate four-season climate, a variety of hotels and restaurants, and plenty of cultural opportunities. It is a city where banjo pickers are as revered as violinists, where mountain folks mix with city slickers, and where everyone finds a common ground in a love for the city.

Getting Around

By Plane The Asheville Airport is served by three major air carriers: **American**–American Eagle, **Delta**–ASA, and **USAir.**

By Car I–40 runs east and west through the city. I–26 runs from Charleston to Asheville. I–240 forms a perimeter around the city. U.S. 23-19A is a major north and west route.

By Bus **Greyhound / Trailways** (tel. 704/253–5353).

Guided Tours

Three companies provide group tours: **Travel Professionals, Inc.** (tel. 704/298–3438), **Western Carolina Tours** (tel. 704/254–4603), and **Young Tour Service** (tel. 800/622–5444 in NC or 800/528–9007 in the Southeast).

Important Addresses and Numbers

Tourist The **Visitor Information Center** (151 Haywood St., tel. 704/258–
Information 6100) and the **Asheville Convention and Visitors Bureau** (Box 1011, 151 Haywood St., Asheville 28802, tel. 800/548–1300 in NC or 800/257–1300 outside NC).

Emergencies Dial 704/252–1110. (A 911 emergency number is being installed, but is not yet available.)

Exploring Asheville

Downtown Asheville is noted for its eclectic architecture. The **Battery Park Hotel,** built in 1924, is neo-Georgian; the **Flatiron Building** (1924) is neoclassical; the **Church of St. Lawrence** (1912) is Spanish Baroque; **Old Pack Library** (1925) is in Italian Renaissance–style; the **S & W Cafeteria** (1919) is Art Deco. A brochure entitled "Asheville Heritage Tour," details six different historic districts in the city. A guided walking tour is given every Sunday at 2 PM from June through mid-October. For details, contact the Preservation Society of Asheville and Buncombe County (Box 2806, Asheville 28802, tel. 704/254–2343).

The **Thomas Wolfe Memorial** (48 Spruce St.), built in 1880 in the Queen Anne style, is one of the oldest houses in downtown Asheville. Wolfe's mother ran a boarding house here for years, and he used it as the setting for his novel *Look Homeward, Angel.* Family pictures, clothing, and original furnishings fill the house, now a state historic site. Guided tours are available. *Tel. 704/253–8304. Admission: $1 adults, students 50¢. Open Apr.–Oct. Mon.–Sat. 9–5, Sun. 1–5; Nov.–Mar. Tues.–Sat. 9–4, Sun 1–4.*

From downtown, follow I–40 east to Exit 50 (U.S. 25). The entrance to the architecturally famous **Biltmore Estate** faces Biltmore Village, about three blocks from the interstate. Built as the private home of George Vanderbilt, the 250-room French Renaissance château is today a museum. Richard Morris Hunt designed the castle, and Frederick Law Olmsted landscaped the 125,000-acre estate. It took 1,000 men five years to complete the gargantuan project. On view are the priceless antiques and art treasures collected by the Vanderbilts, and 17 acres of gardens. *Tel. 704/255–1776. Admission: $17.50 adults, $13.50 students ages 12–17. Open daily 9–5. Evening candlelight tours during the Christmas holidays.*

Take U.S. 19-23 Bypass north, off I-240, from Asheville to Weaverville, a distance of about 18 miles. The **Zebulon B. Vance Birthplace** is located on Reems Creek Road (Route 1103). This state historic site, which includes a two-story log cabin and several outbuildings, is where Vance—North Carolina's governor during the Civil War—grew up. Crafts and chores typical of his period are often demonstrated. Picnic facilities are available. *Tel. 704/645–6706. Admission free. Open Apr.–Oct., Mon.–Sat. 9–5, Sun. 1–5; Nov.–Mar., Tues.–Sat. 9–4, Sun. 1–4.*

Time Out Enjoy fresh mountain trout or chicken with pineapple raisin sauce in the turn-of-the-century **Weaverville Milling Company,** near the Vance Homestead. Waitresses dress in gingham. The craft shop on the premises sells locally made quilts and quilted pillows. *Tel. 704/645–4700. Reservations suggested. Open Mon., Tues., Thurs., Fri., 5–9, weekends 5–9:30. Closed Wed., Jan.–Mar., Mon. and Tues. MC, V. Moderate.*

Flat Rock About 20 miles south of Asheville, Flat Rock can be reached via I-26. This vacation-retirement community, long popular with Charlestonians, is home to the Flat Rock Playhouse and to the estate of poet and Lincoln biographer Carl Sandburg. **Connemara** is the home where the great Pulitzer Prize winner spent the last years of his life with his wife Lilian. The house is at same time warm and austere. Guided tours are given by the National Park Service, which manages the property. "The World of Carl Sandburg" and "Rootabaga Stories" are presented here by the Vagabond Players during the summer. *Tel. 704/693–4178. Admission free. Open daily 9–5.*

What to See and Do with Children

Sliding Rock. Slide for 150 wet and wild feet on a natural water slide located north of Brevard, off Highway 276, in Pisgah National Forest. Wear old jeans and tennis shoes and bring a towel. *Tel. 704/877–3265. Open 10–6 late May–Labor Day.*

Off the Beaten Track

Riverside Cemetery (Birch St., off Montford Ave. north of I-240 in Asheville) is the final resting place of Thomas Wolfe, O. Henry (William Sydney Porter), Zebulon Vance, and early founders and settlers of Asheville. *Open daylight hours.*

Shopping

Crafts **The Folk Art Center** (Milepost 382 on the Blue Ridge Parkway) is the best place to find authentic quality mountain crafts. *Tel. 701/298–7928. Open mid–June–early Sept. daily 9–8; 9–5 remainder of year.*

Qualla Arts and Crafts (U.S. 441 and Drama Rd., in Cherokee) features authentic Cherokee Indian crafts, as well as items from other American tribes. *Tel. 704/497–3103. Open daily 9–5.*

Biltmore Village, built by George Vanderbilt outside the entrance to his magnificent estate, houses more than 20 antique, craft, clothing, and gift shops. Be sure to check out **New Morning Gallery,** which features quality art and crafts.

Biltmore Homespun Shop, located on the grounds of the Grove Park Inn and established by Mrs. George Vanderbilt, features woven goods made on the premises. *Macon St., tel. 704/253–7651. Open Apr.–Oct., Mon.–Sat. 9–5:30; Nov.–Mar., Mon.–Sat. 9–4:30.*

Participant Sports

Camping   For information on state parks, national forests, and designated sites along the Blue Ridge Parkway and in the Great Smoky Mountains National Park, request the free *NC Camping and Outdoors Directory* from the NC Travel & Tourism Division (tel. 919/733–4171 in NC or 800/847–4862 outside NC).

Canoeing/White   The Nolichucky, French Broad, Nantahala, Ocoee, and Green
Water Rafting   Rivers offer Class I–IV rapids. About 10 outfitters serve the Asheville area, including **Cherokee River Trips** (Box 516, Cherokee, 28719, tel. 704/488–3373) and **Nantahala Outdoor Center** (U.S. 19W, Box 41, Bryson City, 28713, tel. 704/488–2175).

Gem Mining   Franklin has at least a dozen mines where you can get up to your elbows in common mud in search of precious rubies, sapphires, garnets, and other stones. There are many gem shops in the area where you can have your "finds" appraised. *Location maps are available from the Franklin Chamber of Commerce (180 Porter St., Franklin 28734, tel. 704/524–3161). Admission: $4–$5 for adults, $1–$2 for children. Most mines are open mid-May–Oct. 8 to 5 or dusk.*

Golf   Some 15 challenging courses are within a 60-minute drive of Asheville. Public courses are located in Asheville, Black Mountain, Brevard, Hendersonville, Lake Lure, Old Fort, and Waynesville. *Contact the Asheville Convention & Visitors Bureau (Box 1010, Asheville, 28802, tel. 800/548–1300 in NC or 800/548–1300 in Eastern USA) for a listing.*

Hiking   There are hundreds of trails along the Blue Ridge Parkway and in the Great Smoky Mountains National Park. The Appalachian Trail runs along the crest of North Carolina's highest mountains. *For trail maps, contact the Superintendent (Blue Ridge Parkway, BB & T Bank Bldg., 1 Pack Sq., Asheville 28801, tel. 704/259–0779), or the Superintendent Great Smoky Mountains National Park, Gatlinburg, TN (37738, tel. 615/436–9564).*

Skiing   Ski resorts in the Asheville area include **Cataloochee** (Rte. 1, Box 500, Maggie Valley 28751, tel. 704/926–0285), **Fairfield–Sapphire Valley** (Rte. 70, Box 80, Sapphire Valley 28774, tel. 704/743–3441), and **Wolf Laurel** (Rte. 3, Mars Hill, 28754, tel. 704/689–4111).

Dining

As you might expect in a resort city, dining choices are many: upscale gourmet restaurants, middle-of-the-road country fare, and fast-food establishments.

Category	Cost*
Very Expensive	over $25
Expensive	$15–$25
Moderate	$8–$15
Inexpensive	under $8

per person without tax (4.5%), service, or drinks

The following credit-card abbreviations are used: AE, American Express; CB, Carte Blanche; DC, Diners Club; MC, MasterCard; V, Visa.

Very Expensive **The Market Place.** Nouvelle cuisine is served in a relaxed atmosphere, part chintz, part bamboo. Vegetables and herbs are regionally grown, and bread, pasta, and pastries are made on the premises. The menu changes about every 10 days. The Grille downstairs, where everything is prepared over a fire, offers a more casual atmosphere and somewhat lower prices. *10 N. Market St., tel. 704/252-4162. Reservations must be confirmed by 4 PM. No lunch. Closed Sun. and major holidays. AE, MC, V.*

Moderate **Steven's Restaurant.** International cuisine is offered in an elegant Victorian setting. The restaurant is known for its rack of lamb, freshly baked breads and desserts, and extensive wine list. *157 Charlotte St., tel. 704/253-5348. Dress: informal. Reservations recommended. Sun. brunch. AE, MC, V.*

Inexpensive– **Black Forest Restaurant.** Enjoy traditional German dishes in a
Moderate Bavarian setting. Specialties include sauerbraten, knockwurst, schnitzel, and Kassler rippchen. The restaurant celebrates Oktoberfest in the fall. *U.S. 25, tel. 704/684-8160. Reservations suggested. AE, MC. V. Closed Mon. and Christmas Day.*

Inexpensive **Bill Stanley's Barbecue and Bluegrass.** Overalls and crinoline skirts are the order at this local establishment known for its clogging, bluegrass music, barbecue, and rustic atmosphere. The locals who hang out here make everyone, including tourists and convention delegates, feel welcome. *20 Spruce St., tel. 704/253-4871. Reservations advised on weekends. Cover is $3 on weekends and $2 on weekdays. Closed Sun. and Mon. AE, DC, MC. Inexpensive.*

J & S Cafeteria. People come by the busloads to enjoy this above-average cafeteria. After you clean your plate, you can look for more bargains in the outlet stores that occupy the same shopping center. *800 Fairview Rd., in River Ridge Market Pl., tel. 704/298-0507. Closed Christmas Day.*

Lodging

Lodging options range from posh resorts to mountain cabins, country inns, and economy chain motels. There's a bed for virtually every pocketbook.

Category	Cost*
Very Expensive	over $100

Expensive	$60–$100
Moderate	$30–$60
Inexpensive	under $30

* double room; add 7.5% for taxes

The following credit card abbreviations are used: AE, American Express; CB, Carte Blanche; DC, Diners Club; MC, MasterCard; V, Visa.

Hotels and Motels
Expensive

Great Smokies Hilton. Play golf or tennis, go swimming, or just enjoy the mountain views at this complete hotel resort. Rooms are spacious and recently renovated; the Thomas Wolfe Room is a favorite. *1 Hilton Dr. (U.S. 19/23) near Westgate Shopping Center, tel. 704/254–3211. 280 rooms. Facilities: restaurant, coffee shop and lounge, 2 pools, sauna, golf, tennis, complimentary airport shuttle. AE, CB, MC, V.*

Grove Park Inn and Country Club. This is Asheville's premier resort, and it's just as beautiful and exciting as it was the day it opened in 1913. The guest list has included Henry Ford, Thomas Edison, Harvey Firestone, and Warren G. Harding. Novelist F. Scott Fitzgerald stayed here while his wife Zelda was in a nearby sanitorium. His room was no. 441. In the past five years the hotel has been completely renovated. The two new wings are in keeping with the original design. Facilities include four restaurants. *290 Macon Ave., tel. 800/438–5800. 510 rooms and suites. Facilities: meeting rooms, pool, sauna, whirlpool, putting green, fitness center, golf, tennis, racquetball, parking garage, airport shuttle, children's program, social program. AE, CB, MC, V.*

Inns and B&Bs
Moderate–Expensive

Cedar Crest Inn. This beautiful cottage was constructed by Biltmore craftsmen as a private residence around the turn of the century. Jack and Barbara McEwan have lovingly restored it as a bed-and-breakfast inn and filled it with Victorian antiques. Guests are treated to afternoon tea, evening coffee or chocolate, and a breakfast of fruits, pastries, and coffee. *674 Biltmore Ave., 28803, tel. 704/252–1389. 11 rooms. AE, MC, V.*

Moderate

Flynt Street Inns. These B&Bs are located in Asheville's Montford Park. Rick and Lynne Vogel, and Rick's mother, Marion, treat guests to a full breakfast. *100 & 116 Flint St., 28801, tel. 704/253–6723. 8 rooms. AE, MC, V.*

North Carolina High Country

Majestic peaks, meadows, and valleys characterize the North Carolina High Country (Alleghany, Ashe, Avery, Mitchell, and Watauga counties) in the Blue Ridge Mountains. Once remote, the area has boomed in the past 25 years following the introduction of snowmaking equipment. Now North Carolina is both the Southern ski capital and a summertime playground for hiking, bicycling, camping, fishing, and canoeing. Luxury resorts now dot the valleys and mountaintops. The building of a 10-story concrete condo monolith on Sugar Mountain in Banner Elk caused a public outcry and resulted in the passage of a mountain ridge protection law to restrict this type of construction. On the other hand, the Linn Cove Viaduct on Grandfather Mountain, a bridge that circumvents the peaks and valleys without disturbing them, has received rave reviews from virtually everyone, including environmentalists. The bridge, which opened in 1987, is the final link in the Blue Ridge Parkway. Visitors to the hills take advantage of the many crafts shops, music festivals, theater, and special events such as the Grandfather Mountain Scottish Games. The passing of each season is a special visual event in the High Country, with autumn's colors being the most spectacular of all.

Getting Around

By Plane **USAir Express** (tel. 800/251–5720) serves the Hickory Airport, about 40 miles from the High Country.

By Car The closest interstate is I–40, which is intersected by U.S. 321 at Hickory, NC 181 at Morganton, and U.S. 221 at Marion, leading to the High Country. U.S. 421 is a major east-west artery. The Blue Ridge Parkway, a slowly winding road, goes from Shenandoah National Park in Virginia to Great Smoky Mountains National Park in North Carolina and Tennessee, and passes over the crests of mountains in the High Country.

By Bus Service from Charlotte to Boone is provided by **Greyhound/ Trailways** (tel. 704/262–0501), with arrivals and departures from the Appalcart Bus Station on Winklers Creek Road, off U.S. 321 in Boone.

Important Addresses and Numbers

Tourist Information **North Carolina High Country Host** (701 Blowing Rock Rd., Boone 28607, tel. 800/222–7515 in NC or 800/438–7500 in the eastern U.S.).

Emergencies Dial 911 for emergency assistance or go to the emergency room at **Watauga County Hospital** in Boone (tel. 704/262–4100), **Cannon Memorial Hospital** in Banner Elk (tel. 704/898–5111), or the **Blowing Rock Hospital** in Blowing Rock (tel. 704/295–3136).

Exploring North Carolina High Country

Blowing Rock, a tourist mecca since the 1880s, has retained the flavor of a quiet mountain village. Only a few hundred people are permanent residents, but the population swells each summer. The town is named for a large outcropping of rock, which has become the state's oldest tourist attraction. The town of Blowing Rock boasts some of the best restaurants in the High Country and offers a variety of accommodations.

The Blowing Rock (off U.S. 321, on the southern outskirts of town), looms 3,000 feet over the Johns River Gorge. If you throw your hat over the sheer precipice, it may come back to you, should the wind gods be playful. The story goes that a Cherokee brave and a Chickasaw maiden fell in love. Torn between returning to his tribe or staying with her, he jumped from the cliff. Her prayer to the Great Spirit resulted in his safe return to her. During the Depression of the '30s, a local family by the name of Robbins who owned the big rock decided to make it a tourist attraction and charge admission to see it. The formula worked. The family also owns the Tweetsie Railroad theme park. Today's visitors to the Blowing Rock enjoy views from an observation tower and a garden landscaped with mountain laurel, rhododendron, and other native plants. *Tel. 704/295–7111. Admission: $3 adults, $1 children 6–11. Open daily Apr.–May 9–6, June–Oct. 8–8.*

From downtown Blowing Rock, follow U.S. 221 one mile south to the **Blue Ridge Parkway**—a scenic asphalt ribbon that stretches over mountain crests from northern Virginia to Tennessee and North Carolina. Here are quiet vistas, dramatic mountain ranges, and remnants of pioneer life. Mileposts help tourists find the sites. Consider a stop at the **Moses H. Cone Park** (Mileposts 297.7–295) to see the manor house where the textile magnate lived.

If you want to go hiking, canoe on a mountain lake, fish for trout in a rushing stream, or pitch a tent, head for the 4,000 acres of forest in **Julian Price Park** (Mileposts 295.1–298). Keep driving south and you'll come to Grandfather Mountain, Linville Falls, Asheville, and Cherokee; head north from the park and you'll soon be at Doughton Park, the Peaks of Otter, and Roanoke. The Blue Ridge Parkway is open year-round, but it often closes during heavy snows. Maps and information are available at visitor centers along the highway. *For more information, contact the Superintendent (Blue Ridge Pkwy., BB & T Bldg., 1 Pack Sq., Asheville 28801, tel. 704/259–0779).*

From Blowing Rock, head north toward Boone, via U.S. 321, until you come to **Tweetsie Railroad,** a theme park popular with young children. In its heyday, Tweetsie provided passenger service between Johnson City, Tennessee, and Boone, but the tracks were washed away in a flood in the '40s and never rebuilt. In 1956, the train was placed on a three-mile track and opened as an attraction. The park also features a petting zoo, rides, gold panning, a saloon show, and concessions. *Tel. 704/264–9061. Admission: $10 adults, $8 children ages 4–12. Open late May–Labor Day daily 9–6; Sept.–Oct. weekdays 9–5 and weekends 9–6.*

Boone, named for frontiersman Daniel Boone, is a city of several thousand residents at the convergence of three major highways—U.S. 321, U.S. 421, and NC 105. **"Horn in the West,"** a project of the Southern Highlands Historical Association, is an outdoor drama that traces the story of Boone's life. *The amphitheater is located off U.S. 321, tel. 704/264–2120. Admission: $8 adults, $4 children under 13. Curtain time is 8:30 nightly except Mon. mid-June through mid-Aug.*

To reach **Ashe County (Jefferson-West Jefferson),** travel five miles east on U.S. 421 to the Blue Ridge Parkway, and follow the parkway north for about 15 miles to Milepost 258.6 near Glendale Springs. The scene quickly changes from commercial strips to mountain vistas and rural landscapes dotted with manicured farms and quiet villages.

The **Blue Ridge Mountain Frescoes** at Glendale Springs and Beaver Creek were painted by North Carolina artist Ben Long. Long found the abandoned churches and painted four big-as-life frescoes, applying rich earthy pigments to wet plaster. "The Last Supper" (measuring 17 × 19.5 feet) is in the Glendale Springs Holy Trinity Church. The others are in St. Mary's Episcopal Church at Beaver Creek, including "Mary, Great with Child," which won the Leonardo da Vinci International Award. *Tel. 919/982–3076. Admission free. Open 24 hours a day. Guide service available 9:30–4:30.*

You can go in another direction from Boone by following NC 105 south (about 14 miles) to NC 184, which leads to **Banner Elk.** This college and ski resort town is surrounded by the lofty peaks of Grandfather, Hanging Rock, Beech, and Sugar. Banner Elk is home to Elk River Club, fast becoming one of the most prestigious residential developments on the East Coast.

Linville, eight miles from Banner Elk at the intersection of U.S. 221 and NC 105, sits at the base of Grandfather Mountain. This resort town, distinguished by its chestnut bark homes and lodges, has not changed much since it was built in the 1880s.

Grandfather Mountain is long known for its mile-high **Swinging Bridge,** stretching between two prominent peaks. Two big events draw record crowds to the mountain. The annual Singing on the Mountain is an opportunity to hear old-time gospel music and preaching in late June. Scottish clans from all over North America gather for athletic events and Highland dancing in July. At other times of the year the mountain is a great place for hiking and picnicking. *Blue Ridge Parkway and US 221, Linville 28646, tel. 704/733–2013. Admission to the Swinging Bridge: $6 adults, $3 children ages 4–12. Hiking permits are $3 per day and may be obtained at the gate or at the Scotchman on NC 105. Open Apr.–mid-Nov., 8 until dusk; mid-Nov. –Mar., 9–4, weather permitting.*

Follow U.S. 221 south for about 10 miles to **Linville Caverns,** the only caverns in the Carolinas. The caverns go 2,000 feet underground and have a year-round temperature of 51 degrees. *Tel. 704/756–4171. Admission: $3 adults, $1.50 children 5–11. Open Apr.–Oct., daily 9–6; Nov.–Mar., weekends 9–5.*

What to See and Do with Children

Emerald Village. Grab a bucket of dirt and get muddy while looking for gems at this old mine that was established by the Bon Ami Company years ago. Then go to the Mining Museum on the site and try to identify your treasures. *Located on Rtes. 1002 and 1100, off U.S. 19E, near Spruce Pine, tel. 704/765–6463. Admission: $3 adults, $2 students and senior citizens. Open May–Oct., 9–5.*

Off the Beaten Track

You'll find everything from ribbons and calico to brogans and overalls in the **Mast Store,** an authentic general store that has been the center of the Valle Crucis community for over 100 years. *NC 194 in Valle Crucis, tel. 704/963–6511. Open Mon.– Sat. 6:30–6:30, Sun. 12:30–7.*

Shopping

Crafts   High-quality handmade brooms, quilts, pottery, jewelry, and other items made by members of the Southern Highland Handicraft Guild can be found at the **Parkway Craft Center,** which operates out of the Moses H. Cone mansion. *Moses H. Cone Park, tel. 704/295-7938. Open daily 9-5:30.*

Handwoven Goods   The **Goodwin Weavers** create bedspreads, tablecloths, and afghans on Civil War–era looms and then sell them in their shop. *Off U.S. 321 Bypass, Blowing Rock, tel. 704/295-3577. Open Mon.-Sat. 9-5, Sun. 1-5.*

Wicker and Wood   Factory-made household items produced in the Boone area are sold at the **American Wicker and Wood Factory Outlet and Gift Shop.** *NC 105 S., Boone, tel. 704/264-8136. Open Mon.-Sat. 10-6, Sun. 1-6.*

Participant Sports

Canoeing   The wild and scenic New River (Class I and II) provides hours of excitement, as do the Watauga River (Class I and II), Wilson Creek, and Toe River (Class II and III). Outfitters include **Edge of the World Outfitters** (Banner Elk, tel. 704/898-9550) and **Wahoo's Wild Whitewater Rafting** (Boone, tel. 704/262-5774).

Golf   The High Country has 18 golf courses, including **Boone Golf Club** (tel. 704/264-8760), **Hanging Rock Golf Course** at Seven Devils/Foscoe (tel. 704/963-6565), and **Mountain Glen Golf Club** at Newland (tel. 704/733-5804). A list of golf courses is available from NC High County Host, 701 Blowing Rock Rd. (U.S. 321), Boone 28607, tel. 800/438-7500 or 800/222-7515 in NC.

Hiking   Trails abound in wilderness areas of national forests and near the Blue Ridge Parkway. The Boone Fork Trail in Julian Price Park, near Blowing Rock, is an easy hike for most people; Shanty Springs, on Grandfather Mountain, is more difficult. The Appalachian Trail follows the not-too-distant North Carolina–Tennessee border. Trail maps are available at the entrance gate of Grandfather Mountain (tel. 704/733-4337) at the Scotchman at NC 105; or from the Superintendent (Blue Ridge Pkwy., 700 BB & T Bldg., 1 Pack Sq., Asheville 28801, tel. 704/259-0779).

Rock Climbing   One of the most challenging climbs in the country is the Linville Gorge, off NC 181. Permits are available from the District Forest Ranger's Office in Marion (tel. 704/652-2144) or from the Linville Falls Texaco Station on U.S. 221. **Appalachian Mountain Sports** in Boone (tel. 704/264-3170) provides instruction and guided trips.

Skiing   The High Country offers six alpine ski areas, plus many cross-country opportunities. For ski conditions, call 800/438-7500 in the eastern U.S. or 800/222-7515 in North Carolina. Downhill skiing is available at **Appalachian Ski Mountain** (Box 106, Blowing Rock 28605, tel. 704/295-7828), **Ski Beech** (Box 1118, Beech Mountain 28604, tel. 704/387-2011), **Ski Hawksnest** (Rte. 1, Box 256, Banner Elk 28604, tel. 704/963-6561), **Hound Ears Club** (Box 188, Blowing Rock 28605, tel. 704/963-4321), **Sugar Mountain** (Box 369, Banner Elk 28604, tel. 704/898-4521), and **Ski Mill Ridge** (U.S. 105 at Foscoe, tel. 704/963-4500). Cross-country skiing is offered at **Moses Cone Park** and at **Linville Falls** on the Blue Ridge Parkway (tel. 704/295-7591), and **Roan Mountain** (tel. 615/772-3303) or **Appalachian Mountain Sports** (tel. 704/264-3170).

Dining and Lodging

Dining   In the past 25 years the High Country has seen a tremendous
increase in restaurants, from upscale gourmet restaurants to
fast-food establishments. Many now serve alcoholic beverages
in various ways (restrictions of previous years have been
lifted). Boone has beer/wine and brown bagging (carrying your
own in a paper bag); Blowing Rock and Beech Mountain, beer/
wine and liquor by the drink; Banner Elk, wine and brown bagging.

Category	Cost*
Very Expensive	over $25
Expensive	$15–$25
Moderate	$8–$15
Inexpensive	under $8

per person without tax (4.5%), service, or drinks

Lodging   Overnight lodging in the High Country ranges from mom-and-
pop motels to luxurious mountaintop condos and chalets. Contact North Carolina High Country Host (tel. 800/438–7500
in eastern U.S. or 800/222–7515 in NC) for complete information.

Category	Cost*
Very Expensive	over $100
Expensive	$60–$100
Moderate	$30–$60
Inexpensive	under $30

double room; add 7.5% for taxes

The following credit-card abbreviations are used: AE, American Express; CB, Carte Blanche; DC, Diners Club; MC,
MasterCard; V, Visa.

Blowing Rock   **Green Park Inn.** This 100-year-plus Victorian charmer on the
Dining and Lodging   eastern continental divide offers spacious, luxurious rooms,
wide porches with rocking chairs, and large public rooms deco-
rated in bright colors and wicker. Old photographs and
mementoes highlight the illustrious history of the grand hotel.
The bilevel restaurant has won high ratings and is often the setting for dinner theater productions and murder mystery
weekends. *U.S. 321, Box 7, 28605, tel. 704/295–3141. Open
May–Dec. 88 rooms. Facilities: pool, golf, tennis, meeting
rooms. MC, V. Expensive–Very Expensive.*
Hound Ears Club. This Alpine inn, overlooking Grandfather
Mountain and a lush golf course, offers comfortable, well-kept
rooms dressed in Waverly print fabrics. *Off NC 105, 8 mi from
Boone; Box 188, 28605, tel. 704/963–4321. Open Apr.–Feb. 27
rooms. Facilities: restaurant, pool, golf, tennis. MC, V. Very
Expensive (price includes meals).*
Ragged Garden Inn. Rooms in this intimate inn are decorated in
a Colonial style. Continental breakfasts and northern Italian
dishes are prepared by owner/chef Joe Villani. Breakfast is

served only to inn guests, but the dining room is open to the public. *Sunset Dr., Box 1927, 28605, tel. 704/295–9703. Dinner reservations suggested. Open Apr.–Jan. AE, MC, V. Expensive.*

Sunshine Inn. Guests love the warmth and charm of this restored country inn, which has a family-style restaurant open to the public. *Sunset Dr., Box 528, 28605, tel. 704/295–3487. Open May–Nov. 5 rooms. MC, V. Inexpensive.*

Boone   **Claire's.** Formerly in Blowing Rock, this Colonial-style restau-
Dining   rant has moved to Boone. The menu features veal, marinated beef tenderloin, grilled breast of chicken, shrimp creole, fresh mountain trout, and other dishes. *101 N. King St., tel. 704/264–6152. Dress: casual. Dinner reservations suggested. Open for lunch and dinner Apr. 15–Feb., Fri. and Sat. dinner only Mar.–Apr. 15. MC, V, Moderate–Expensive.*

Witch's Hollow Restaurant This 9,000-square-foot log cabin, decorated in Colonial-style furnishings, serves Continental cuisine. Specialties are veal and mountain trout. *NC 105, 8 mi south of Boone, tel. 704/963–4365. Reservations suggested. Casual dinner attire. No lunch. Closed Sun. and Dec.–Apr. AE, MC, V. Moderate.*

Lodging   **Broyhill Inn.** Though primarily a conference center, this contemporary hotel on the ASU campus is attractive to individual travelers who enjoy a university atmosphere. The dining room offers a great view of the mountains. *96 Bodenheimer Dr., 28607, tel. 800/222–8636 or 800/438–6022. 83 rooms. Facilities: meeting rooms, restaurant. AE, MC, V. Moderate.*

Banner Elk   **Stonewalls.** This contemporary rustic restaurant enjoys one of
Dining   the best views of Beech Mountain. Fare includes steak, prime rib, fresh seafood, chicken, and homemade desserts. *Hwy. 184, tel. 704/898–5550. Reservations required for groups of 7 or more. Casual dinner attire. AE, MC, V. No lunch. Moderate.*

Lodging   **Holiday Inn.** Convenient to all the ski slopes, this inn is situated on an old farm in Moon Valley. Rooms are standard for this hotel chain, and attractively decorated. *NC 184, Box 1478, 28604, tel. 704/898–4571 or 800/HOLIDAY. 102 rooms. Facilities: restaurant, lounge, pool, horseshoes, soccer, badminton. AE, CB, DC, MC, V. Moderate.*

Linville   **Eseeola Lodge and Restaurant.** Built in the 1880s, this lodge is
Dining and Lodging   the cornerstone of Linville. Rich chestnut paneling and stonework grace the interior rooms. *U.S. 221, tel. 704/733–4311. 28 rooms. Facilities: restaurant, lounge, golf, tennis, pool. Open June–Labor Day. MC, V. Very Expensive.*

Wilmington and Cape Fear Country

There was much to celebrate in the old seaport town of Wilmington during its recent 250th birthday. The once-decadent downtown has been revitalized, thanks to efforts led by the Downtown Area Revitalization Effort (DARE). *Henrietta II*, a paddle wheeler similar to those that used to ply the waters of the Cape Fear River, has been put into service as a tourist vessel. Visitors are drawn to the new Coastline Convention Center complex reminiscent of old railroad days and to the charms of Chandler's Wharf and the Cotton Exchange, now shopping and entertainment centers. They also come to Wilmington for special annual events such as the Azalea Festival, North Carolina Jazz Festival, Christmas candlelight tours, and fishing tournaments. And in surrounding Cape Fear Country visitors tour old plantation houses and azalea gardens, study sea life at the state aquarium, and bask in the sun at nearby beaches.

Getting Around

Visitors can get to Wilmington and Cape Fear Country via car, plane, bus, or boat. Several cruise lines dock in the Port of Wilmington on their way to Bermuda or the Caribbean. Though the city was once a rail center, there is no train service anymore.

By Plane US Air (tel. 919/763–3615) and **American Eagle** (tel. 919/762–1847) serve the recently expanded New Hanover County Airport (tel. 919/341–4333) 2.5 miles from downtown Wilmington.

By Car U.S. Highways 421, 74, 76, 17, and 117 serve Wilmington. When completed in the 1990s, I–40 will link the city with I–95. A state-run ferry connects Fort Fisher with Southport.

By Bus **Greyhound Lines** serves the Union Bus Terminal, located at 201 Harnett Street (tel. 919/762–6625). The **Wilmington Transit Authority** provides service every day except Sunday. There is also taxi service.

By Boat Public boat access is offered at Atlantic Marina, Carolina Beach State Park, Masonboro Boat Yard and Marina, Seapath Transient Dock, Wrightsville Gulf Terminal, and Wrightsville Marina. The Wilmington Hilton, Blockade Runner, Harbor Inn, and Summer Sands provide docking facilities for their guests. A river taxi runs (mid-June until Labor Day) across the Cape Fear River between the USS *North Carolina Battleship Memorial* and downtown Wilmington. The fare is $1 roundtrip.

Guided Tours and Guides

"Guide Map of Historic Downtown Wilmington" is available from the Cape Fear Coast Convention and Visitors Bureau in the restored New Hanover Courthouse (24 N. 3rd St.) and at the Visitor Information Booth at the foot of Market Street (during the summer). The bureau can suggest one-, two-, and three-day itineraries and can arrange tours of local industries upon advance request. (The area is known for its sailboat-building industry and is popular with seagoing celebrities such as former CBS newsman Walter Cronkite.) Write to the North Carolina State Ports Authority (Box 9002, Wilmington 28402) for more information.

Historic Wilmington House Tours offers guided tours of some of Wilmington's most prestigious old homes, including the Burgwin-Wright House (224 Market St.), the Zebulon Latimore House (126 N. 3rd St.), and Thalian Hall (305 Princess St.). (The latter is currently closed for renovation.) *Tickets available at either of the 2 houses that are open. Admission: $2.50 adults, $1 children, at each site.*

The Wilmington Adventure Tour Company offers guided walking tours of old Wilmington and other tours of the Lower Cape

Fear Region year-round. *Tel. 919/763–1785. Admission: $3 adults, $2 children 6–12.*

Sightseeing Tours by Horse Drawn Carriage, given by John and Janet Pucci of Springbrook Farms, during the summer and off-season on weekends, depart from Water & Market streets. *Tel. 919/251–8889. Admission: $5 adults, $3 children.*

Cape Fear Riverboats, Inc., operated by Capt. Carl Marshburn, offers a variety of cruises aboard a stern-wheel riverboat that departs from Riverfront Park. *Tel. 919/343–1611. Sightseeing tours: adults $6, children $4. Dinner cruises: $30 per person, including tip and tax. Sightseeing tour departs Apr.–May and Sept.–Oct., Tues.–Sun. 2:30 P.M.; June–Aug., Tues.–Sun. 11 A.M. and 2:30 P.M.. Dinner cruises depart during spring and fall, Thurs.–Sat. 7 P.M.; during summer, Fri.–Sun. 7 P.M..*

The Captain J. N. Maffitt Harbor Tour is a half-hour cruise of the harbor. *Tel. 919/343–1776. Admission: $3 adults, $1.50 children. Tours depart daily May–Sept.*

Custom tours for groups can be arranged by a number of tour companies, including Blockade Runner Tour and Travel (tel. 800/722–5809 in NC; 800/541–1161 in eastern U.S.), Cape Fear Tours (tel. 919/763–8747), Family Vacation Seminars (tel. 919/392–0724), and Jane Price Tours (tel. 919/791–2700).

Important Addresses and Numbers

Tourist Information Cape Fear Coast Convention and Visitors Bureau (24 N. 3rd St., Wilmington 28401, tel. 919/341–4030 or 800/922–7117 in NC, 800/222–4757 in eastern U.S.

Emergencies Tel. 911.

Coast Guard Tel. 919/256–3469.

Exploring Wilmington and Cape Fear Country

Orientation Because Wilmington is central to Cape Fear Country, we will begin the tour in the heart of the historic downtown and then go on a driving tour of the area. Pick up a copy of the "Guide Map of Historic Downtown Wilmington" and see a 10-minute orientation video at the Cape Fear Coast Convention and Visitors Bureau, located in the restored New Hanover County Courthouse on North Third Street. The Queen Anne structure was built in 1892. You probably won't have time to see everything, but make the USS *North Carolina Battleship Memorial* a top priority if possible.

Wilmington USS *North Carolina Battleship Memorial,* a battleship that participated in every major naval offensive in the Pacific during World War II, can be reached by driving to the site off U.S. 421 or by taking the river taxi from Riverfront Park. The self-guided tour takes about two hours, and a 10-minute film is shown throughout the day. Narrated tours on cassette are available for rent. The 70-minute sound-and-light spectacular "The Immortal Showboat," presented nightly at 9 from early June until Labor Day, will leave you spellbound. *USS North Carolina Battleship Memorial, Box 417, Wilmington 28402, tel. 919/762–1829. Admission: $5 adults, $2.50 children 6–12. Open daily 8–sunset.*

The **Wilmington Railroad Museum** is located at the corner of Red Cross and Water streets, a few blocks from Riverfront Park. The museum traces the days of the Wilmington and Weldon Railroad (about 1840) to the present. Children love climbing on the steam locomotive and caboose. The building is a part of the Coastline Convention Center complex. *Tel. 919/763-2634. Free admission. Open Mar.-Oct., Mon.-Sat. 10-5, Sun. 1-5; Oct.-Mar. Tues.-Sat. 10-3, Sun. 1-5, closed Mon.*

From the museum and convention center, follow Red Cross Street one block toward downtown and turn right on Front Street. On the second block is the **Cotton Exchange,** a shopping-dining complex housed in restored buildings that have flourished as a trading center since the pre–Civil War days. *Tel. 919/343-9896. Open Mon.-Sat. 10-5:30, Sun. 1-5.*

Continue east on Grace Street until you reach Third Street and then go south to Chestnut Street, to the **New Hanover County Public Library.** The North Carolina Room in the library attracts researchers and genealogists from all over the country. *201 Chestnut St., tel. 919/341-4390. Admission free. Open weekdays 9-9, Sat. 9-5, Sun. 1-5.*

Follow Chestnut Street to 4th Street, then go two blocks to Market Street. On that corner is the **St. James Graveyard,** which contains the headstones of many early settlers who were members of the St. James Episcopal Church.

In the next block of South Fourth Street is the **Temple of Israel,** the oldest Jewish place of worship in the state.

Continue several blocks north on Market Street to the **New Hanover County Museum of the Lower Cape Fear,** which traces the natural and social history of Cape Fear River Country from its beginnings to the present day. The museum includes an exhibit on some of Wilmington's superstars, including Michael Jordan, David Brinkley, Charles Kuralt, Charlie Daniels, Sammy Davis Jr., Mary Baker Eddy, Anna McNeill Whistler, President Woodrow Wilson, and others. *814 Market St., tel. 919/341-4350. Admission free. Open Tues.-Sat. 9-5, Sun. 2-5. Closed holidays.*

Several blocks west on Market Street is the **Burgwin-Wright House.** This historic structure was built in 1770 on the foundations of a jail. This colonial restoration, which includes a period garden, is maintained by the National Society of the Colonial Dames of America and by the State of North Carolina. *224 Market St., tel. 919/762-0570. Admission: $2.50 adults, $1 children. Open Tues.-Sat. 10-4.*

Go two more blocks on Market to North Third Street, where you'll find the **Zebulon Latimer House.** Built in 1852 in the Italianate style. *126 N. 3rd St., tel. 919/762-0492. Open Tues.-Sat. 10-5. Admission: $2.50 adults, $1 children.*

Wind up your tour at **Chandler's Wharf** on Water Street. Originally a complex of warehouses, Chandler's Wharf offers quaint shops as well as some of Wilmington's best seafood restaurants (Elijah's and the Pilot House). This is a great place to conclude your tour of downtown Wilmington.

Cape Fear Country   Go three blocks east to U.S. 17, then south on U.S. 421 to the Southport–Fort Fisher Ferry. You can see some of the children's attractions in the Fort Fisher area along the way, as well as explore the beaches (*see* What to See and Do With Children and Beaches, below). After you cross the Cape Fear River by ferry, head north on Route 133 to the suggested attractions, then make your return to Wilmington.

On the way out of town, stop at **Greenfield Lake and Gardens,** located on South Third Street (U.S. 421). The park offers picnicking and canoe- and paddle-boat rentals on a scenic lake bordered by cypress trees laden with Spanish moss. *Open daily. Free admission.*

Follow U.S. 17 north for 14 miles until you reach **Poplar Grove Historic Plantation.** The home of the Foy family for generations, the 1850 Greek Revival plantation was opened to the public in 1980. You can tour the manor house and outbuildings, see craft demonstrations, shop in the country store, pet the farm animals, ride a horse (reservations required), go on a hayride, and enjoy a gracious homecooked meal in the Manor House Restaurant. *14 mi northeast of Wilmington on U.S. 17, tel. 919/686–9989 (restaurant 919/686–9503). Open Mon.–Sat. 9–5, Sun. 12–6. House tours: $4 adults, $3 senior citizens, $2 students and children 5–18.*

Head south on U.S. 17 until you reach Military Cut-off Road, which leads to **Airlie Gardens** (8 miles east of Wilmington). The gardens are open only in spring, when the azaleas explode with color. *Tel. 919/763–9991. Admission: $3 adults, children under 10 free.*

Take Route 76 to U.S. 132 south; continue to U.S. 421 south, and follow Route 421 to **Southport-Fort Fisher Ferry,** some 20 miles south of Wilmington. The car-ferry trip is an enjoyable river ride between Old Federal Point and the quaint town of Southport. You can see the "Old Baldy" lighthouse en route. *Ferries run year-round 8–6. Fare: $3 per standard-size vehicle. (The privately owned ferry to Bald Head Island runs from Southport 8–7.)*

After you get off the ferry, take Route 87 to the **Carolina Power and Light Company Nuclear Visitors Center.** Here you can learn about nuclear power through exhibits and movies and then enjoy the picnic area. *Tel. 919/457–6041. Free admission. Open June–Aug., weekdays 9–5, weekends 1–5; Sept.–May, weekdays 9–5. Closed holidays.*

Follow Route 87 to Route 133 and you will arrive at **Orton Plantation Gardens.** The house is not open to the public, but the gardens may be toured anytime. *Tel. 919/371–6851. Admission: $5 adults, $2.50 children 6–12. Open Mar.–Aug., daily 8–6, Sept.–Nov., daily 8–5.*

Continue south on Route 133 to **Brunswick Town State Historic Site,** where you can explore the excavations of this colonial town. *Tel. 919/371–6613. Free admission. Open Apr.–Oct., Mon.–Sat. 9–5, Sun. 1–5; Nov.–Mar., Tues.–Sat. 10–4, Sun. 1–4. Picnicking available.*

To complete the loop and return to Wilmington, follow Route 133 north to U.S. 74-76 and then U.S. 17.

What to See and Do with Children

Fort Fisher State Historic Site was the largest and one of the most important earthenwork fortifications in the South during the Civil War. Children like climbing the extensive earthworks and looking at Civil War relics and artifacts from sunken blockade-runners. *U.S. 421 at Kure Beach, tel. 919/458–5538. Admission free. Open Apr.–Oct., Mon.–Sat. 9–5, Sun. 1–5; Nov.–Mar., Tues.–Sat. 10–4, Sun. 1–4.*

The **North Carolina Aquarium at Fort Fisher,** one of three state aquariums, features a 20,000-gallon shark tank, a touch pool (where you can handle starfish, sea urchins and the like), whale exhibit, and other attractions. You can also visit the World War II bunker that stood guard against sea attacks from the Atlantic. Field trips and workshops for groups can be arranged. *U.S. 421 at Kure Beach, tel. 919/458–8257. Admission free. Open Mon.–Sat. 9–5, Sun. 1–5.*

Also see under **Exploring:**

Poplar Grove Historic Plantation
USS *North Carolina Battleship Memorial*
Wilmington Railroad Museum

Off the Beaten Track

Military history buffs get a bang out of **Moore's Creek National Military Park,** where American patriots defeated the Loyalists on Feb. 27, 1776. *20 mi northwest of Wilmington on Rte. 210, tel. 919/283–5591. Admission free. Open daily 8–5.*

Tryon Palace at New Bern, about 100 miles north of Wilmington, is an ideal overnight trip. The reconstructed Georgian-style palace, considered the most elegant government building in the country in its time, served as the colonial capital and the home of Royal Governor William Tryon in the 1770s. It was rebuilt according to architectural drawings of the original palace and furnished in English and American antiques as listed in Governor Tryon's inventory. Costumed interpreters give tours of the house; tours of the 18th-century formal gardens are self-guided. During the summer, actors in period dress give monologues describing a day in the life of Governor Tryon. Special events are held periodically throughout the year, and craft demonstrations are given daily. The stately John Wright Stanly House (circa 1783) and Dixon-Stevenson House (circa 1826) are a part of the Tryon Palace Complex. An audio-visual orientation is offered in the Visitor Reception Center. *610 Pollock St. (80 mi north of Wilmington), New Bern 28560, tel. 919/638–1560. Open Mon.–Sat. 9:30–4, Sun. 1:30–4. Closed New Year's Day, Thanksgiving, and Dec. 24–26. Admission (to palace and gardens only): $8 adults, $4 K–12 students. Combination tour of all buildings and gardens: $12 adults, $6 students. Garden tour only: $4 adults, $3 students.*

Shopping

Visitors will find it easy to restrict their shopping to Chandler's Wharf and the Cotton Exchange, but the city also offers shopping malls and discount outlets. Wilmington is the home of **Dorothy's Ruffled Originals,** a must-see for decorators. You can visit her showroom on U.S. 17 north of the city. *Tel. 919/791–1296 or 800/334–2593 in NC. Open Mon.–Sat. 9–5.*

Beaches

Three beaches—**Wrightsville, Carolina,** and **Kure**—are within a few minutes' drive from Wilmington, and miles and miles of beach stretch northward to the Outer Banks and southward to South Carolina. The beaches offer a full gamut of activities, from fishing to sunbathing to snorkeling, and a choice of accommodations, including weathered cottages, resorts, condos, and motels. Wrightsville, about 7 miles southeast of Wilmington, is a quiet family beach with a number of outstanding restaurants nearby. Carolina and Kure beaches, about 20 miles south, have an old-fashioned Coney Island look. Camping and picnicking are available at Carolina Beach State Park. There are approximately 100 points of public access along the shoreline. Marked by orange-and-blue signs, these points offer parking, restrooms, and outdoor showers. Some of the smaller beaches have lifeguards on duty, and many are accessible to the handicapped. A number of fishing piers are also open to the public. Additional beaches line the coast between Wilmington and Morehead City, a port city south of the Outer Banks.

Participant Sports

Biking Those who enjoy jogging, swimming, and bicycling can join in the annual **Wilmington Triathlon** in the fall. Participants swim across Banks Channel to Wrightsville Beach, then bicycle to Carolina Beach and back to Wilmington, and then run from there back to Wrightsville Beach.

Fishing Surf fishing is popular on the piers that dot the coast. Charter boats and headboats are available for off-shore fishing. Four major fishing tournaments are held each year—the **Cape Fear Marlin Tournament** (tel. 919/256-6550), the **Wrightsville Beach King Mackeral Tournament** (tel. 919/256-3581), **East Coast Open King Mackeral Tournament** (tel. 919/458-8434), and the **U.S. Open King Mackeral Tournament** (tel. 919/457-6964).

Golf The city has an 18-hole course designed by Donald Ross. In addition, there are 10 public and semi-private courses in the Greater Wilmington area, including the breathtaking Bald Head Island Golf Course, a George Cobb design. For more information on golf, call the Cape Fear Coast Convention and Visitors Bureau, (tel. 919/341-4030 or 800/922-7117 in NC, 800/222-4757 in eastern U.S.).

Sailboat Racing The Wrightsville Beach Ocean Racing Association sponsors sailboat races for yachts from April through October.

Surfing and Board Sailing These sports are popular at area beaches, and rentals are available at shops in Wilmington, Wrightsville Beach, and Carolina Beach.

Spectator Sports

College Sports Local fans support the University of North Carolina at Wilmington's Seahawk basketball, baseball, and swimming teams. The school belongs to the NCAA Division I Colonial Athletic Association. *For tickets, tel. 919/395-3841.*

Fishing *See* Participant Sports, above.

Rugby The Cape Fear Rugby Tournament is an annual July 4th event, held at UNC–W. *Tel. 919/395–3841.*

Dining and Lodging

Dining Local cuisine is simply seafood. Shrimp (this is where the shrimp boats come in), oysters, Atlantic blue crab, and king mackerel—and lots of it—are prepared in a variety of ways. (You can buy fresh seafood at the Hieronymous family's market —they also operate three local restaurants.) Homegrown fruits and vegetables, too, are used extensively in local cooking. Barbecued pork is another popular dish. International cuisines—from Mexican to Japanese to German—are also represented.

Category	Cost*
Very Expensive	over $25
Expensive	$15–$25
Moderate	$8–$15
Inexpensive	under $8

*per person without tax (4.5%), service, or drinks

Lodging Visitors to Wilmington and Cape Fear Country have over 5,000 rooms to choose from. The selection includes a variety of chains, Mom and Pop motels, condos and resorts overlooking the ocean, and in-town guest houses. In addition to in-town properties, there are many accommodations at Carolina, Kure, and Wrightsville beaches. A complete list is included in the resort directory, available from the Convention and Visitors Bureau.

Category	Cost*
Very Expensive	over $100
Expensive	$60–$100
Moderate	$30–$60
Inexpensive	under $30

Dining **Ferrovia's.** For the most elegant dining and the most delectable
Moderate and eclectic cuisine in Wilmington, this downtown gypsy restaurant operated by Guy and Justine Ferraro is the place to go. Entrées include medallions of filet mignon with bernaise sauce, broiled lamb chops with chutney and mint jelly, sauteed filet of flounder with seasoned butter and lemon sauce, and other delicacies. Live jazz is featured nightly. *Nutt St. at Coast Line Center, tel. 919/763–6677. Dinner reservations required. AE, DC, MC, V.*

The Pilot House. This Chandler's Wharf establishment overlooking the Cape Fear River serves great fresh seafood dishes, including Cape Fear crab and smoked peppered mackerel, in a back-porch atmosphere. *2 Ann St., tel. 919/343–0200. Reservations advised. AE, MC, V.*

Inexpensive **The Chart House.** Come here for the best shrimp in town— broiled, boiled, pan-fried, or deep-fried—plus all other kinds of seafood, steak, chicken, and barbecue. This family-owned restaurant serves no alcoholic beverages, but carry-out food orders are available. A sister restaurant by the same name is located in Whiteville. *N. Kerr Ave., tel. 919/762–8096. Dress: casual. No credit cards. Personal and travelers checks accepted. Closed holidays.*

Lodging
Very Expensive

Bald Head Island Resort, accessible only by ferry, offers privacy in a luxurious isolated setting. Guests have their own rental condo or house. Despite the quiet surroundings, there's always something to do on the resort island—from golf to tennis to fishing. One of the favorite pastimes is watching the loggerhead turtles. Naturalist-conducted tours are also avilable. *Bald Head Island, tel. 800/722–6450. 90 rental condos and homes. Facilities: pool, canoes, bicycles, golf, tennis, fishing, nature walks. AE, DC, MC, V. Three-night minimum. Ferry transportation from Southport $12–$20 per person, tel. 800/ 443–0382.*

Expensive

Shell Island Resort Hotel, an all-suite hotel, is one of the newest and most luxurious properties in the area. *2700 N. Lumina Ave., Wrightsville Beach 28480, tel. 800/522–8575 in NC or 800/ 826–0347 outside NC. 169 suites. Facilities: outdoor and indoor pool, fitness center, restaurant, lounge. AE, DC, MC, V.*

Wilmington Hilton Inn, overlooking the Cape Fear River on one side and the city on the other, is one of the most convenient places to stay in town. The spacious inn has a dining room and lounge. *301 N. Water St., Wilmington 28401, tel. 919/763–5900. 179 rooms and suites. Facilities: outdoor pool, meeting rooms, complimentary airport transportation. AE, MC, V.*

Moderate

Blockade Runner Resort Hotel is widely known for both its food and lodging. Refurbished rooms overlook either the inlet or the ocean. The hotel caters to the special needs of visitors and can arrange customized tours of the area. The Ocean Terrace Restaurant located in the hotel, serves three meals a day but attracts the largest crowd to its Saturday seafood-buffet and Sunday brunch. Regular dishes here include grilled New York strip steak with bourbon-shallot butter; sautéed almond-bread flounder with shrimp; sautéed chicken breast with toasted pecans, pears, and apples. *275 Waynick Blvd., Wrightsville Beach, tel. 919/256–2251. 150 rooms and suites. Facilities: restaurant (reservations advised), pool, health spa, meeting rooms, sailing center, bike rentals, golf privileges. AE, DC, MC, V.*

The Arts and Nightlife

The arts are very much a part of Wilmington life. Theatrical productions are staged by the **Thalian Association, Opera House Productions,** and **Academy Players.** The city has its own symphony orchestra, oratorio society, civic ballet and concert association; and the **North Carolina Symphony** makes four appearances here each year. The annual **Wilmington Jazz Festival,** held in February, is always a sell-out.

The Arts

St. John's Museum of Art is known for its collection of 13 prints by Cassatt, as well as for its works by North Carolina artists. The museum is housed in three buildings, including the 1804 Masonic Lodge Building, the oldest such lodge in the state. There is also a sculpture garden. *114 Orange St., tel. 919/763– 0281. Admission free. Open Tues.–Sat. 10–5.*

The Museum of World Cultures (601 S. College Rd., tel. 919/395–3411), at the University of North Carolina at Wilmington, exhibits its collections of African art, pre-Columbian textiles, Chinese ceramics, and Middle Eastern artifacts at various locations around the campus.

Nightlife Wilmington nightlife is centered in hotel lounges. The **Ocean Terrace Dining Room** in the Blockade Runner Hotel (*see* Dining and Lodging, above) features live entertainment Thursday through Sunday, with nationally known acts in the **Comedy Zone.**

Southern Pines–Pinehurst and Sandhills

Because of their sandy soil—once the beaches of the Atlantic Ocean—the Sandhills weren't of much use to early farmers, most of whom switched to lumbering and making turpentine for a livelihood. Since the turn of the century, however, this area has proven ideal for golf and tennis. Today promoters call it the Golf Capital of the World, and there's even a museum here that honors the sport. World-class resorts are centered around more than three dozen golf courses, including the famed Pinehurst Number 2.

The Highland Scots, who settled the area, left a rich heritage that is perpetuated through festivals and gatherings. In Colonial times English potters were attracted to the rich clay deposits in the soil, and today their descendants and others turn out beautiful wares that are sold in more than 30 local shops.

Getting Around

By Plane Visitors can fly into the Raleigh-Durham Airport, the Piedmont Triad International Airport, or the Charlotte-Douglas International Airport. The drive from each airport to the Sandhills takes approximately one to two hours. Rental cars are available at each terminal.

By Car U.S. 1 runs north–south through the Sandhills and is the recommended route from the Raleigh-Durham area, a distance of about 70 miles. Another alternate is U.S. 15–501 from Chapel Hill. Route 27 leads east from Charlotte and intersects U.S. 15–501 near Carthage, about 10 miles from Pinehurst and Southern Pines. U.S. 74 from Charlotte intersects U.S. 1 at Rockingham, south of Southern Pines. The 100-mile drive from Charlotte takes about two hours.

By Train **Amtrak** (tel. 919/692–6305 or 800/872–7245) southbound and northbound trains, one daily from each direction, stop in Southern Pines.

Important Addresses and Numbers

Tourist Information **Pinehurst Area Convention and Visitors Bureau** (600 SW Broad St. Annex, Box 2270, Southern Pines 28387, tel. 919/692–3330 or 800/346–5362).

Emergencies Dial 919/947–2911 for police and ambulance, or go to the emergency room of the Moore Regional Hospital in Pinehurst or the Sandhills Urgent Care Clinic in Southern Pines.

Exploring

Southern Pines **Southern Pines,** the center of the Sandhills, is a good place to start a tour. Lunch and afternoon tea are served at the Shaw House (W. Broad St. and Morganton Rd., tel. 919/692–2051). Built in 1842, it is the oldest structure in town.

Weymouth Center is headquarters for the Moore County Historical Society. (E. Vermont Ext., tel. 919/692–6261). **Weymouth Woods Nature Preserve** (tel. 919/692–2167), on the eastern outskirts of town, is a 531-acre wildlife preserve with a state-operated museum.

Pinehurst **Pinehurst** lies 8 miles west of Southern Pines via U.S. 15-501 or Midland Road. The New England–style village, with its quiet, shaded streets and immaculately kept cottages, was laid out in the late 1800s in a wagon-wheel fashion, by landscape genius Frederick Law Olmsted. It is a mecca for sports enthusiasts, retirees, and tourists.

The **PGA/World Golf Hall of Fame** traces the history of golf from the 1600s to the present day. It has been renovated recently and the Out of Bounds gift and memorabilia shop added. *PGA Blvd., tel. 919/295–6651. Admission: $3 adults, $2 students age 10–18. Open Mon.–Sat. 9–5, Sun. 1–5 (hours vary according to season).*

Aberdeen From Pinehurst, take U.S. 15–501 south for 5 miles to the intersection of U.S. 1 and then follow that route for 3 miles to **Aberdeen,** a town of Scottish ancestry with a beautifully restored turn-of-the-century train station and two working shortline freight railroads (the Aberdeen & Briarpatch and the Aberdeen & Rockfish lines).

Follow Bethesda Road east past the Aberdeen & Rockfish Railroad to **Bethesda Presbyterian Church** on the outskirts of town. The church was founded in 1788 and the present wooden structure, which is used for weddings, funerals, and reunions, was built in the 1860s. The cemetery, where many early settlers are buried, is always open.

Continue on Bethesda Road for a short distance and you will come to the **Malcolm Blue Farm,** where Scots gather in September for a festival that recalls life here in the 1800s. The buildings are open only during the festival, but you're welcome to stroll the grounds anytime.

From Aberdeen take routes 5 and 211 northwest to the intersection of U.S. 220, just east of Candor. Follow U.S. 220 north to the **North Carolina Zoological Park** at Asheboro. This 1,400-acre natural habitat for animals is one of the up-and-coming zoos of the late-20th century. The park includes the African Pavilion, an aviary, and a new gorilla habitat. *Tel. 919/879–5606. Admission: $3 adults, $1 senior citizens and children 2–15. Tram ride: $1. Open weekdays 9–5, weekends 10–6.*

Shopping

Antiques Shop for antiques in **Cameron,** which hasn't changed much since the 19th century, when it was a commerce center for the dewberry crop. Approximately 60 antique dealers operate out of seven stores. The town itself has been declared a historic district. *Tel. 919/245–7042. Most shops open Wed.–Sat. 10–5.*

Herbs and Wildflowers **Sandhills Farms,** 12 miles east of Cameron off Highway 24, is a one-of-a-kind operation offering herbs, wildflowers, wreaths, crafts, and oils. *Tel. 919/499–4753. Open Wed.–Sat. 10–5.*

Pottery Mugs, bowls, pitchers, platters, and sometimes clay voodoo heads can be found in about 30 shops scattered along and off Route 705 and U.S. 220. The work of some local potters is exhibited in national museums, including the Smithsonian. A map locating the various potteries is available at most shops. *For information, tel. 919/873–7887. Most shops open Mon.–Sat. 8:30–5.*

Participant Sports

Golf More than three dozen courses await you in this golfers' paradise, including **Pinehurst, Pine Needles, Mid-Pines,** and other famous links. Several Southern Pines courses are open to the public, including **Hyland Hills** (tel. 919/692–3752), **Knollwood Fairways** (tel. 919/692–3572), **Southern Pines Country Club** (tel. 919/692–6551), and **The Pit** (tel. 919/944–1600). A complete list of golf courses is available from the Pinehurst Area Convention and Visitors Bureau (tel. 919/692–3330 or 800/346–5362).

Tennis Facilities are available at various resorts. Pinehurst, Seven Lakes, Mid Pines, and the Country Club of North Carolina offer regular clinics. Public courts can be found in Aberdeen, Carthage, Pinebluff, and Southern Pines and at Sandhills Community College. For details, contact the Pinehurst Area Convention and Visitors Bureau (tel. 919/692–3330 or 800/346–5346).

Horseback Riding English and Western-style riding instruction is available by appointment at the Pinehurst Riding Stables. Escorted trail rides can also be arranged. *Hwy. 5, Pinehurst, tel. 919/295–6811. Open daily 9–4.*

Dining and Lodging

Dining There's no particular local cuisine that typifies the Sandhills, but a number of sophisticated restaurants are located in the area.

Category	Cost*
Very Expensive	over $25
Expensive	$15–$25
Moderate	$8–$15
Inexpensive	under $8

*per person without tax (5%), service, or drinks

Lodging Most lodging options in the Sandhills are in the luxury resort category, featuring full amenities and services. However, there are a few chains such as Econo-Lodge, Hampton Inn, Quality Inn, and Sheraton in Southern Pines.

Category	Cost*
Very Expensive	over $100
Expensive	$60–$100
Moderate	$30–$60
Inexpensive	under $30

double room; add 8% for taxes

Pinehurst **The Pinehurst Hotel and Country Club.** This venerable resort
Dining and Lodging hotel, in operation since the turn of the century, has never lost the charm that founder James Tufts intended it to have. Civilized decorum rules in the spacious public rooms, on the rocker-lined wide verandas, and amid the lush gardens of the surrounding grounds. Guests can play lawn croquet, shoot skeet, or tee off on one of seven premier golf courses. The Carolina Dining Room is known for its gourmet cuisine. *Carolina Vista, Box 4000, Pinehurst 28374, 800/672–4644 in NC, 800/334–9560 outside NC. 310 rooms and 125 condos. Facilities: pool, golf, tennis, croquet, horseback riding, sailing, fishing, boating, wind surfing, biking, trap and skeet shooting, meeting rooms. AE, CB, DC, MC, V. Very Expensive.*
Holly Inn. This renovated wooden inn, built in 1895, is testimony to James Tufts' success as an hotelier. It was so popular that he was forced to build a bigger structure—now the Pinehurst Hotel. Guests at the inn enjoy their own pool, restaurant, and lounge. *Cherokee Rd., Box 2300, Pinehurst 28374, tel. 800/682–6901 in NC, 800/533–0041 outside NC. 77 rooms and suites. AE, CB, MC. Very Expensive.*
The Manor Inn. This small village hotel features contemporary furnishings. Guests have privileges at 18 area golf courses. *Magnolia and Community Rds., Box 3610, Pinehurst 28374, tel. 919/295–2700. 49 rooms and suites. AE, DC, MC, V. Expensive.*
Pine Crest Inn. Formerly owned by golfing great Donald Ross, this small village inn was recently refurbished. Chefs Carl and Peter Jackson whip up some great dishes, including homemade soups; fresh seafood dishes; and the house special, stuffed pork chops. Guests have golf and tennis privileges at local clubs. *Dogwood Rd., Box 879, Pinehurst 28374, tel. 919/295–6121. 43 rooms and suites. Rates include two meals per day. AE, MC, V. Moderate.*

Southern Pines **Antoine's.** Dishes of veal, seafood, filet mignon, chicken, and
Dining lamb (prepared tableside), dramatically capped with flambéed desserts, make dining in this family-owned French restaurant an experience to remember. The restaurant features mirrored walls, a black ceiling, and peach-tone accents. *S.W. Broad St. tel. 919/692–5622. Reservations advised. Jacket required at dinner. AE, MC, V. No lunch. Closed Sun. and Mon. Expensive.*
The Lob Steer Inn. Come hungry for broiled seafood and prime rib dinners, complemented with salad and dessert bars. The restaurant is upscale, with brass accents a part of the decor. *U.S. 1S, Southern Pines, tel. 919/692–3503. Dress: casual.*

Reservations advised on weekends. AE, MC, V. Closed lunch. Moderate–Expensive.

Mannie's Dinner Theatre. Guests can see Broadway shows here on weekends, after a dinner of prime rib or shrimp scampi. The same menu is available throughout the week. *W. Penn. Ave., tel. 919/692–8400. Dress: casual. Reservations required for dinner theatre. AE, MC, V. Closed Sun. $19.50 per person for dinner theater; otherwise Moderate.*

Silver Bucket Oyster Bar. You can order just about any kind of fish—plus steaks, ribs, barbecue, and some Italian dishes—for a tasty and satisfying meal. The atmosphere is trés casual. *S.E. Broad St., tel. 919/692–6227. AE, MC, V. Closed lunch and Sun. Inexpensive–Moderate.*

Lodging **Pine Needles Lodges and Country Club.** One of the bonuses of staying at this informal lodge is the chance to meet Peggy Kirk Bell, a champion golfer and golf instructor. She built the resort with her late husband, and she continues to be involved in its operation. The rooms here are spacious. The lodge is done in a rustic style, with exposed beams in many rooms. *Box 88, Midland Rd., Southern Pines 28387, tel. 919/692–7111. 67 rooms. Facilities: pool, sauna, whirlpool, lighted tennis courts, steambaths, golf, airport transportation, restaurant. No credit cards. Personal and traveler's checks accepted. Very Expensive.*

Mid Pines Resort. This resort community, now a Clarion Resort, features an 18-hole golf course designed by Donald Ross that has been the site of numerous tournaments, including the 1988 Women's Eastern Amateur. *1010 Midland Rd., Southern Pines 28387, tel. 919/692–2114 or 800/323–2114. 118 rooms. Facilities: pool, sauna, lighted tennis courts, golf, airport transportation, restaurant, meeting rooms. AE, CB, MC, V. Expensive.*

The Jefferson Inn. Located in the heart of downtown Southern Pines, this small hotel has been refurbished to serve as a bed-and-breakfast inn. Guest rooms are compact and decorated with a subdued country flair. *W. New Hampshire Ave., Southern Pines 28387, tel. 919/692–6400. 22 rooms. Facilities: golf and tennis privileges. MC, V. Moderate.*

4 South Carolina

Introduction

*by Edgar and
Patricia Cheatham*

*Award-winning
travel writers
Edgar and Patricia
Cheatham are
based in Charlotte,
North Carolina.
They are members
of the Society of
American Travel
Writers and the
American Society
of Journalists and
Authors.*

From its Low Country shoreline, with wide sand beaches, spacious bays, and forests of palmettos and moss-strewn live oaks, South Carolina extends into an undulating interior region rich with fertile farmlands, then reaches toward the Blue Ridge Mountains, studded with scenic lakes, forests, and wilderness hideaways. What this smallest of Southern states lacks in land area it makes up in diversity.

The historic port city of Charleston, lovingly preserved, links past with present. Many of its treasured double-galleried antebellum homes were built at right angles to the streets to conserve space and catch ocean breezes. Some are now authentically furnished house museums where visitors savor gracious early-era eloquence. Culturally vibrant, the city nurtures theatre, dance, music, and visual arts, showcased each spring during the internationally acclaimed Spoleto Festival USA.

Myrtle Beach is the hub of the Grand Strand, a 55-mile stretch of wide golden-sand beaches and countless family entertainment and recreational activities (especially golf, a top attraction throughout the state). To the south, tasteful, low-key Hilton Head—a sea island tucked between the Intracoastal Waterway and the ocean and divided into several sophisticated, self-contained resorts—also offers beautiful beaches and some of the world's best golf and tennis. Nearby is the port city of Beaufort, where the most rewarding activity is wandering the lovely streets dotted with preserved 18th-century homes, live oaks, and palmettos.

Columbia, the state capital, is a lively (and of course historic) city cleaved by a rushing river. In addition to several museums, a good minor-league baseball team, and a library of Movietonews film clips, the city has one of the country's top zoos. It is also home to the newly opened State Museum and one of the South's finest new performing arts complexes, Koger Center for Performing Arts. Nearby lakes and state parks offer abundant outdoor recreation and first-rate fishing.

Thoroughbred Country, centered around the town of Aiken, is a peaceful area of rolling pastures where some of the world's top race horses are trained. It is also notable for magnificent mansions built by wealthy Northerners who vacationed here at the turn of the century.

Upcountry South Carolina, at the northwestern tip of the state, is less visited than most of the rest of the state but well repays time spent with dramatic mountain scenery, excellent hiking, and challenging white-water rafting.

Since 1670, when the British established the first permanent European settlement at Charleston, the history of the Palmetto State has been characterized by periods of great prosperity contrasted with eras of dismal depression. This vibrant past—from the pioneer, Colonial, Revolutionary, and antebellum periods through the bitter Civil War and Reconstruction years and beyond—is preserved in cherished traditions and an enduring belief in family that give resonance to the optimism and vitality of today's South Carolina.

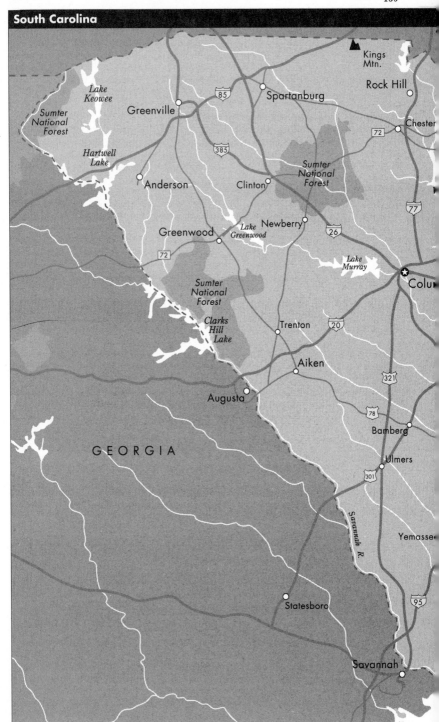

South Carolina

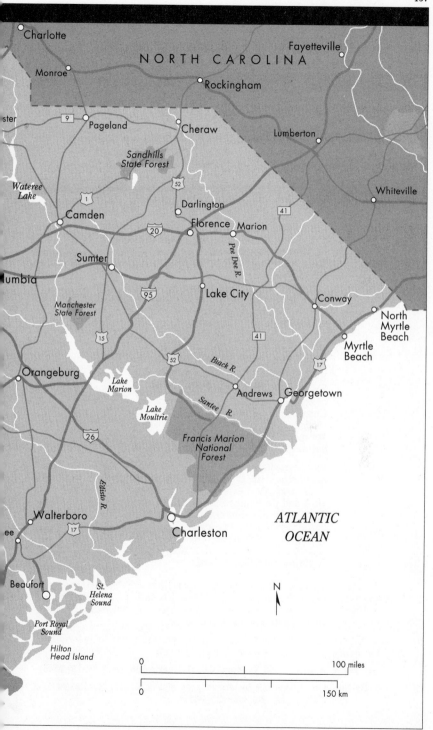

Charlotte

Fayetteville

NORTH CAROLINA

Monroe

Rockingham

ster

9

Pageland

Cheraw

Lumberton

Sandhills State Forest

Whiteville

Wateree Lake

1

52

Camden

Darlington

41

20

Florence

Marion

Sumter

Pee Dee R.

umbia

95

Manchester State Forest

Lake City

Conway

North Myrtle Beach

15

41

52

Black R.

Myrtle Beach

Orangeburg

Lake Marion

17

Lake Moultrie

Santee R.

Andrews

Georgetown

26

Francis Marion National Forest

Edisto R.

Walterboro

17

ee

Charleston

ATLANTIC OCEAN

N

Beaufort

St. Helena Sound

Port Royal Sound

Hilton Head Island

| 0 | | 100 miles |

| 0 | | 150 km |

Charleston

At first glimpse, Charleston resembles an 18th-century etching come to life. Its low-profile skyline is punctuated with the spires and steeples of 181 churches, representing 25 denominations that have sought out Charleston as a haven (it was known for having the most liberal provisions for religious freedom of the 13 original colonies). Parts of the city appear stopped in time. Block after block of old downtown structures have been preserved and restored for both residential and commercial use. After three centuries of epidemics, earthquakes, fires, and hurricanes, Charleston has prevailed, and it is today one of the South's best-preserved cities.

Along the Battery, on the point of a narrow peninsula bounded by the Ashley and Cooper rivers, handsome mansions surrounded by gardens face the harbor. Called the "Charleston style," this distinctive look is reminiscent of the West Indies, and for good reason. Before coming to the Carolinas in the late 17th century, many early British colonists had first settled on Barbados and other Caribbean islands. In that warm and humid climate they had built homes with high ceilings and rooms opening onto broad piazzas at each level to catch welcome sea breezes. In Charleston, the settlers adapted these designs for other practical reasons. One new twist—building narrow two-to four-story houses (called single houses) at right angles to the street—emerged partly because of the British Crown's policy of taxing buildings according to frontage length. To save money (as well as to catch the prevailing winds), shrewd Charlestonians faced their houses to the side.

Each year, from mid-March to mid-April, the city opens its homes to visitors. In addition to tours of private homes, gardens, and churches, the Festival of Houses celebrates Charleston's heritage with symphony galas in stately drawing rooms, plantation oyster roasts, candlelight tours, and more. For more information, write to the Historic Charleston Foundation (51 Meeting St., Charleston 29401, tel. 803/722–3405).

But Charleston is more than a carefully polished and preserved relic of the past. It is a city with a vibrant cultural life, which finds its greatest expression in the renowned Spoleto Festival USA and its companion festival, Piccolo Spoleto, when hundreds of local and international artists, musicians, and other performers fill the city streets and buildings with sound and spectacle (see The Arts).

Arriving and Departing

By Plane
Airports and
Airlines
Charleston International Airport, in North Charleston, opened new terminal facilities in 1985. It's on I–26, 12 miles west of downtown Charleston, and is served by **American, Bankair, Delta, Eastern, United,** and **USAir.**

Between the Airport
and Center City
Taxis average $13, plus tip. By **car,** take I–26S to its terminus, at U.S. 17, near the heart of the city.

By Train
Amtrak (4565 Gaynor Ave., N. Charleston, tel. 800/872–7245).

By Bus
Greyhound (89 Society St., tel. 803/722–1115), **Trailways** (100 Calhoun St., tel. 803/723–8649).

By Car I–26 traverses the state from northwest to southeast and terminates at Charleston. A favorite coastal route for north-south travelers is U.S. 17, which passes through Charleston.

By Boat Charleston harbor is along the Intracoastal Waterway.

Getting Around

By Taxi Fares within the city vary from company to company but average $2–$3 per trip. Companies include Everready Cab Co. (tel. 803/722–8383), Yellow Cab (tel. 803/577–6565), Safety Cab (tel. 803/722–4066), and Limo-Taxi (tel. 803/767–7111).

By Bus Regular bus service within the city is provided by **SCE&G** (South Carolina Electric and Gas Company) between 5:35 AM and 10 PM and to North Charleston until 1 AM. The cost is 50¢; at peak hours (9:30–3:30), senior citizens and disabled persons pay 25¢. Exact change is needed, and free transfers are available. SCE&G also operates the **DASH** (Downtown Area Shuttle) buses, new trolley-style vehicles that provide fast service on weekdays in the main downtown areas. The fares are the same. For schedule information, call 803/724–7368 (DASH) or 803/722–2226 (regular service).

Important Addresses and Numbers

Tourist Information **Visitor Information Center,** 85 Calhoun St., tel. 803/722–8338. Open weekdays 8:30–5:30, weekends 8:30–5.

Emergencies Dial 911 for emergency assistance.

Hospital The emergency rooms are open all night at **Charleston Memorial Hospital** (326 Calhoun St., tel. 803/577–0600) and **Roper Hospital** (316 Calhoun St., tel. 803/724–2000).

Dentist The **Dental Center** (86 Rutledge Ave., tel. 803/723–7242) provides dental care on short notice.

Guided Tours

Orientation Tours **Adventure Sightseeing** (tel. 803/762–0088), **Carolina Lowcountry Tours** (tel. 803/797–1045), and **Gateway Tours** (tel. 803/556–7059) offer van or motor-coach tours of the historic district. **Gray Line** (tel. 803/722–4444) offers similar motor-coach tours, plus seasonal tours to gardens and plantations.

Special-Interest Tours **Historically Speaking** (tel. 803/571–1787) offers a 100-minute van tour of the historic district with complimentary refreshments. **Livin' in the Past** (tel. 803/871–0791 or 723–0933) offers historically oriented van and minibus tours of the city and the plantations.

Carriage Tours **Charleston Carriage Co.** (tel. 803/577–0042) offers 40- to 50-minute horse-drawn-carriage tours through the historic district. **Old South Carriage Co.** (tel. 803/723–9712) has similar tours, but conducted by guides in Confederate uniforms. **Old Towne Carriage Co.** (tel. 803/722–1315) has carriage tours as well as semiprivate surrey tours. **Palmetto Carriage Tours** (tel. 803/723–8145) offers one-hour horse- and mule-drawn-carriage tours of the historic district.

Cassette Tours **Charles Towne Tours** (tel. 803/883–3320) and **Charleston Carriage Co.** (tel. 803/577–0042) rent self-paced cassette tours of the historic district.

Personal Guides Contact **Associated Guides of Historic Charleston** (tel. 803/724–6419); **Charleston Guide Service** (tel. 803/747–3111); **Charleston Hospitality Tours** (tel. 803/722–6858), whose walking, car, and bus tours may include dinner and/or cocktails in antebellum homes; **Parker Limousine Service** (tel. 803/723–7601), which offers chauffeur-driven luxury limousine tours; or **Tours of Historic Charleston** (tel. 803/722–0026).

Walking Tours Guided tours are given by **Charleston Carriage Co.** (tel. 803/577–0042), **Charleston Strolls** (tel. 803/766–2080), **Charleston Tea Party Walking Tour** (tel. 803/577–5896; includes tea in a private garden), and **Civil War Walking Tour** (tel. 803/722–7033).

Boat Tours **Charles Towne Princess Gray Line Water Tours** (tel. 803/722–1112) and **Charleston Harbor Tour** (tel. 803/722–1691) offer non-stop harbor tours. **Fort Sumter Tours** (tel. 803/722–1691) includes a stop at Fort Sumter in its harbor tour. It also offers Starlight Dinner Cruises aboard a luxury yacht.

Exploring Charleston

Numbers in the margin correspond with points of interest on the Charleston map.

If you have just a day to spend in Charleston, you might begin with a carriage tour for the tidbits of history and humor that the driver-guides provide as they take you through the main streets of the historic district. This is the best way to decide where to go on your own. Next, browse through the shops of the Old Market area, where most of the carriage tours begin and end. After that, walk south along East Bay Street, past Rainbow Row (a row of pastel-painted houses near Tradd Street), or along any side streets on your way to your choice of the area's four house museums. Spend the rest of the day wandering the cool, palmetto-shaded streets, peeking into private gardens and churches of every stripe, discovering all the little surprises that reveal themselves only to those who seek them out.

If you have more time (and you really should), you can expand your itinerary by adding more sights within the same area; by adding a shopping excursion at the Shops at Charleston Place or along King Street; by including the Marion Square area, which has an excellent art museum and a house museum; or by adding excursions to magnificent plantations and gardens west of the Ashley River or to major historic sites east of the Cooper. There are also boat excursions and some very nice beaches for days when you just want to relax.

For a good overview of the city before you begin touring, drop by the Visitor Information Center to view *The Charleston Adventure*, a 30-minute film. *Admission: $3 adults; $1.50 children 6–12, under 6 free. Shown daily 9–5 on the half-hour.*

For another perspective, see *Dear Charleston: The Motion Picture.* This audacious 42-minute film depicts the city's unique history and personality through the voices of its residents, and through scenes from D. W. Griffith's *Birth of a Nation. Shown at two locations: Historic Preservation Society Visitor Center, 142 King St., tel. 803/723–4381; and Old Exchange and Provost Dungeon, 122 E. Bay St., tel. 803/792–5020. Admission: $3 adults; $1.50 children 7–12, under 7 free. Shown daily at both locations at 10, 11, noon, 2, 3, and 4.*

Marion Square to the Battery

❶ ❷

Starting at the **Visitor Information Center,** where there's free parking (for two hours; 50¢ per hour thereafter), head down Calhoun Street to Marion Square. Facing the square is the **Old Citadel Building,** built in 1822 to house state troops and arms. Here began the famed South Carolina Military College—The Citadel—now located on the banks of the Ashley River.

❸

At 350 Meeting Street is one of Charleston's fine house museums, and a National Historic Landmark, the **Joseph Manigault Mansion.** An outstanding example of Adam-style architecture, it was designed by Charleston architect Gabriel Manigault in 1803 and is noted for its carved-wood mantels and elaborate plasterwork. Furnishings are British, French, and Charleston antiques, including rare tricolor Wedgwood pieces. *Tel. 803/723–2926. Admission: $3 adults; $1.50 children 3–12, under 3 free. Open Mon.–Sat. 10–5, Sun. 1–5.*

❹

Across John Street, housed in a $6-million contemporary complex, is the oldest city museum in the United States. The **Charleston Museum,** founded in 1773, is one of the Southeast's major museums and is especially strong on South Carolina decorative arts. The 500,000 items in the collection—in addition to Charleston silver, fashions, toys, snuff boxes, etc.—include objects relating to natural history, archaeology, and ornithology. *360 Meeting St., tel. 803/722–2996. Admission: $3 adults; $1.50 children 3–12, under 3 free. Open Mon.–Sat. 9–5, Sun. 1–5. Three historic homes—the Joseph Manigault House, the Aiken-Rhett Mansion, and the Heyward-Washington House—are part of the museum, and a combination ticket can be bought for either all three and the museum ($9 adults) or any two ($5) or three ($7) houses at any of the four locations.*

❺

Walk up Meeting Street to Wragg Street and take a right to reach the 1817 **Aiken-Rhett Mansion.** Furnished in a variety of 19th-century styles, with a heavy, ornate look overall, the house is still undergoing restoration and is especially interesting for that reason. *48 Elizabeth St. tel. 803/723–1159. Admission: $3 adults; $1.50 children 3–12, under 3 free. Open daily 10–5.*

❻

If you've left your car at the visitor center, return now to retrieve it. From here you can either take an excursion to see the lovely **College of Charleston** (founded in 1770 as the nation's first municipal college, with a graceful main building constructed in 1828 after a design by famed Philadelphia architect William Strickland) and/or make a shopping tour of King Street, or you can proceed directly to the market area.

❼

When you're ready for the market area, head for one of the many centrally located parking garages. Now is the time for a carriage tour, many of which leave from here (*see* Guided Tours). Our tour picks up again at **Congregation Beth Elohim** (90 Hassell St.), considered one of the nation's finest examples of Greek Revival architecture. It was constructed in 1840 to replace an earlier temple—the birthplace of American Reform Judaism in 1824—that was destroyed by fire. Visitors are welcome weekdays 10 AM–noon.

❽

Follow Meeting Street south to Market Street, and at the intersection on the left you'll see **Market Hall.** Built in 1841 and modeled after the Temple of Nike in Athens, the hall is a National Historic Landmark. Here you'll find the **Confederate Museum,**

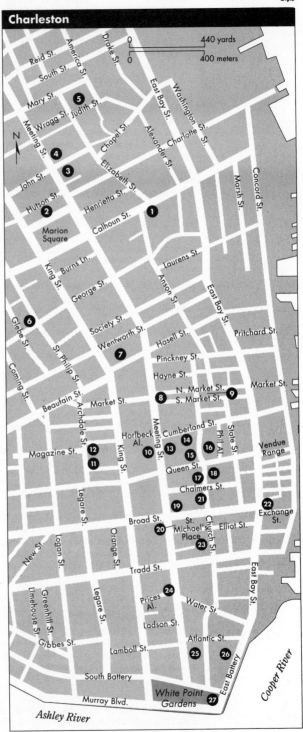

Charleston

Aiken-Rhett Mansion, **5**

American Military Museum, **21**

Calhoun Mansion, **25**

Charleston Museum, **4**

Circular Congregational Church, **13**

City Hall, **19**

College of Charleston, **6**

Congregation Beth Elohim, **7**

Dock St. Theatre, **17**

Edmonston-Alston House, **26**

Exchange Bldg./Provost Dungeon, **22**

French Huguenot Church, **18**

Gibbes Art Gallery, **10**

Heyward-Washington House, **23**

Joseph Manigault Mansion, **3**

Market Hall, **8**

Nathaniel Russell House, **24**

Old Citadel Bldg., **2**

Old City Market, **9**

Old Powder Magazine, **14**

St. John's, **12**

St. Michael's, **20**

St. Philip's, **16**

Thomas Elfe Workshop, **15**

Unitarian Church, **11**

Visitor Info., **1**

White Point Gardens, **27**

where the Daughters of the Confederacy preserve and display flags, uniforms, swords, and other memorabilia. *188 Meeting St., tel. 803/723–1541. Museum admission: $1 adults; 25¢ children 6–12, under 6 free. Hours vary.*

Between Market Hall and East Bay Street is a series of low sheds that once housed produce and fish markets. Called **Old City Market,** the area now features restaurants and shops. There are still vegetable and fruit vendors here, too, along with local "basket ladies" busy weaving and selling distinctive sweet-grass, pine-straw, and palmetto-leaf baskets—a craft inherited from their West African ancestors—which are fast becoming collectors' items.

Time Out This is a great area for some serious time out. Pick up batches of Charleston's famed benné (sesame) seed wafers at **Olde Colony Bakery** in the open-air market. Choose from 13 gourmet food stands in **The Gourmetisserie** in the Market Square shopping complex across South Market Street. Or indulge the urge to munch on oysters on the half-shell, steamed mussels, and clams at **A.W. Shucks** in nearby State Street Market.

Across the street is the **Omni Hotel at Charleston Place** (130 Market St.). You might wander over to peer at the lobby or have cocktails or tea in the intimate Lobby Lounge. The city's only world-class hotel is flanked by a four-story complex of upscale boutiques and specialty shops (*see* Shopping).

Heading south on Meeting Street, we come to the **Gibbes Art Gallery.** Its collection of American art includes notable 18th- and 19th-century portraits of Carolinians and an outstanding group of more than 300 miniature portraits. Don't miss the miniature rooms—intricately detailed with fabrics and furnishings and nicely displayed in shadow boxes inset in dark-paneled walls—or the Tiffany-style stained-glass dome in the rotunda's 30-foot ceiling. *135 Meeting St., tel. 803/722–2706. Admission: $2 adults, $1 senior citizens and college students, 50¢ children under 18. Open Tues.–Sat. 10–5, Sun. and Mon. 1–5.*

For a little detour, head south on Meeting Street to Queen Street, then west to Archdale. At no. 8 is the **Unitarian Church,** built in 1774. The building was remodeled in the mid-19th century after plans inspired by the Chapel of Henry VII in Westminster Abbey, including the addition of an unusual Gothic fan-tracery ceiling. *No regular visiting hours. Call 803/723–4617 10–noon weekdays in winter, Mon. and Fri. only in summer, to see whether someone can unlock the church.*

At the corner of Clifford and Archdale streets is the Greek Revival–style **St. John's Lutheran Church,** built in 1817. Notice the fine craftsmanship in the delicate wrought-iron gates and fence. Organ aficionados may be interested in the 1823 Thomas Hall organ case. The church is open weekdays 9–1. Back at Meeting Street, across from the Gibbes is the unusual **Circular Congregational Church.** Legend has it that its corners were rounded off so the devil would have no place to hide. The inside of this Romanesque-style church is simple but pretty, with a beamed, vaulted ceiling. It is open weekdays 9–1.

On Cumberland Street, one of Charleston's few remaining cobblestoned thoroughfares, is the **Old Powder Magazine,** built in 1713, used as a powder storehouse during the Revolutionary War, and now a museum with costumes, furniture, armor, and other artifacts from 18th-century Charleston. *79 Cumberland St., tel. 803/722–3767. Admission: $1 adults, 50¢ students. Open weekdays 9:30–4.*

⓯ It's a few steps down Church Street to the **Thomas Elfe Workshop,** the home and workplace of one of the city's famed early furniture makers. Inside this restored miniature "single house," original and replica Elfe furniture is on display. *54 Queen St., tel. 803/722–2130. Admission: $3. Tours weekdays 10–4:30, Sat. 10–noon. Closed Sun., holidays.*

⓰ At 146 Church Street is graceful **St. Philip's Episcopal Church.** The late Georgian–style structure, the second on the site, was completed in 1838. In its serene graveyard are buried some legendary native sons, including statesman John C. Calhoun and DuBose Heyward, the author of *Porgy*.

⓱ The **Dock Street Theatre,** across Queen Street, was built on the site of one of the nation's first playhouses. It combines the reconstructed early Georgian playhouse and the preserved Old Planter's Hotel (ca. 1809). *135 Church St., tel. 803/723–5648. Open weekdays noon–6 for tours ($1).*

⓲ At 110 Church Street is the Gothic-style **French Huguenot Church,** the only U.S. church still adhering to the original Huguenot liturgy. A French-liturgy service is held each spring. *Tel. 803/722–4385. Donations accepted. Open to visitors weekdays 10–12:30 and 2–4. Closed weekends, holidays, Jan.*

The intersection of Meeting and Broad streets is known as the Four Corners of Law, because structures here represent federal, state, city, and religious jurisdiction. The County Court House and the U.S. Post Office and Federal Court occupy two corners.

⓳ The Council Chamber of the graceful 1801 **City Hall,** on the northeast corner, has interesting historical displays as well as fine portraits, including John Trumbull's famed 1791 portrait of George Washington and Samuel F. B. Morse's likeness of James Monroe. *Admission free. Open weekdays 9–5. Closed holidays.*

⓴ On the last corner is **St. Michael's Episcopal Church,** modeled after London's St. Martin's-in-the-Field. Completed in 1761, this is Charleston's oldest surviving church. Climb the 186-foot steeple for a panoramic view. *Open Mon., Tues., Thurs., Fri. 9–4:30; Wed. 9–3:30; Sat. 9–noon.*

From the Four Corners, head down Broad Street toward the **㉑** Cooper River. The **American Military Museum** displays hundreds of uniforms and artifacts from all branches of service, dating from the Revolutionary War. *115 Church St., tel. 803/ 723–9620. Admission: $2 adults, $1 children under 12, military in uniform no charge. Open Mon.–Sat. 10–6, Sun. 1–6.*

㉒ At the corner of East Bay Street stands the **Exchange Building/Provost Dungeon.** The building itself was originally a customs house. The dungeon was used by the British to confine prisoners during the Revolutionary War; today, a tableau of lifelike wax figures recalls this era. *East Bay and Broad Sts., tel. 803/792–5020. Admission: $2.50 adults, $2 senior citizens, $1 children, Open Mon.–Sat. 9:30–5. Closed major holidays.*

Returning to Church Street and continuing south, you'll come
㉓ to the **Heyward-Washington House.** Built in 1772 by rice king
Daniel Heyward, it was the residence of President George
Washington during his 1791 visit. The mansion is notable for
fine period furnishings by such local craftsmen as Thomas Elfe
and includes Charleston's only restored 18th-century kitchen
open to visitors. *87 Church St., tel. 803/722-0354. Admission:
$3 adults; $1.50 children 3-12, under 3 free. Open Mon.-Sat.
10-5, Sun. 1-5.*

㉔ At 51 Meeting Street is the **Nathaniel Russell House,** headquarters of the Historic Charleston Foundation. Built in 1808, it is
one of the nation's finest examples of Adam architecture. The
interior is notable for its ornate detailing, its lavish period furnishings, and a "flying" circular staircase that spirals three
stories with no apparent support. *Tel. 803/723-1623. Admission: $3.50, children under 6 free. Open Mon.-Sat. 10-5, Sun.
2-5. A combination ticket with the Edmonston-Alston House
can be purchased at either location for $5.*

Continuing south, you'll come into an area where somewhat
㉕ more lavish mansions reflect a later era. The **Calhoun Mansion,**
at 16 Meeting Street, is opulent by Charleston standards, an
interesting reflection of Victorian taste. Built in 1876, it's notable for ornate plasterwork, fine wood moldings, and a 75-foot
domed ceiling. *Tel. 803/722-8205 or 577-9863. Admission: $5
adults; $4.50 senior citizens over 62; $3 children 6-13, under 6
free. Open daily 10-4, other times by appointment.*

㉖ The **Edmonston-Alston House,** at 21 East Battery, is an imposing 1828 Greek Revival structure with a commanding view of
Charleston harbor. It is tastefully furnished with antiques,
portraits, Piranesi prints, silver, and fine china. *Tel. 803/722-
7171. Admission: $3.50, children under 6 free. Open Mon.-
Sat. 10-5, Sun. 2-5.*

㉗ After all this serious sightseeing, relax in **White Point Gardens,**
on Battery Point, facing the harbor. It's a tranquil spot, shaded
by palmettos and graceful live oaks.

East of the Across the Cooper River Bridges, via U.S. 17, is the town of
Cooper River **Mt. Pleasant.** Here, along Shem Creek, where the area's fishing fleet brings in fresh daily catches, seafood restaurants
attract visitors and locals alike. Mt. Pleasant is home to **Patriots Point,** the world's largest naval and maritime museum.
Berthed here are famed aircraft carrier *Yorktown,* nuclear
merchant ship *Savannah,* vintage World War II submarine
Clamagore, and destroyer *Laffey.* Missiles, airplanes, and
weapons are also displayed. Tours are offered in all vessels, and
the film *The Fighting Lady* is shown regularly aboard the *Yorktown. Tel. 803/884-2727 or 800/327-5723. Admission: $7
adults; $6.50 senior citizens and military in uniform; $3.50
children 6-11, under 6 free. Open daily 9-6 Apr.-Oct., 9-5 rest
of year.*

From the docks here, Fort Sumter Tours' boats leave for 2¼-
hour cruises that include an hour-long stop at **Fort Sumter National Monument.** (The company also has boats leaving from
the Municipal Marina, on Charleston's west side.) This is the
only way to get there, as the fort is on a man-made island in the
harbor. *Tel. 803/722-1691. Cost: $7.50 adults; $3.75 children
6-12, under 6 free. Tours depart daily at 9, 10:15, noon, 1:30,*

2:30, 4 Easter weekend and June 15–Labor Day; call for schedules rest of year.

It was at Fort Sumter that the first shot of the Civil War was fired, when Confederate forces at Fort Johnson (now defunct) across the way opened fire on April 12, 1861. After a 34-hour bombardment, Union forces surrendered and Confederate troops occupied Sumter, which became a symbol of Southern resistance. The Confederacy managed to hold the fort—despite almost continual bombardment—for nearly four years, and when it was finally evacuated, Fort Sumter was a heap of rubble. Today National Park Service rangers conduct free guided tours of the restored structure, which includes a museum (also free) with historical displays and dioramas.

Continuing north out of Mt. Pleasant along U.S. 17, you'll find more "basket ladies" at roadside stands. If you have the heart to bargain, you *may* be able to purchase the baskets at somewhat lower costs than in Charleston.

SC 703 will take you to Sullivan's Island and **Fort Moultrie,** completed in 1809 and the third fort on this site. Here Colonel William Moultrie's South Carolinians repelled a British assault in one of the first Patriot victories of the Revolutionary War. The interior has been restored. A film and slide show tell the history of the fort. *W. Middle St., Sullivan's Island, tel. 803/883–3123. Admission free. Open daily 9–6 summer, 9–5 winter. Closed Christmas.*

Back on U.S. 17, about eight miles out of Charleston, is the 1681 **Boone Hall Plantation,** approached via one of the South's most majestic avenues of live oaks. The primary attraction is the grounds, with formal azalea and camellia gardens, as well as the original slave quarters—the only "slave street" still intact in the Southeast—and cotton-gin house. Visitors may also tour the first floor of the classic columned mansion, which was built in 1935 incorporating woodwork and flooring from the original house. *Tel. 803/884–4371. Admission: $4.50 adults; $1 children 6–12, under 6 free. Open Mon.–Sat. 8:30–6:30, Sun. 1–5 Apr.–Labor Day; Mon.–Sat. 9–5, Sun. 1–4 rest of year. Closed holidays.*

West of the Ashley River Vestiges of the Old South—and Charleston's beginnings—beckon as you cross the Ashley River Bridge. Take SC 171 north to reach **Charles Towne Landing State Park,** commemorating the site of the original Charleston settlement, begun in 1670. There's a reconstructed village and fortifications, English park gardens with bicycle trails and walkways, and a replica 17th-century vessel moored in the creek. In the animal park roam species native to the region for three centuries. A pavilion includes exhibits and a film about the region. Bicycle and kayak rentals and cassette and tram tours are available. *1500 Old Towne Rd., tel. 803/556–4450. Admission: $4 adults; $2 children 6–14, under 6 free; $2 senior citizens. Open daily 9–6 June–Aug.; 9–5 rest of year.*

Nine miles west of Charleston via the Ashley River Road (SC 61) is **Drayton Hall,** built between 1738 and 1742. A National Historic Landmark, it is considered the nation's finest example of Georgian Palladian architecture. The mansion is the only plantation house on the Ashley River to have survived the Civil War intact and serves as an invaluable lesson in history as well as architecture. It has been left unfurnished to highlight the original plaster moldings, opulent hand-carved woodwork, and other ornamental details. *Tel. 803/766–0188. Admission: $6 adults, $3 students, children under 6 free. Guided tours daily 10–4 Mar.–Oct. 10–3 rest of year. Closed major holidays.*

A mile or so farther on SC 61 is **Magnolia Plantation and Gardens.** The 50-acre informal gardens, begun in 1686, boast one of the continent's largest collections of azaleas and camellias and were proclaimed the "most beautiful garden in the world" by John Galsworthy. Nature lovers may canoe through the 125-acre Waterfowl Refuge, explore the 30-acre swamp garden along boardwalks and bridges, or walk or bicycle over 500 acres of wildlife trails. Tours of the manor house, built during the Reconstruction period, depict plantation life. Several nights weekly the gardens are open for strolls along lighted paths. There is also a petting zoo and a mini-horse ranch. *Tel. 803/571–1266. Admission: $7 adults; $6.50 senior citizens; $5 teens; $3 children 4–12, under 4 free. House tours $3 extra. Mar. 15–May 15, all prices $1 additional. Open daily 8–5.*

Middleton Place, four miles farther north on SC 61, has the nation's oldest landscaped gardens, dating from 1741. Design highlights of the magnificent gardens—ablaze with camellias, magnolias, azaleas, roses, and flowers of all seasons—are the floral *allées,* terraced lawns, and ornamental lakes. Much of the mansion was destroyed during the Civil War, but the south wing has been restored and houses impressive collections of silver, furniture, paintings, and historic documents. The stableyard is a living outdoor museum: here craftsfolk, using authentic tools and equipment, demonstrate spinning, blacksmithing, and other domestic skills from the plantation era. Farm animals, peacocks, and other creatures roam free. Rides in a vintage horse-drawn wagon are offered. *Tel. 803/556–6020. Gardens and stableyard open daily 9–5. Admission: $7 adults; $3.50 children 4–12, under 4 free. Prices slightly higher mid-Mar.–mid-June. House tours Tues.–Sun. 10–4:30, Mon. 1:30–4:30; $4 extra.*

The picturesque town of **Summerville,** about 25 miles northwest of Charleston via I–26 (Exit 199), is a pleasant place for a drive or stroll. Built by wealthy planters as an escape from hot-weather malaria, it's a treasure trove of mid-19th-century and Victorian buildings—many of which are listed in the National Register of Historic Places—with colorful gardens of camellias, azaleas, and wisteria. Streets often curve around tall pines, since a local ordinance prohibits cutting them down. This is a good place for a bit of antiquing in attractive shops.

Last but not least, about 24 miles north of Charleston via U.S. 52 is **Cypress Gardens,** a swamp garden created from what was once the freshwater reserve of a vast rice plantation. Explore the inky waters by boat, or walk along paths lined with moss-draped cypress trees, azaleas, camellias, daffodils, wisteria, and dogwood. Peak season is late March into April. *Tel. 803/553–0515. Admission (not including boat ride) Feb. 15–Apr. 30: $5 adults; $4 senior citizens; $2 children 6–16, under 6 free. Rest of year, $1 less and boat ride included in admission cost. Open daily 9–5.*

Charleston for Free

The Citadel Corps of Cadets Dress Parade. Visitors are welcome at the military college's parade at Summerall Field every Friday at 3:45 PM during the school year.

The Citadel Memorial Military Museum. Military documents and relics relating to the Civil War, the college, and its graduates are on display at this on-campus museum. *Tel. 803/792–6846. Open weekdays 2–5, Sat. 9–5, Sun. 10–5.*

Hampton Park Concerts in the Park. These concerts, held often on Sunday afternoons, are free. *For information, call the visitors bureau, tel. 803/723–7641 or 800/845–7108.*

Monday Night Recital Series. The College of Charleston (tel. 803/792–8228) presents guests and faculty artists in free musical performances during the school year.

What to See and Do with Children

American Military Museum (*see* Marion Square to the Battery in Exploring Charleston).
Boat Ride to Fort Sumter (*see* East of the Cooper River in Exploring Charleston).
Charles Towne Landing Animal Forest (*see* West of the Ashley River in Exploring Charleston). Birds, alligators, bison, pumas, bears, wolves, and many other animals roam in natural environments. Children's Days are held during the last two weeks of December.
Charleston Museum (*see* Marion Square to the Battery). The Discover Me Room, designed just for children, has computers and other hands-on exhibits.
Herbie's Antique Car Museum. Nearly 100 vehicles are on display. *2140 Van Buren Rd., N. Charleston, tel. 803/747–7207. Admission: $4, children under 12 free. Open daily 11–8.*
Magnolia Plantation and Gardens (*see* West of the Ashley River). The petting zoo and mini-horse ranch appeal to the young at heart of all ages.
Middleton Place (*see* West of the Ashley River). At this plantation, youngsters can ride in a horse-drawn wagon, pet farm animals, and watch craftsfolk demonstrate their skills.
Palmetto Islands County Park. This family-oriented nature park has a Big Toy playground, a two-acre pond, a canoe trail, an observation tower, and marsh boardwalks. Bicycles, pedal boats, and canoes can be rented in season. *On U.S. 17N, ½ mi past Snee Farm, turn left onto Long Point Rd., tel. 803/884–0832. Admission: $1. Open daily 10–6 Apr. and Sept., 10–7 May–Aug., 10–5 Oct.–Mar. Closed major holidays.*
Shelling. Kiawah Island has excellent shelling. If you're not staying at the private resort, you can shell at **Beachwalker Park,** the public beach at the west end of the island. *Tel. 803/762–2172. Parking fee: $2. Open daily 9:30–6:30 June–Aug.; weekends only Apr., May, Sept., Oct.*

Off the Beaten Track

Angel Oak. Reportedly the oldest living thing east of the Rockies, this 1,500-year-old giant has a 25½-foot circumference and a 151-foot limb spread. *From SC 700 turn left onto Bohicket*

Rd.; after about 1 mi, turn right at sign and follow dirt road, tel. 803/559–3496. Nominal fee. Visitors welcome daily 10–6.

Francis Marion National Forest. About 40 miles north of Charleston via U.S. 52, this site comprises 250,000 acres of swamps, vast oaks and pines, and little lakes thought to have been formed by meteors—a good place for picnicking, camping, boating, and swimming. (tel. 803/336–3248 or 887–3311). At the park's **Rembert Dennis Wildlife Center** (off U.S. 52 in Bonneau, tel. 803/825–3387), deer, wild turkey, and striped bass are reared and studied.

St. James Church. At Goose Creek, about 19 miles north of Charleston, is this remarkably well preserved church, built between 1708 and 1719. Not in use since 1808, it retains the original box pews, slave gallery, and pulpit. The British royal arms are still visible above the chancel. The sexton's house is nearby, and he will open the church on request. *U.S. 52N to U.S. 78; at junction, turn right at stoplight and bridge and drive to top of hill. Donation.*

Shopping

Most downtown Charleston shops and department stores are open from 9 or 10 AM to 5 PM. The malls are open 10–9 and on Sunday, 1–6. The sales tax is 5%. Generally, banks are open Monday through Thursday 8:30–5 and Friday from 8:30 to 6.

Shopping Districts. One of the most interesting shopping experiences awaiting visitors to Charleston is the colorful produce market in the two-block **Old City Market** at East Bay and Market streets. Adjacent to it is the **open-air flea market,** with crafts, antiques, and memorabilia. Here (and at stands along U.S. 17 north of Charleston, near Mt. Pleasant) women weave and sell baskets of grass (*see* Marion Square to the Battery in Exploring Charleston). A portion of the Old City Market where cotton was once auctioned, now called **The Market,** has been converted into a complex of specialty shops and restaurants. Other such complexes in the area are **Rainbow Market** (in two interconnected 150-year-old buildings), **Market Square,** and **State Street Market.** Also, some of Charleston's oldest and finest shops are on the main downtown thoroughfare, **King Street.**

Antiques Charleston is one of the South's major cities for antiques shopping. King Street is the center. **Coles & Company** (84 Wentworth St., tel. 803/723–2142, and 185 King St., tel. 803/722–3388) is a direct importer of 18th- and 19th-century English antiques. **Livingston Antiques,** dealers in 18th- and 19th-century English and Continental furniture, clocks, and bric-a-brac, has two locations: a large one west of the Ashley (2137 Savannah Hwy., tel. 803/556–6162) and a smaller one in the historic district (163 King St., tel. 803/723–9697). **Vendue House Antiques** (9 Queen St., tel. 803/577–5462) sells 18th- and 19th-century English antiques and distinctive objets d'art.

Art Galleries The **Birds I View Gallery** (119-A Church St., tel. 803/723–1276 or 795–9661) sells bird paintings and prints by Anne Worsham Richardson. The **Elizabeth O'Neill Verner Studio & Museum** (79 Church St., tel. 803/722–4246) is located in a 17th-century house where the late artist, one of Charleston's most distinguished, had her studio. The studio is now open to the public, as is a gallery of her pastels and etchings. Prints of her work are on sale at adjacent **Tradd Street Press** (38 Tradd St., tel. 803/722–4246). The **Virginia Fouché Bolton Art Gallery** (127 Meeting St., tel. 803/577–9351) has original paintings and limited-edition lithographs of Charleston scenes.

Gift Shops **Charleston Collections** (142 E. Bay St., tel. 803/722–7267, and Bohicket Marina Village, between Kiawah and Seabrook resorts, tel. 803/768–9101) has Charleston chimes, prints, and candies, T-shirts, and more. **Charleston Ornaments** (188 Meeting St., The Market, tel. 803/723–6945) carries Christmas ornaments, plus cotton-boll and other novelty items.

One of a Kind Over two dozen upscale boutiques are clustered in a luxurious complex adjoining the Omni Hotel called **The Shops at Charleston Place** (130 Market St., tel. 803/722–4900). Included are branches of Jaeger, Laura Ashley, Gucci, Banana Republic, Polo/Ralph Lauren, Brookstone, Godiva, and Crabtree & Evelyn. Also here is Charleston's and London's own Ben Silver, premier purveyor of blazer buttons, with over 800 designs struck from hand-engraved dies, including college, monogram, British regimental, and specialty motifs. (Ben Silver also sells British neckties, embroidered polo shirts, and blazers.)

Period Reproductions **Historic Charleston Reproductions** (105 Broad St., tel. 803/723–8292) has superb reproductions of Charleston furniture and accessories, all authorized by the Historic Charleston Foundation. Royalties from sales contribute to restoration projects. At the **Thomas Elfe Workshop** (54 Queen St., tel. 803/722–2130), you'll find excellent 18th-century reproductions and objets d'art, Charleston rice beds, handmade mirrors, and Charleston pieces in silverplate, pewter, or porcelain. At the **Old Charleston Joggling Board Co.** (tel. 803/723–4331), these Low Country oddities can be purchased.

Participant Sports

Beaches South Carolina's climate allows swimming from April through October. There are public beaches at **Beachwater Park,** on Kiawah Island; **Folly Beach County Park** and **Folly Beach,** on Folly Island; **Isle of Palms;** and **Sullivan's Island.** Resorts with extensive private beaches are **Fairfield Ocean Ridge,** on Edisto Island; **Kiawah Island Resort; Seabrook Island;** and **Wild Dunes Resort,** on the Isle of Palms. This is definitely not a "swingles" area; all public and private beaches are family oriented.

Bicycling The **historic district** is level and compact, ideal for bicycling, and many city parks have biking trails. **Palmetto Islands County Park** also has trails. Bikes can be rented at **The Bicycle Shop** (tel. 803/722–8168), which offers a self-guided tour of the district; and at the **Charleston Carriage Co.** (tel. 803/577–0042), which also rents tandem bikes. **Pedal Carriage Co.** (tel. 803/722–3880) rents a sort of pedal "surrey with the fringe on top" for two riders (plus two children) and offers a 40-minute self-guided tour of the historic district; it also rents one-speed balloon-tire bikes.

Boardsailing Instructions are provided by **Sailsports** in Mt. Pleasant (tel. 803/884–1508) and **Time Out Sailing** at the Charleston marina (tel. 803/577–5979).

Fishing Fresh- and saltwater fishing is excellent along 90 miles of coastline. Surf fishing is permitted on many beaches, including

Palmetto Islands County Park's. Charter fishing boats offering partial- or full-day sails to individuals include the *J. J.* at Charleston marina (tel. 803/766–9816) and **Blue Water Sportfishing Charter** (tel. 803/554–5280. **Bohicket Yacht Charters** on Johns Island (tel. 803/768–1280) arranges charters for groups of four to six for full- or half-day sportfishing, shark fishing, flat-bottom-boat marsh fishing, shrimping, crabbing, shelling, and nature-observing expeditions.

Golf Public courses include **Charleston Municipal** (tel. 803/795–6517), **Patriots Point** (tel. 803/881–0042), **Plantation Pines** (9 holes; tel. 803/599–2009), and **Shadowmoss** (tel. 803/556–8251). **Kiawah Island** (tel. 803/768–2121) and **Wild Dunes** (tel. 803/886–6000) offer golf to nonguests on a space-available basis.

Jogging Jogging paths wind through **Palmetto Islands County Park,** and **Hampton Park** has a fitness trail.

Miniature Golf There are also three 18-hole **Putt-Putt Golf Courses** (tel. 803/797–7874) in the area and 36 holes of miniature golf at **Classic Golf** (tel. 803/881–9614).

Sailing Boats can be rented and yachts chartered from **Bohicket Yacht Charters** on Johns Island (tel. 803/768–1280).

Tennis Courts are open to the public at **Farmfield Tennis Courts** (tel. 803/724–7402), **Shadowmoss** (tel. 803/556–8251), **Kiawah Island** (tel. 803/768–2121), and **Wild Dunes** (tel. 803/886–6000).

Spectator Sports

Baseball The **Charleston Rainbows,** the San Diego Padres' minor-league team, play at College Park Stadium (701 Rutledge Ave., tel. 803/723–7241). For other sporting events, see the "Database" column in the sports section of the daily *News and Courier.*

Dining

by Eileen Robinson Smith

Formerly a travel editor for Ziff-Davis Publishing in New York and more recently the editor of Charleston Magazine, Ms. Smith, still Charleston-based, is a freelance food and travel writer.

Known for its Low Country specialties—she-crab soup, sautéed shrimp and grits, and variations on pecan pie—Charleston is also a hotbed of new American cuisine. Its chefs are busy creating marriages of the classical and the contemporary, of down-home cooking and haute cuisine. With the strong national interest in both seafood and Southern cooking, Charleston was chosen as the host city for the American Seafood Challenge. For the last three years, chefs from more than 30 states have competed in what has been called the "toughest hot food competition in the country." Locally, chefs and restauranteurs took advantage of the learning experience the Challenge provided.

82 Queen has not only just opened 102 North Market as a steakhouse. Robert Dickson, chef/opera singer, has moved his famous supper club to larger quarters at Planters Inn, 122 North Market. In his former location in the Rainbow Market is an elegant new restaurant, Chouinards.

Near St. Philip's Episcopal Church, at 158 Church Street, once the address of Le Madeleine, Pierre, the first maître'd at the Omni's Shaftesbury Room, has opened his own restaurant, calling it the obvious, Pierre's. For the college crowd, which can't get enough of the buffalo wings and pitchers of Killian's South African dark beer, there's now Humps at 14 Market Street.

Across the East Cooper Bridge, in the trendy suburb of Mount Pleasant, the Village Cafe, opened by chef Scott Roark whose talent kept Supper At Seven so well–booked, is a culinary oasis. Directly across the street, A.W. Shucks new mega-restaurant fronting Shem Creek (Mt. Pleasant's waterfront restaurant row) is a total renovation of the old Crab Net. Out on Folly Beach, the Sugar Reef Cafe, once just a luncheonette up from the surf shop, now has a chef, Terry Gouallard, and on week–ends, it is a feat to secure a table.

Things change and this year no business in Charleston is so exciting to watch as the hospitality industry.

The most highly recommended restaurants in each price category are indicated by a star ★.

Category	Cost*
Expensive	over $30
Moderate	$20–$30
Inexpensive	under $20

per person without tax (5% in South Carolina), service, or drinks

The following credit-card abbreviations are used: AE, American Express; CB, Carte Blanche; DC, Diners Club; MC, MasterCard; V, Visa.

Expensive
Low Country/
Continental
★

The Shaftesbury Room. Under the direction of master chef Joel Gourio de Bourgonnier (previously with Wild Dunes), an updated Charleston cuisine with an emphasis on seafood is featured. In addition to the regular menu is a moderately priced table d'hôte with entrees such as petite filet mignon with bordelaise and quail stuffed with cornbread and shellfish served with a peach sauce. Still formal, with its hardwood paneling and Venetian-glass chandeliers, the place has lightened up, thanks in part to the jazz combo, but the cuisine continues to be world-class. Still offered is the ever-so-special smoked-meat cart from which diners choose such appetizers as Norwegian salmon, chicken with apricot sauce, and tenderloin with horseradish cream. *130 Market St., tel. 803/722–4900. Jackets suggested. Reservations preferred. Dinner only. AE, CB, MC, V.*

Moderate
American
★

82 Queen. This popular restaurant, part of a complex of pink stucco buildings dating to the mid-1800s, is the unofficial headquarters for many of the city's annual events; during Spoleto, musicians perform in the courtyard garden. At the outdoor raw bar, tourists can meet and mingle with the locals. Low Country favorites like crab cakes are served with basil tartar sauce. The traditional commingles with innovations like scallops simmered in leek sauce over spinach fettuccine, garnished with toasted pine nuts. Ask about the homemade relishes, particularly the passion fruit/kiwi chutney. For dessert, the strawberry mocha mousse is exceptional. *82 Queen St., tel. 803/723–7591. Dress: informal. Reservations preferred for dinner. AE, MC, V.*

Low Country

The Moultrie Tavern. This reconverted brick warehouse, dating from 1833, is filled with artifacts and artwork from the Civil War era. Chef/owner Robert Bohrn, who greets guests in a

Dining
Athens, **1**
Barbadoes Room, **17**
Calif. Dreaming, **2**
Carolina's, **27**
82 Queen, **12**
Henry's, **23**
Moultrie Tavern, **25**
Queen St. Seafood Inn, **22**
Rusty Anchor, **8**
Shaftesbury Room, **11**
Shem Creek Bar & Grill, **9**

Lodging
Battery Carriage House, **18**
Best Western King Charles, **14**
Days Inn Hist. Dist., **16**
Econo Lodge, **4**
Elliott House Inn, **13**
Hampton Inn Airport, **5**
Heart of Charleston, **20**
Holiday Inn, Mt. Pleasant, **10**
Indigo Inn, **19**
Lodge Alley Inn, **24**
Meeting St. Inn, **15**
Mills House, **17**
Motel 6, **6**
Omni Hotel, **11**
Planters Inn, **21**
Sheraton Charleston, **3**
Sword Gate Inn, **7**
Vendue Inn, **26**

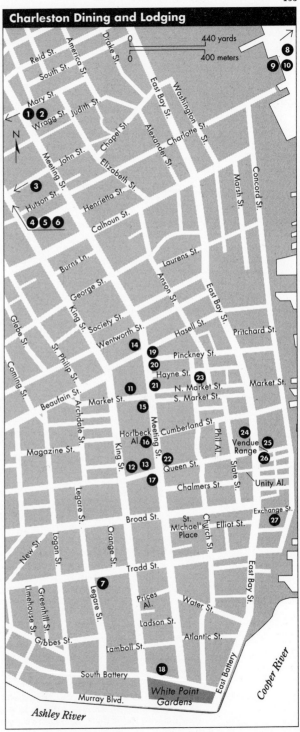

Charleston Dining and Lodging

Confederate uniform, is a historian and unearths his own relics. The fife-and-drum music plays continuously and the food and spirits are authentically 1860s. Try an early Southern specialty: baked oyster and sausage pie with puff pastry. *18 Vendue Range, tel. 803/723–1862. Dress: informal. Dinner reservations recommended. AE, MC, V. Closed Sat. lunch and Sun.*

Carolina's. European chic with its black lacquer, white, and peach decor, Carolina's is the brainchild of German restaurateurs Franz Meier and Chris Weihs. Many come here for the "appeteasers" and the late-night (until 1 AM) offerings, which include everything from baby back smoked ribs to pasta with crawfish and tasso (spiced ham) in cream sauce. Dinner entrees are selections from the grill: Carolina quail with goat cheese, sun-dried tomatoes and basil; salmon with cilantro, ginger, and lime butter; and lamb loin with jalapeño chutney. *10 Exchange St., tel. 803/724–3800. Dress: informal. Reservations suggested. AE, MC, V. Dinner only. Closed Sun.*

New American
★
Henry's. Henry Hesselmer opened a grocery store here with a second-story bordello and gambling room in 1928. Total renovation has restored the decor to a "late Prohibition" style; the Art Deco black-and-white-tile floors have been saved. Red-hot action has returned upstairs—though this time around with live jazz. Original items served at Henry's over the last 30 years have been re-created, for example, shrimp wando—shrimp, oysters, blue crab, and lobster in a veloute sauce served over fried grits. The new chef, Karl Schwerzler, formerly with Baker's Cafe, is incorporating his own creations, such as linguine Matriciana with bacon, peppers, onions, peppers, tomatoes, and parmesan cheese. *54 Market St., tel. 803/723–4363 or 723–4084. Dress: informal. Dinner reservations suggested. AE, MC, V.*

Seafood
Barbadoes Room. This large, airy plant- and light-filled space has a sophisticated island look and a view out to a cheery courtyard garden. Entrees include such Charleston traditions as Middleton Shrimp—large shrimp sautéed in white wine with garlic and Dijon mustard and blended with heavy cream. A new treatment of Caesar salad, called South Caroline salad is prepared tableside, with spinach and romaine, toasted local pecans, and bleu cheese crumbles tossed with a Caesar-style dressing. There's an elegant and extensive Southern-style breakfast menu and a popular Sunday brunch. *115 Meeting St., tel. 803/577–2400. Jacket and tie suggested at dinner. Reservations required for Sun. and holiday brunch, suggested for dinner in season. AE, CB, DC, MC, V.*

Queen Street Seafood Inn. Surrounded by a white picket fence, it was converted from a two–story residence, c. 1880. Classical music is played and there is dining in the courtyard, weather permitting. The rooms are intimate, with period furnishings and decor—Victorian black and pink upstairs, lighter and softer downstairs. Especially recommended is a puff-pastry concoction called Bouche à la Reine; the filling varies from day to day—perhaps scallops and mushrooms in a cream sauce. For dinner try the duckling with loquart (sweeter cousin to the kumquat), sauce. The new chef, Hank Yaden, masterfully combines spices for such specials as sea trout broiled with lemon butter, and finishes with a dusting of lavender flowers. The peach crisp is a dense, moist, cinnamony delight, served hot with vanilla ice cream. The kitchen is very accommodating to those on restricted diets. *68 Queen St., tel. 803/723–7700. Jack-*

et and tie optional. Reservations recommended. AE, CB, DC, MC, V.

★ **Rusty Anchor.** Executive chef Terence McKelvey has a refreshing outlook on local American cuisine, which shows in his grilled fish served in a simple island style—for instance, the shrimp-and-scallops brochette in a garlic-and-lemon-butter sauce—and his Sullivan Island sauté: clams, oysters, shrimp, scallops, and dolphin in a sauce similar to a Mediterranean bouillabaise. All preparation is done in view of the diners, either in the open display kitchen or at the raw bar. Closed Sun. and Mon. *2213 Middle St. and Station 22½, Sullivan's Island, tel. 803/883–9131. Dress: informal. Reservations suggested, particularly for large parties and on weekend nights. AE, MC, V.*

Inexpensive **California Dreaming.** The floor-to-ceiling windows of this
American heavy-volume restaurant, in an impressive stone fort on the Ashley River, look out at night on the lights of the harbor. The crowds come for the great view, low prices, and bountiful platters of food, such as Texas smoked ribs, barbecued chicken, prime rib, and catch of the day. To make the wait bearable, take to the bar for a frothy frozen margarita. *1 Ashley Pointe Dr. (5 min from downtown), tel. 803/766–1644. Dress: informal. No reservations. AE, MC, V.*

Greek **Athens.** Located just six minutes from downtown, a sojourn here is like a Greek holiday. The *bouzouki* music is straight from the *Plaka* in Athens. George Koutsogiannaks, one of three owners, is the vocalist on tape. The *kalamari lemonato* (baby squid in lemon) is like that served in the *tavernas* on the isle of Hydra. Traditional dishes moussaka and pasticcio are mainstays, but in keeping with current health trends, the freshest of seafood appears on the special board and a vegetarian plate with eggplant, pita, feta cheese, stuffed grape leaves, and *spanakopita* (spinach pie) has been added. The homemade Greek pizza with 12 different spices is Charleston's best. *325 Folly Rd., Cross Creek Shopping Center, James Island, tel. 803/795–0957. AE, MC, V. Closed Sun. lunch.*

Seafood **Shem Creek Bar & Grill.** This pleasant dockside spot is perennially popular for its oyster bar and light fare (until 10 Mon.–Wed., until 1 AM Thurs.–Sun.). There's also a wide variety of seafood entrees, including a steam pot—dobsters, clams, oysters, and sausages with melted lemon butter or hot cocktail sauce—big enough fmr twm. *508 Mill St., Mt. Pleasant, tel. 803–884–8102. Dresq: indmrmal. No reservatiols. AE, MC, T.*

Lodging

Hotels and inls on the peninsula are generally more expensive. Also, rates tend to increase during the Spring Festival of Houses (mid-March to mid-April) and the Spoleto Festival USA (late May to early June); at those times, reservations are essential. During Visitors' Appreciation Days, from mid-November to mid-February, discounts of up to 50% may apply. For a Courtesy Discount Card, write to the **Charleston Trident Convention and Visitors Bureau** (Box 975, Charleston 29402, tel. 803/723–7641 or 800/845–7108).

Three organizations offer rooms in homes, cottages, and carriage houses: **Charleston East Bed and Breakfast League** (1031 Tall Pine Rd., Mt. Pleasant 29464, tel. 803/884–8208), **Charles-**

ton Society Bed & Breakfast (84 Murray Blvd., Charleston
29401, tel. 803/723–4948), and **Historic Charleston Bed and
Breakfast** (43 Legare St., Charleston 29402, tel. 803/722–
6606). Those interested in renting condominiums or houses on
the beach on the Isle of Palms—some with private pools and
tennis courts—might contact **Island Realty** (Box 157, Isle of
Palms 29451, tel. 803/886–8144 or 800/845–2546).

The most highly recommended properties in each price category are indicated by a star ★. For a map pinpointing locations,
see Dining.

Hotel/Motel Category	Cost*
Very Expensive	over $100
Expensive	$75–$100
Moderate	$50–$75
Inexpensive	under $50

*double room; add 7% for taxes

The following credit-card abbreviations are used: AE, American Express; CB, Carte Blanche; DC, Diners Club; MC,
MasterCard; V, Visa.

Hotels and Motels
Very Expensive
★
Mills House Hotel. Antique furnishings and period decor give
great charm to this luxurious Holiday Inn property, a reconstruction of a historic hostelry on its original site in the historic
district. There's a lounge with live entertainment, and excellent dining in the Barbadoes Room (*see* Dining). *115 Meeting
St., 29401, tel. 803/577–2400 or 800/465–4329. 215 rooms. Facilities: pool. AE, CB, DC, MC, V.*

★
Omni Hotel at Charleston Place. The city's newest luxury hotel,
this graceful, low-rise structure in the historic district is
flanked by upscale boutiques and specialty shops (*see* Shopping). The lobby features a magnificent hand-blown Venetian
glass chandelier, an Italian marble floor, and antiques from
Sotheby's. Rooms are furnished with period reproductions.
*130 Market St., 29401, tel. 803/722–4900 or 800/228–2121. 443
units, including 46 suites. Facilities: fitness center with heated
pool, sauna, whirlpool, Nautilus; concierge floor; restaurants;
lounges with entertainment. AE, CB, DC, MC, V.*

Expensive
Best Western King Charles Inn. This inn in the historic district
has spacious rooms furnished with period reproductions. *237
Meeting St., 29401, tel. 803/723–7451 or 800/528–1234. 91
rooms. Facilities: pool, dining room, lounge. AE, CB, DC,
MC, V.*

*Moderate–
Expensive*
Sheraton Charleston Hotel. Some rooms and suites in this 13-
story hotel outside the historic district overlook the Ashley
River. Spacious rooms and suites are highlighted with Queen
Anne furnishings, and there's concierge service. Live entertainment and dancing contribute to the lounge's local
popularity. *170 Lockwood Dr., 29403, tel. 803/723–3000 or 800/
325–3535. 337 rooms. Facilities: 4 lighted tennis courts, pool,
jogging track, coffee shop, dining room. AE, CB, DC, MC, V.*

Moderate
★
Days Inn Historic District. This inn is well located and attractively furnished. *155 Meeting St., 29401, tel. 803/722–8411 or*

800/325–2525. 124 units. Facilities: pool, dining room. AE, DC, MC, V.

Heart of Charleston Motor Inn. This long-established motor hotel draws loyal repeat visitors for its convenient courtyard parking and location across from the Charleston Convention Center. *200 Meeting St., Box 460, 29402, tel. 803/723–3451 or 800/845–2504. 118 rooms. Facilities: pool, coffee shop, lounge, beauty shop. AE, CB, DC, MC, V.*

Holiday Inn Charleston/Mt. Pleasant. Just over the Cooper River Bridge, a 10-minute drive from the downtown historic district, is this new full-service hotel. Everything has been graciously done: brass lamps, crystal chandeliers, Queen Anne-style furniture. Two suites have Jacuzzis. "High-tech suites" offer PC cable hookups, large working areas, glossy ultramodern furniture, and refrigerators. *250 U.S. 17 Bypass, Mt. Pleasant 29464, tel. 803/884–6000 or 800/465–4329. 158 rooms. Facilities: outdoor pool, sauna, exercise room, cable TV/ movies, meeting facilities and ballroom, concierge floor, laundry, restaurant, raw bar, lounge with DJ.*

Inexpensive **Econo-Travel Motor Hotel.** This budget-chain unit is eight miles from downtown. Contemporary-style rooms are spacious and well maintained. *4725 Arco Ln., N. Charleston 29405, tel. 803/ 747–3672 or 800/446–6900. 48 rooms. Facilities: cable TV/free movies. Senior citizen, military/government discounts. AE, CB, DC, MC, V.*

Hampton Inn Charleston Airport. This economy arm of Holiday Inns offers lower rates with full service amenities. Rooms are decorated in contemporary style. *4701 Arco Ln., N. Charleston 29418, tel. 803/554–7154 or 800/426–7866. 125 rooms. Facilities: pool, cable TV/free movies, suite for small meetings. AE, CB, DC, MC, V.*

Motel 6. This well-maintained motor inn, part of a budget chain, is 10 miles from the downtown historic district. The decor is cheerful, colorful, and contemporary. *2551 Ashley Phosphate Rd., N. Charleston, 29418, tel. 803/572–6590. 126 rooms. Facilities: pool, cable TV/movies. DC, MC, V.*

Inns and Guest Houses The charms of historic Charleston can be enhanced by a stay at one of its many inns, most housed in restored structures. Some are reminiscent of European inns; one is tastefully contemporary, tucked away on the grounds of a famous garden estate. For all, double-room rates range from $85 to $145 in peak season. For complete listings, consult the "Charleston Area Visitors Guide," published by the Charleston Trident Convention & Visitors Bureau (Box 975, 17 Lockwood Blvd., Charleston 29402, tel. 803/723–7641 or 800/845–7108).

Historic District **Battery Carriage House.** This small luxury guest house—one of Charleston's first inns—has handsomely furnished rooms with period furniture and kitchenettes. *20 S. Battery St., 29401, tel. 803/723–9881 or 800/845–7638. 10 rooms. Facilities: pool. AE, MC, V.*

★ **Indigo Inn.** All the rooms here focus on the picturesque interior courtyard and are furnished with 18th-century antiques and reproductions. The trademark "hunt breakfast" consists of homemade breads, ham biscuits, fruit, and coffee. There are six slightly more expensive suites—one with a Jacuzzi—in the nearby **Jasmine House,** a pre–Civil War Greek Revival structure. These have high ceilings, fireplaces, and Oriental rugs. *1*

Maiden Ln., 29401, tel. 803/577–5900 or 800/845–7639. 40 rooms. AE, MC, V.

Lodge Alley Inn. All of the various accommodations here are luxuriously appointed in traditional Charleston fashion with Oriental carpets and period reproduction furnishings. Room refrigerators are stocked with complimentary wine. The French Quarter Restaurant features a grand rotisserie. Adjacent is a lounge with an ornate bar. *195 E. Bay St., 29401, tel. 803/722–1611 or 800/845–1004. 34 rooms, 37 suites with kitchens, 1 2-bedroom penthouse. AE, MC, V.*

Meeting Street Inn. The rooms in this handsome 1870 structure are furnished in period. Each has a reproduction four-poster rice bed, and all open onto a piazza. Guests mingle in the courtyard garden for complimentary afternoon champagne and for evening cocktails and chamber music. *173 Meeting St., 29401, tel. 803/723–1882 or 800/845–7638. 54 rooms. Facilities: whirlpool, boardroom suite for meetings. AE, MC, V.*

★ **Planters Inn.** Rooms and suites here are beautifully appointed with opulent fabrics and furnishings, including mahogany four-poster beds and marble baths. There's a concierge and 24-hour room service. *112 N. Market St., 29401, tel. 803/722–2345 or 800/845–7082. 46 rooms and suites. AE, CB, DC, MC, V.*

Sword Gate Inn. Rooms in this, Charleston's oldest inn, are all furnished in antiques, including a large plantation bed or two. The four downstairs rooms have private entrances off the courtyard. A traditional Charleston breakfast is highlighted by host Walter Barton's cheese grits, and complimentary wine and cheese are served afternoons in the expansive ballroom. *111 Tradd St., 29401, tel. 803/723–8518. 6 rooms. AE, MC, V.*

★ **Vendue Inn.** Near the waterfront, this European-style inn in a renovated 1828 warehouse offers antiques-furnished public areas and guest rooms, with canopied four-poster beds and Oriental rugs. The adjacent **Vendue West,** in a restored 1800 house, has deluxe suites with fireplaces, wet bars, Jacuzzis, and marble baths. Complimentary wine and cheese are served afternoons in the courtyard, accompanied by chamber music. Concierge service is offered, and there is an elegant restaurant, Morton's. *19 Vendue Range, 29401, tel. 803/723–9980 or 800/845–7900. 30 rooms and suites. AE, MC, V.*

West of the Ashley **Middleton Inn and Conference Center.** This contemporary-style
★ lodge with sumptuously furnished rooms is located on the grounds of Middleton Place Plantation. Floor-to-ceiling windows are hung with wooden shutters, and working fireplaces are serviced by tools forged by the estate's blacksmith. There is a cafe. *Ashley River Rd. (U.S. 61), Middleton Place, 29407, tel. 803/556–0500. 55 rooms. Facilities: pool, tennis courts. AE, MC, V.*

Resort Islands The semitropical islands dotting the South Carolina coast near Charleston are home to some of the nation's finest resorts. A wide variety of packages makes them more affordable than you would imagine. Peak-season rates (during spring and summer vacations) range from $100 to $250 per day, double occupancy. Costs often drop considerably off-season.

Kiawah Island Resort. Choose from 150 inn rooms, 48 suites, and 500 completely equipped one- to four-bedroom villas in two luxurious resort villages on 10,000 wooded acres. There are 10 miles of fine broad beaches, two championship golf courses, two complete tennis centers, jeep and water safaris, land sailing, canoeing, surfcasting, fishing, and children's programs.

There's also a general store and shops. Dining options are many and varied: Low Country specialties in the Jasmine Porch and Veranda, Indigo House; Continental cuisine in the Charleston Gallery; lagoonside dining at the Park Cafe; casual dining in the Sand Wedge, Sundancers, Jonah's. *On Kiawah Island, 21 mi from Charleston (take U.S. 17S to Main Rd., take left and follow signs), Box 12910, Charleston 29412, tel. 803/768–2121 or 800/354–2924. AE, DC, MC, V.*

Seabrook Island Resort. There are 360 completely equipped one- to three-bedroom villas, cottages, and beach houses. Beach Club and Island Club, open to all guests, are centers for dining and leisure activities. Amenities include championship golf, tennis and equestrian centers, bicycling, water sports, pools, children's programs. *On Seabrook Island, 23 mi from Charleston (take U.S. 17S to SC 171S to SC 700, then follow signs), Box 32099, Charleston 29417, tel. 803/768–1000 or 800/845–5531. AE, CB, DC, MC, V.*

★ **Wild Dunes.** This lavish, 1,500-acre resort has 350 villa accommodations, each with a fully equipped kitchen and washer and dryer. There are two widely acclaimed championship golf courses, a racquet club, a yacht harbor on the Intracoastal Waterway, bicycling, nature trails, surfcasting, water sports, and children's programs. Guests enjoy beef specialties at The Club House and fresh seafoods at The Island House, where all dishes are created by a French master chef. There's a lounge with live entertainment. *On the Isle of Palms, 12 mi northeast of Charleston (take U.S. 17 to SC 703), Box 1410, Charleston 29402, tel. 803/886–6000 or 800/845–8880. AE, CB, DC, MC, V.*

The Arts

Pick up the comprehensive Schedule of Events at the Visitors Information Center (85 Calhoun St.) or at area hotels, inns, and restaurants. For an advance copy, contact **Charleston Trident Convention and Visitors Bureau** (Box 975, Charleston 29402, tel. 803/723–7641 or 800/845–7108). Also see "Tips for Tourists" each Saturday in *The News & Courier/The Evening Post*. And the weekend ARTSline (tel. 803/723–2787) gives information on arts events for the week.

Arts Festivals **Spoleto Festival USA.** Founded by renowned maestro Gian Carlo Menotti in 1977, Spoleto has become one of the world's greatest celebrations of the arts. For two weeks, from late May to early June, opera, dance, theater, symphonic and chamber music performances, jazz, and the visual arts are showcased in concert halls, theaters, parks, churches, streets, and gardens throughout the city. For information: Spoleto Festival USA (Box 704, Charleston, SC 29402, tel. 803/722–2764).

Piccolo Spoleto Festival. The spirited companion festival of Spoleto Festival USA showcases the best in local and regional talent from every artistic discipline. There are about 700 events—from jazz performances to puppet shows—held at 60 sites in 17 days, from mid-May through early June, and most performances are free. For a program, available May 1 each year, contact the Office of Cultural Affairs, Piccolo Spoleto Festival (133 Church St., Charleston 29401, tel. 803/724–7305).

Moja Arts Festival. Theater, dance, and music performances, art shows, films, lectures, and tours celebrating the rich heritage of the African continent are held at sites throughout the historic district the first two weeks in October. For information: The Office of Cultural Affairs (133 Church St., Charleston 29401, tel. 803/724–7305).

Concerts The College of Charleston has a **Monday Night Recital Series** (*see* Charleston for Free). The **Charleston Symphony Orchestra** (tel. 803/723–7528) presents its Classics Concerts Series at Gaillard Municipal Auditorium (77 Calhoun St., tel. 803/577–4500). Its Brass Quintet plays at the Charleston Museum Auditorium (360 Meeting St., tel. 803/722–2996) and the Garden Theatre (371 King St., tel. 803/722–6230). Its Woodwind Quintet also performs at the Charleston Museum Auditorium. Guest artists at **Sarah Johnson & Friends** (tel. 803/577–0536)—a chamber music series held fall through spring at the Dock Street Theatre (135 Church St., tel. 803/723–5648)—have included Paula Robison and Eliot Fisk.

Dance The **Charleston Ballet Theatre** (tel. 803/723–7334) and the **Charleston Civic Ballet** (tel. 803/722–8779 or 577–4502) perform at Gaillard Municipal Auditorium. The **Robert Ivey Ballet Company** (tel. 803/556–1343), a student group at the College of Charleston, gives a fall and spring program of jazz, classical, and modern dance at the Simons Center for the Arts.

Theater The **Footlight Players,** the **East Cooper Theater,** and the **Young Charleston Theatre Co.** stage performances at the Dock Street Theatre. The East Cooper Theatre also stages some performances at the Garden Theatre. Performances by the College of Charleston's drama department and guest theatrical groups are presented during the school year at the **Simons Center for the Arts** (tel. 803/792–8228).

Nightlife

Beach Bar **Windjammer** (tel. 803/886–8596), on the Isle of Palms, is an oceanfront spot featuring live rock music.

Dance Clubs In the market area, there's **Fannigans** (tel. 803/722–6916), where a DJ spins Top-40 hits, and the best of beach music. The "shag", South Carolina's state dance, popularized in the early '60s, is alive and well here. **Juke Box** (tel. 803/723–3431), with a DJ, '50s and '60s music, and a '50s look (waitresses wear cheerleader outfits); and **Myskyns** (tel. 803/577–5595), with live rock, reggae, R&B, or other bands most nights and an 8-by-10 video screen.

Hotel Bars The **Best Friend Lounge** (tel. 803/577–2400), in the Mills House Hotel, has a guitarist playing easy-listening tunes Monday–Saturday nights. **Water Colors** (tel. 803/722–4900), in the Omni Hotel at Charleston Place, has dancing Monday–Saturday nights, with a DJ, Top-40 hits, and videos.

Restaurant Lounges **A.W. Shucks** (tel. 803/723–1151) is a popular spot for relaxed evenings set to taped easy-listening. **Cafe 99** (tel. 803/577–4499) has laid-back '60s and '70s music indoors and out by vocalists and guitarists. **East Bay Trading Co.** (tel. 803/722–0722) has a small dance floor in its lively bar and a DJ playing Top 40s Friday and Saturday nights.

Dinner Cruise For an evening of dining and dancing afloat on the luxury yacht *Spirit of Charleston,* call 803/722–2628. *The Southern Star,* a reconverted paddlewheeler, also has dinner cruises and sails from the Ripley Light Marina near California Dreaming. Call

Bill Miller, 803/722–6182. *The Pride* operates from the same dock and is an 84-foot gaff-topsail schooner available for daily harbor excursions and cruises to Savannah, Georgia. Phone Capt. Bob, 803/795–1180.

Myrtle Beach and the Grand Strand

The Grand Strand, a resort area along the South Carolina coast, is one of the Eastern Seaboard's megafamily-vacation centers, and the state's top tourist area. The main attraction, of course, is the broad, beckoning beach—55 miles of it, stretching from the North Carolina border south to Georgetown, with Myrtle Beach at the hub. But the Strand has something for everyone: 48 championship golf courses, designed by such legends as Arnold Palmer, Robert Trent Jones, and Tom and George Fazio; excellent seafood restaurants; giant shopping malls and factory outlets; amusement parks, water slides, and arcades; a dozen shipwrecks for divers to explore; fine fishing; nine private campgrounds, most on the beach; plus paddlewheeler cruises, antique-car and wax museums, the world's largest sculpture garden, a version of the Grand Ole Opry, an antique pipe organ and merry-go-round, a minor-league baseball team, and a museum dedicated entirely to rice.

Getting Around

By Plane The Myrtle Beach Jetport is served by **American, American's American Eagle** affiliate; **Atlantis, Eastern's** affiliate; **Delta** and its **Atlantic Southeast** Airlines affiliate; and **USAir.**

By Car Located midway between New York and Miami, the Grand Strand can be reached from all directions via Interstates 20, 26, 40, 77, 85, and 95, which connect with U.S. 17, the major north–south coastal route through the Strand.

By Train **Amtrak** service for the Grand Strand is available through a terminal in Florence. Buses connect with Amtrak there for the 70-mile drive to Myrtle Beach.

By Bus Public transportation is provided by **Coastal Rapid Transit Authority** (tel. 803/248–7277). It operates daily between 6 AM and 1:15 AM. The fare is 75¢, exact change required.

By Taxi Service is provided by **Coastal Cab Service** in Myrtle Beach (tel. 803/448–4047).

Guided Tours

Palmetto Tour & Travel in Myrtle Beach (tel. 803/626–2660) and **Leisure Time Unlimited** in Myrtle Beach (Gray Line) (tel. 803/448–9483) offer tour packages, guide service, and charter service. At the **Georgetown County Chamber of Commerce and Information Center** (U.S. 17, tel. 803/546–8436), you can pick up free driving- and walking-tour maps or rent cassette walking tours. Also from here (Mar.–Oct.), you can take three different tours of historic areas: by tram, by 1840 horse-drawn carriage, or by boat.

Important Addresses and Numbers

Tourist **Georgetown County Chamber of Commerce and Information**
Information **Center** (U.S. 17, Georgetown 29442, tel. 803/546–8436). **Myrtle**
Beach Area Chamber of Commerce (Box 2115, 1301 N. Kings
Hwy., Myrtle Beach 29578, tel. 803/626–7444 or for literature
only 800/356–3016).

Emergencies Dial 911 for emergency assistance.

Hospital The emergency room is open 24 hours a day at the **HCA Grand**
Strand General Hospital (off U.S. 17 at 809 82nd Ave. Pkwy.,
Myrtle Beach, tel. 803/449–4411).

Dentist For emergency service, call **Sexton's Dental Clinic** (901 Medical
Plaza, 82nd Ave. Pkwy., Myrtle Beach, tel. 803/449–0431).

Exploring the Grand Strand

Myrtle Beach—whose population of 26,000 increases to about
350,000 in summer—is the center of activity in the Grand
Strand. It is here that you find the amusement parks and other
children's activities that make the area so popular for family
vacations, as well as most of the nightlife that keeps parents
and teenagers happy after beach hours. North of Myrtle
Beach, in the North Strand, there is Little River, with a thriving fishing and charter boat industry, and the several
communities—each with its own small-town flavor—that make
up North Myrtle Beach. In the South Strand, Surfside Beach
and Garden City are family retreats of year-round and summer
homes and condominiums. Farther south are Murrells Inlet,
once a pirate's haven and now a popular fishing port, and
Pawleys Island, one of the East Coast's oldest resorts. Historic
Georgetown, the state's third-oldest city, forms the Strand's
southern tip.

Our tour begins in **Myrtle Beach.** At the **Myrtle Beach Pavilion**
and Amusement Park, you'll find activities for all ages and interests: thrill and kiddie rides, including the Carolinas' largest
flume, plus video games, a teen nightclub, specialty shops, antique cars, and sidewalk cafes. *Ninth Ave. N and Ocean Blvd.,*
tel. 803/448–6456. Fees for individual attractions; family dis-
count book available. Open daily 1 PM–midnight late May–
Sept., weekends rest of year.

Nearby, at the **Guinness Hall of World Records,** fantastic human and natural phenomena spring to life through videotapes,
replicas, and other displays. *911 N. Ocean Blvd., tel. 803/448–*
4611. Admission: $3.95 adults; $2.95 children 7–12, under 7
free. Open daily 10 AM–midnight mid-Mar.–early Oct. Closed
rest of year.

More of the unusual awaits at **Ripleys Believe It or Not Museum.**
Among the more than 750 exhibits is an eight-foot, 11-inch wax
replica of the world's tallest man. *901 N. Ocean Blvd., tel. 803/*
448–2331. Admission: $4.95 adults; $2.95 children 6–12, under
6 free. Open daily 10 AM–10 PM First week Mar.–mid-Oct.
Closed rest of year.

Drama, sound, and animation highlight religious, historical,
and entertainment sections in the **Myrtle Beach National Wax**
Museum. *1000 N. Ocean Blvd., tel. 803/448–9921. Admission:*

$4.50 adults; $2 children 6–12, under 6 free. Open daily 9 AM–9 PM Feb.–mid-Oct. Closed rest of year.

When your family's appetite for more raucous amusements has been sated, it's time to head out of town. Going south on Kings Highway, you'll come to **Murrells Inlet,** a picturesque little fishing village that boasts some of the most popular seafood restaurants on the Grand Strand. It's also a great place for chartering a fishing boat or joining a half- or full-day group excursion.

Three miles south, on the grounds of a Colonial rice plantation, is the largest outdoor collection of American sculpture, with works by such American artists as Frederic Remington and Daniel Chester French. **Brookgreen Gardens** was begun in 1931 by railroad magnate/philanthropist Archer Huntington and his wife, Anna, herself a sculptor. Today, more than 400 works are set amid beautifully landscaped grounds, with avenues of live oaks, reflecting pools, and over 2,000 plant species. Also on the 9,000-acre site is a wildlife park, an aviary, a cypress swamp, nature trails, and an education center. It's a lovely, soothing place for a picnic. *18 mi south of Myrtle Beach off U.S. 17, tel. 803/237–4218. Admission: $4 adults; $1 children 6–12, under 6 free. Tape tours, $1 extra. Open daily 9:30–4:45 except Christmas.*

Across the highway is **Huntington Beach State Park,** the 2,500-acre former estate of the Huntingtons. The park's focal point is the Moorish-style "castle" Atalaya, once the Huntingtons' home, now open to visitors in season. In addition to the splendid beach, there is surf fishing, nature trails, an interpretive center, a salt-marsh boardwalk, picnic areas, a playground, concessions, and a campground. *Tel. 803/237–4440. Admission free; parking fee in peak months; incidentals fees. Open daily during daylight hours.*

Farther south is one of the first summer resorts on the Atlantic coast, **Pawleys Island.** Prior to the Civil War, wealthy planters and their families summered here to avoid malaria and other fevers that infested the swampy coastal region. Four miles long and a half-mile wide, it's made up mostly of weathered old summer cottages nestled in groves of oleander and oak trees. The famed Pawleys Island hammocks have been handmade here since 1880. In several shops, you can watch them being fashioned of rope and cord by local craftsfolk (*see* Shopping).

Bellefield Nature Center, south on U.S. 17, is at the entrance of Hobcaw Barony, the vast estate of the late Bernard M. Baruch. Here he consulted with such guests as President Franklin D. Roosevelt and Prime Minister Winston Churchill. The nature center, operated by the Belle W. Baruch Foundation, is used for teaching and research in forestry and marine biology. *Tel. 803/546–4623. Admission free. Open weekdays 10–5, Sat. 1–5.*

Georgetown, on the shores of Winyah Bay, was founded in 1729 by a Baptist minister and soon became the center of America's Colonial rice empire. A rich plantation culture took root here and developed on a scale comparable to Charleston's. Today, oceangoing vessels reach Georgetown's busy port through a deepwater channel, and the town's prosperity is based on industry (such as its paper mill and an iron foundry) and tourism.

In the heart of town, the graceful market-meeting building, topped by an 1842 town clock and tower, has been converted into the **Rice Museum,** which traces the history of rice cultivation through maps, tools, and dioramas. *Front and Screven Sts., tel. 803/546-7423. Admission: $2 adults, $1 military, students free. Open weekdays 9:30-4:30, Sat. 10-4:30 (until 1 PM Oct.-Mar.), Sun. 2-4:30 PM. Closed major holidays.*

Nearby, **Prince George Winyah Episcopal Church,** named after King George II, still serves the congregation established in 1721. It was built in 1737 with bricks brought over from Mother England. *Broad and Highmarket Sts., tel. 803/546-4358. Donation suggested. Visitors welcome weekdays 9-4.*

Overlooking the Sampit River from a high bluff is the **Harold Kaminski House** (ca. 1760). It's especially notable for its collections of regional antiques and furnishings, and for its Chippendale and Duncan Phyfe furniture, Royal Doulton vases, and silver. *1003 Front St., tel. 803/546-7706. Admission: $4 adults; $3 senior citizens; $2 children 12-16, under 12 free. Open weekdays 10-5, tours hourly. Closed holidays, 2 weeks at Christmas.*

Twelve miles south of Georgetown, **Hopsewee Plantation,** surrounded by moss-draped live oaks, magnolias, and tree-size camellias, overlooks the North Santee River. The mansion is notable for its fine Georgian staircase and hand-carved Adam candlelight moldings. *U.S. 17, tel. 803/546-7891. Admission: $3 adults; $1 children 6-18, under 6 free. Open Tues.-Fri. 10-5 Feb.-Oct., other times by appointment. Grounds only, including nature trail, $1 per car.*

Hampton Plantation State Park, at the edge of the Francis Marion National Forest (*see* off the Beaten Track in Charleston section), preserves the home of Archibald Rutledge, poet laureate of South Carolina for 39 years until his death in 1973. The 18th-century plantation house is an excellent example of a Low Country mansion. The exterior has been restored; cutaway sections in the finely crafted interior show the changes made through the centuries. The grounds are landscaped, and picnic areas are available. *Off U.S. 17, tel. 803/546-9361. Admission: $1 adults; 50¢ children 6-18, under 6 free. Grounds free; open Thurs.-Mon. 9-6. House open Sat. 10-3, Sun. noon-3.*

What to See and Do with Children

Brookgreen Gardens (*see* Exploring the Grand Strand).

Huntington Beach State Park (*see* Exploring).

Myrtle Beach Grand Prix. Auto-mania heaven, it offers Formula 1 race cars, go-carts, bumper boats, mini-go-carts, kiddie cars, and mini-bumper boats for adults and children age 3 and up. *Two locations: U.S. 17 Bus., Myrtle Beach, across from Air Force base, tel. 803/238-2421; and Windy Hill, U.S. 17N, N. Myrtle Beach, tel. 803/272-6010. Rides priced individually, average ride $3.50. Open daily 10 AM-11 PM Mar. 10-Oct. 31.*

Myrtle Beach Pavilion and Amusement Park (*see* Exploring).

Myrtle Waves Water Park. There's splashy family fun for all ages in 17 rides and activities. *U.S. 17 Bypass and 10th Ave. N, Myrtle Beach, tel. 803/448-1026. Cost: $10.92, $8.27 after 3 PM, $5.25 after 5 PM Tues.-Thurs., children under 3 free. Open*

*daily 9:30–6 (Tues.–Thurs. until 8) Memorial Day weekend–
Labor Day, weekends only rest of May, after Labor Day–Sept.
30. Closed rest of year.*

Shopping

Malls **Myrtle Square Mall** (2502 N. Kings Hwy., Myrtle Beach, tel.
803/448–2513) is an upscale complex with 71 stores and restaurants, and a new 250-seat Food Court. **Briarcliffe Mall** (10177
N. Kings Hwy., Myrtle Beach, tel. 803/249–2819) has 100 specialty shops, JC Penney, and K-mart. Both malls, the area's
largest, are open Monday–Saturday 10–9:30 (until 9 in winter),
Sunday 1–6.

Discount and Off-price shopping outlets abound in the Grand Strand.
Off-Price Outlets **Waccamaw Pottery and Outlet Park** (U.S. 501 at the Waterway,
Myrtle Beach, tel. 803/236–1100) is one of the nation's largest.
In several buildings, over three miles of shelves are stocked
with china, glassware, wicker, brass and pewter, and countless
other items. Outlet Park has about 50 factory outlets with
clothing, furniture, books, jewelry, and more. Open Monday
through Saturday 9–10. The **Hathaway Factory Outlet** (tel. 803/
236–4200), across from Waccamaw, offers menswear by Christian Dior, Ralph Lauren, and Jack Nicklaus and women's wear
by White Stag and Geoffrey Beene, among others. Open daily
9–6 (until 8 Mon.–Sat. in summer).

Specialty Shops **The Hammock Shops at Pawleys Island** is a handsome complex
of 17 boutiques and gift shops built with old brick brought from
England as ballast. In one shop, summer visitors can see rope
hammocks being made. Other wares include jewelry, toys, antiques, and designer fashions. The shops are open daily 10–5 in
winter; Monday–Saturday 9:30–9, Sunday 12:30–6 in summer.

Beaches

All the Grand Strand beaches are family oriented, and almost
all are public. The widest expanses are in North Myrtle Beach,
where the sand stretches for up to an eighth of a mile from the
dunes to the water at low tide. Those who wish to combine their
sunning with nightlife and amusement-park activities can enjoy it all at Myrtle Beach. Vacationers seeking a quieter day
head for the South Strand communities of Surfside Beach and
Garden City, or historic Pawleys Island. All along the Strand,
you can enjoy shell hunting, fishing, swimming, sunbathing,
sailing, surfing, jogging, or just strolling.

Participant Sports

Fishing Because offshore waters along the Grand Strand are warmed
by the Gulf Stream, fishing is usually good from early spring
through December. Anglers can walk out over the Atlantic
from 10 piers and jetties to try for amberjack, sea trout, and
king mackerel. Surfcasters may snare bluefish, whiting, flounder, pompano, and channel bass. In the South Strand, salt
marshes, inlets, and tidal creeks yield flounder, blues, croak-
ers, spots, shrimp, clams, oysters, and blue-claw crabs. Some
conveniently located marinas that offer both half- and full-day
fishing and sightseeing trips are **Capt. Dick's** (U.S. 17 Bus.,
Murrells Inlet, tel. 803/651–3676), **Flying Fisherman** (U.S. 17
Bus., Murrells Inlet, tel. 803/651–5700), and **Hurrican Fleet,**

Vereen's Marina (U.S. 17 at 11th Ave. N, N. Myrtle Beach, tel. 803/249-3571).

The annual **Grand Strand Fishing Rodeo** (Apr.-Oct.) features a "fish of the month" contest, with prizes for the largest catch of a designated species. The October **Arthur Smith King Mackerel Tournament** offers more than $350,000 in prizes and attracts nearly 900 boats and 5,000 anglers.

Golf   The Grand Strand—known as the World's Golf Capital—has 48 public courses. Many are championship layouts by top designers. All share meticulously manicured greens, lush fairways, and challenging hazards. Spring and fall are the busiest seasons because of warm temperatures and off-season rates. An organization called **Golf Holiday** (tel. 803/448-5942), whose members include hotels, motels, condominiums, and golf courses along the Grand Strand, offers many package plans throughout the year.

Popular courses include: in Myrtle Beach, **Arcadian Shores Golf Club** (tel. 803/449-5217) and **Dunes Golf and Beach Club** (tel. 803/449-5914); in North Myrtle Beach, **Gator Hole** (tel. 803/249-3543), **Oyster Bay Golf Links** (tel. 803/272-6399), and **Robbers Roost Golf Club** (tel. 803/249-1471); and at Little River, **Marsh Harbor Golf Links** (tel. 803/249-3449).

Scuba Diving   In summer, a large variety of warm-water tropical fish find their way to the area from the Gulf Stream. Off the coast of Little River, rock and coral ledges teem with coral, sea fans, sponges, reef fish, anemones, urchins, arrow crabs, and stone crabs. Several outlying shipwrecks are home to schools of spadefish, amberjack, grouper, and barracuda. Instruction and equipment rentals are available from **Myrtle Beach Scuba Center** (U.S. 501W, Myrtle Beach, tel. 803/448-2832).

Tennis   There are over 150 courts throughout the Grand Strand. Facilities include hotel and resort courts, as well as free municipal courts in Myrtle Beach, North Myrtle Beach, and Surfside Beach. Among tennis clubs offering court time, rental equipment, and instruction are **Myrtle Beach Racquet Club** (tel. 803/449-4031), **Myrtle Beach Tennis and Swim Club** (tel. 803/449-4486), and Surfside Beach's **Grand Strand Tennis Club** (tel. 803/650-3330).

Water Sports   Surfboards, Hobie Cats, Jet Skis, Windsurfers, and sailboats are available for rent at **Downwind Sails** (Ocean Blvd. at 29th Ave. S, Myrtle Beach, tel. 803/448-7245).

Spectator Sports

Baseball   Between early April and late August, the **Myrtle Beach Blue Jays,** farm club for the Toronto Blue Jays, play about 70 home games at the 3,500-seat Coastal Carolina Stadium (tel. 803/347-3161), off U.S. 501 less than 10 miles from downtown Myrtle Beach.

Dining

A wealth of seafood, fresh from inlets, rivers, and ocean, graces the tables of coastal South Carolina. Enjoy it in lavish portions, garnished with hush puppies, cole slaw, and fresh vegetables, in many family-style restaurants. Or sample Continental or classic American preparations at elegant resorts and upscale restaurants. The most highly recommended restaurants in each price category are indicated by a star ★.

Category	Cost*
Very Expensive	over $25
Expensive	$15–$25
Moderate	$7–$15
Inexpensive	under $7

*per person without tax (5% in South Carolina), service, or drinks

The following credit-card abbreviations are used: AE, American Express; CB, Carte Blanche; DC, Diners Club; MC, MasterCard; and V, Visa.

Georgetown
Seafood
★

Rice Paddy. This cozy restaurant is apt to be crowded at lunch, when local business folk flock in for homemade vegetable soup, garden-fresh salads, and sandwiches. Dinner is more relaxed, and the menu showcases broiled fresh seafood. Crabmeat casserole is a tasty specialty. So is veal scaloppine. *408 Duke St., tel. 803/546–2021. Dress: informal. Reservations not required. AE, MC, V. Closed Sun. Moderate.*

Murrells Inlet
Seafood
★

Planter's Back Porch. Sip cool drinks in the spring house of a turn-of-the-century farmhouse, then have dinner in a garden setting reminiscent of a 19th-century Southern plantation. Black wrought-iron chandeliers are suspended from high white ceiling beams, and hanging baskets of greenery decorate white latticework archways separating the fireplace-centered main dining room and the airy, glass-enclosed porch. You can't go wrong with baked whole flounder, panned lump crabmeat, or the hearty Inlet Dinner showcasing several fresh daily catches. *U.S. 17 and Wachesaw Rd., tel. 803/651–5263 or 651–5544. Dress: informal. Reservations not required. AE, MC, V. Closed Dec.–mid-Feb. Moderate.*

Myrtle Beach
Mixed Menu

Slug's Choice. A Carolinas tradition, this immensely popular restaurant has a lounge overlooking the Intracoastal Waterway. It does serve fresh local seafood and some veal dishes, but the house specialties are prime rib, and steaks flame-grilled to order. There's a hefty salad bar. The restaurant is under the same management as nearby Slug's Rib, specializing in prime rib. *Slug's Choice: 10131 N. Kings Hwy., tel. 803/272–7781. Jacket and tie suggested. Reservations accepted. May close one month in winter—best to call. AE, CB, DC, MC, V. Moderate–Expensive. Slug's Rib: 9713 N. Kings Hwy., tel. 803/449–6419. Dress: informal. No reservations. AE, CB, DC, MC, V. Moderate–Expensive.*

Seafood
★

Rice Planter's Restaurant. Dine on fresh seafood, quail, or steaks grilled to order in a homey setting enhanced by Low Country antiques, rice-plantation tools and artifacts, and candlelight. Shrimp Creole is a house specialty; among the appetizers, don't miss the crab fingers! Bread and pecan pie are home-baked. *6707 N. Kings Hwy., tel. 803/449–3456 or 449–3457. Dress: informal. Reservations not required. AE, MC, V. Closed Dec. 25 and 26. Moderate.*

Sea Captain's House. At this picturesque restaurant with a nautical decor, the best seats are in the windowed porch room, with its sweeping ocean views. The fireplace in the wood-paneled inside dining room casts a warm glow on cool off-season evenings. Menu highlights include she-crab soup, Low Country crab casserole, and avocado-seafood salad. Breads and desserts are home-baked. *3002 N. Ocean Blvd., tel. 803/448–8082. Also on U.S. 17 Bus., Murrells Inlet, tel. 803/651–2416. Both: Dress: informal. Reservations not required. AE, MC, V. Closed mid-Dec.–mid-Feb. Moderate.*

Southern Suppers. Here's hearty family dining in a cozy farmhouse filled with country primitive art; handmade quilts line the walls. The menu features an all-you-can-eat seafood buffet. You can also order down-home Southern specialties like fried chicken, country-fried steak, and country ham with red-eye gravy and grits. *U.S. 17S, midway between Myrtle Beach and Surfside Beach, tel. 803/238–4557. Dress: informal. Reservations not required. No liquor. MC, V. Closed Oct.–Feb. Moderate.*

Pawleys Island
American Regional
★

Pawleys Island Inn Restaurant and Bar. There are four dining rooms in this 18-year-old antebellum-style inn. It's especially pleasant to dine on the glass-enclosed porch; request this seating when you make reservations. Specialties include snapper sautéed in lemon butter, then baked; broiled lump-crab cakes; and shrimp Provençale with fresh spinach pasta. There's a children's menu, and all breads and desserts are baked on the premises. Under the same ownership is the adjacent Pawleys Island Inn Bakery, which seats 12 and serves sandwiches, salads, picnic boxes, and freshly baked breads. *U.S. 17, in the Hammock Shops at Pawleys Island, tel. 803/237–9033. Dress: informal. Reservations suggested. AE, DC, MC, V. Closed Sun., major holidays. Expensive.*

Lodging

Among other lodgings options, condominiums are popular on the Grand Strand, combining spaciousness and modern amenities and appealing especially to families. You can choose among cottages, villas, and hotel-style high-rise units. Maid service is frequently available. For the free directories *Grand Hotel and Motel Accommodations* and *Grand Condominium and Cottage Accommodations,* write the Myrtle Beach Area Chamber of Commerce (Box 2115, Myrtle Beach 29578, tel. 803/626–7444 or 800/356–3016).

Attractive package plans are available between Labor Day and spring break. Also, see Golf section in Participant Sports regarding golf packages. The most highly recommended properties in each price category are indicated by a star ★.

Category	Cost*
Very Expensive	over $100
Expensive	$65–$100
Moderate	$45–$65
Inexpensive	under $45

*double room; add 7% for taxes

The following credit-card abbreviations are used: AE, American Express; CB, Carte Blanche; DC, Diners Club; MC, MasterCard; and V, Visa.

Georgetown
Inexpensive–
Moderate

Best Western Carolinian. This conveniently located in-town motor inn has spacious rooms with reproduction period furnishings. *706 Church St., 29440, tel. 803/546–5191 or 800/528–1234. 90 rooms. Facilities: pool, cable TV/movies, restaurant, lounge. AE, CB, DC, MC, V.*

Myrtle Beach
Very Expensive
★

Myrtle Beach Hilton and Golf Club. This luxurious high-rise oceanfront property—part of the Arcadian Shores Golf Club— is highlighted by a dramatic 14-story atrium. Spacious, airy rooms, all with sea views, are decorated in chic plum, mauve, gray, and rose tones and accented by ultracontemporary lamps and accessories. Two newly redecorated executive floors offer two-phone rooms and other amenities. *701 Hilton Rd., Arcadian Shores, 29577, tel. 803/449–5000 or 800/445–8667. 392 rooms. Facilities: 600-foot private beach, oceanfront pool, tennis, golf, restaurant, lounges, entertainment, shops, social program. AE, CB, DC, MC, V.*

Radisson Resort Hotel. The Grand Strand's newest luxury property, this 20-story glass-sheathed tower is part of the Kingston Plantation complex of shops, restaurants, hotels, and condominiums set amid 145 acres of oceanside woodlands. Guest rooms are highlighted by bleached-wood furnishings and attractive artworks. The balconied one-bedroom suites have kitchenettes. *9800 Lake Dr., 29577, tel. 803/449–0006 or 800/228–9822. 255 suites. Facilities: 2 restaurants and lounge; privileges at sports/fitness complex offering racquetball, tennis, squash, aerobics, exercise equipment, sauna, pools, whirlpool. AE, CB, DC, MC, V.*

Sheraton Myrtle Beach Martinique. (Formerly Sheraton Myrtle Beach Inn.) The oceanfront rooms in this luxury hotel have been recently remodeled and all have queen-size beds. There's also a grand new lobby. *7100 N. Ocean Blvd., 29578, tel. 803/449–4441 or 800/325–3535. 147 rooms, 86 efficiencies. Facilities: dining and dancing in glass-enclosed rooftop restaurant, live entertainment in bar, laundry, heated pool, wading pool, racquet club privileges, children's activity director. New conference and amenities center has full spa facilities. AE, CB, DC, MC, V.*

Best Western/The Landmark. The rooms in this high-rise oceanfront resort hotel are tastefully decorated in a modern style. Some have balconies and refrigerators. *1501 S. Ocean Blvd., 29577, tel. 803/448–9441 or 800/528–1234. 326 rooms. Facilities: pool, children's activity program, game room, dining rooms, lounges, nightclub, live nightly entertainment (see Nightlife). AE, CB, DC, MC, V.*

The Breakers Resort Hotel. The rooms in this oceanfront resort are airy and spacious, with contemporary decor. Many have balconies and refrigerators. *2006 N. Ocean Blvd., Box 485, 29578–0485, tel. 803/626–5000 or 800/845–0688. 391 rooms. Facilities: restaurant, 3 oceanfront pools, indoor and outdoor whirlpools, saunas, exercise room, restaurant, lounge, laundry, children's programs. AE, CB, DC, MC, V.*

Expensive

Holiday Inn Downtown. This in-town oceanfront inn is right at the heart of the action. The spacious rooms have been newly redecorated in cool sea tones. After beach basking, you can prolong the mood in the inn's spacious, plant-bedecked indoor recreation center. *415 S. Ocean Blvd., 29577, tel. 803/448–4481 or 800/845–0313. 306 rooms. Facilities: oceanfront pool with bar, pool parties, heated indoor pool, snack bar, sauna, whirlpool, game room, restaurant, 2 lounges (1 with live entertainment). AE, CB, DC, MC, V.*

Driftwood-on-the-Oceanfront. Under the same ownership for over 50 years, this facility is popular with families. Some rooms are oceanfront; all have recently been redecorated in sea, sky, or earth tones. *1600 N. Ocean Blvd., Box 275, 29578, tel. 803/448–1544 or 800/448–1544. 90 rooms. Facilities: room refrigerators, 2 pools, laundry. AE, CB, DC, MC, V.*

Moderate– **Comfort Inn.** This new inn, 400 yards from the ocean, is clean,
Expensive well furnished, and well maintained. *2801 S. Kings Hwy., 29577, tel. 803/626–4444 or 800/228–5150. 153 rooms. Facilities: 8 Jacuzzi suites, 6 kitchen suites, outdoor pool, health club with whirlpool and sauna, cable TV, restaurant, par-3 golf course adjacent. AE, CB, DC, MC, V.*

Moderate **Cherry Tree Inn.** This rambling, low-rise oceanfront inn is in a quiet North Strand section and caters to families. It is furnished Scandinavian-style. *5400 N. Ocean Blvd., 29577, tel. 803/449–6425 or 800/845–2036. 35 rooms. Facilities: kitchens, cable TV, Jacuzzi, laundry, video games, heated pool (enclosed in winter). AE, MC, V.*

North Myrtle **Economy Inn.** This hotel, part of a chain, is across from the air-
Beach port and near Waccamaw Pottery. *3301 U.S. 17S, 29582, tel.*
Inexpensive *803/272–6196 or 800/446–6900. 40 rooms. Facilities: pool, cribs, cable TV. AE, CB, DC, MC, V.*

Pawleys Island **Quality Inn Seagull.** This is a very well maintained inn on a golf
Moderate course (excellent golf packages are available). The rooms are spacious, bright, and airy. *U.S. 17S, Box 153, 29585, tel. 803/237–4261 or 800/228–5151. 95 rooms. Facilities: pool, dining room, lounge with entertainment, in-room movies. AE, CB, DC, MC, V.*

The Arts

Theater productions, concerts, art exhibits, and other cultural events are regularly offered at the **Myrtle Beach Convention Center** (21st Ave. N, Myrtle Beach, tel. 803/448–7166) and during the school year at **Coastal Carolina College's** Wheelright Auditorium (U.S. 501, west of Conway, tel. 803/347–6206).

Nightlife

Clubs offer varying fare, including beach music, the Grand Strand's unique sound, which conjures up memories of the 1950s. During summer, sophisticated live entertainment is featured nightly at some clubs and resorts. Some hotels and resorts also have piano bars or lounges featuring easy-listening music.

In Myrtle Beach: **Sandals,** at the Sands Ocean Club (tel. 803/449–6461) is an intimate lounge with live entertainment. **Coquina Club,** at the Best Western Landmark Inn (tel. 803/448–9441), features beach-music bands. **Studebaker's** (tel. 803/626–3855) is one of the area's hot night spots, with live beach music. At The Breakers Hotel, **Top of the Green Lounge and Sidewalk**

Cafe (tel. 803/626–5000) is a popular spot, with nightly dancing and entertainment.

In North Myrtle Beach, the lounge at **Holiday Inn on the Ocean** (tel. 803/272–6153) showcases live bands.

In Murrells Inlet, **Drunken Jack's** (tel. 803/651–2044) is a popular restaurant with a lounge overlooking the docks and fishing fleets.

Carolina Opry offers music, comedy, and a variety show to combine the flavor of the Grand Ole Opry with a dash of Broadway. Entertainment for the whole family. *301 U.S. 17S, Surfside Beach, tel. 803/238–8888. Tickets $8–$10. Show at 8 PM, days vary with season. Closed Dec. 20–early Feb.*

Hilton Head and Beyond

Anchoring the southern tip of South Carolina's coastline is 42-square-mile Hilton Head Island, named after English sea captain William Hilton, who claimed it for England in 1663. It was settled by planters in the 1700s and flourished until the Civil War. Thereafter, the economy declined and the island languished until Charles E. Fraser, a visionary South Carolina attorney, began developing the Sea Pines resort in 1956. Other developments followed, and today Hilton Head's casual pace, broad beaches, wide-ranging activities, and genteel good life make it one of the East Coast's most popular vacation getaways.

Beaufort is a gracious antebellum town with a compact historic district preserving lavish 18th- and 19th-century homes. Southward lies Fripp Island, a self-contained resort with controlled access. And midway between Beaufort and Charleston is Edisto ("ED-is-toh") Island, settled in 1690 and once a notable center for cultivation of silky Sea Island cotton. Some of its elaborate mansions have been restored; others brood in disrepair. About the only contemporary touches on the island are a few cottages in a popular state park and modern villas in Fairfield Ocean Ridge Resort.

Getting Around

By Plane
Hilton Head Island Airport is served by Atlantis, an Eastern affiliate, with nonstop flights to and from Atlanta and Charlotte. Most travelers use the **Savannah International Airport**, about an hour from Hilton Head via transfer bus or limousine, which is served by American, Continental, and United.

By Car
The island is 40 miles east of I–95 (Exit 28 off I–95S, Exit 5 off I–95N).

By Taxi
Yellow Rose Cab (tel. 803/681–6666) provides service in Hilton Head. Cabs here do not have meters; there is a flat rate of $6, plus a preset fare according to zone. For more than two passengers, an additional charge of $2 per person is levied.

Guided Tours

Low Country Adventures (tel. 803/681–8212) and **Regal Limousine of Hilton Head** (tel. 803/785–5466) offer tours as well as transportation from Savannah and Hilton Head Island air-

ports. **Hilton Head Helicopters** (tel. 803/681–9120) offers sightseeing flights as well as shuttle service from Savannah's
airport. Hilton Head's **Adventure Cruises** (tel. 803/785–4558)
offers dinner, sightseeing, and murder-mystery cruises. Self-
guided walking or driving tours are available through the
Beaufort County Chamber of Commerce (tel. 803/524–3163).

Important Addresses and Numbers

Tourist   **Beaufort County Chamber of Commerce,** Box 910, 1006 Bay St.,
Information Beaufort, 29901–0910, tel. 803/524–3163. Open weekdays
9–4:30, Saturday 10–3. **Hilton Head Island Chamber of Commerce,** Drawer 5647, Hilton Head Island, 29938, tel. 803/785–
3673. Open weekdays 8:30–5:30, Saturday (June–Sept.) 10–4.

Emergencies Dial 911 for emergency assistance.

Doctor   For nonlife-threatening emergencies, no appointment is neces-
sary at **Family Medical Center** (South Island Square, U.S. 278,
tel. 803/842–2900); open daily 8–8.

Exploring Hilton Head and Beyond

Lined by towering pines, wind-sculpted live oaks, and palmetto
trees, Hilton Head's 12 miles of beaches are a major attraction
of this semitropical barrier island. And its oak and pine woodlands, meandering lagoons, and temperate ocean climate
provide an incomparable environment for golfing, tennis, water sports, beachcombing, and sea splashing.

Choice stretches of the island are occupied by various resorts,
or "plantations," among them Sea Pines, Shipyard, Palmetto
Dunes, Port Royal, and Hilton Head. In these, accommodations
range from rental vacation villas and lavish private homes to
luxury hotels. The resorts are also private residential communities, although many have restaurants, marinas, shopping
areas, and/or recreational facilities that are open to the public.
All are secured, and visitors cannot tour the residential areas
unless arrangements are made at the visitor or security office
near the main gate of each plantation.

In the south of the island, at the **Newhall Audubon Preserve,**
you'll find unusual native plant life identified and tagged in a
pristine 50-acre site. There are trails, a self-guided tour, and
plant walks seasonally. *Palmetto Bay Rd., tel. 803/671–2008.
Admission free. Open daily during daylight hours.*

Also in the south, and part of the Sea Pines resort, is the **Sea
Pines Forest Preserve,** a 605-acre public wilderness tract. There
are seven miles of walking trails, a well-stocked fishing pond, a
waterfowl pond, and a 3,400-year-old Indian shell ring. Both
guided and self-guided tours are available. *Tel. 803/671–7170.
$3 per-car fee for nonguests. Open daily 7 AM–9:30 PM. Closed
during the Heritage Golf Classic in April.*

The **Whooping Crane Conservancy,** on Hilton Head Plantation
in the north, is home to rare semitropical birds, reptiles, and
mammals. There are self-guided tours on a boardwalk and trail
through the 137-acre black-gum swamp. (The boardwalk, leading through the rookery, is closed during breeding season,
Feb.–July.) From September to March, there are Saturday-
morning bird walks. *Tel. 803/681–5291. Admission free. Open
daily during daylight hours.*

While on Hilton Head Plantation, you might stop to note the earthwork fortifications that mark the site of **Fort Mitchell,** built in 1812 on a bluff overlooking Skull Creek as part of a large system across the island's northern end.

Beach walks are conducted daily in season by the Environmental Museum of Hilton Head for a nominal fee (tel. 803/842-9197; the museum itself is years away from opening).

Off the island, there's the **Waddell Mariculture Research and Development Center,** three miles west. Here methods of raising seafood commercially are studied, and visitors are invited to tour its 24 ponds and the research building to see work in progress. *Sawmill Creek Rd., near U.S. 278-SC 46 intersection, tel. 803/681-8800. Admission free. Tours weekdays at 10 AM and by appointment.*

North of here is the waterfront city of **Beaufort.** Established in 1710, Beaufort achieved immense prosperity toward the close of the 18th century when Sea Island cotton was introduced as a money crop. Many of the lavish houses that the wealthy landowners and merchants built—with wide balconies, high ceilings, and luxurious appointments—today remain, a legacy of an elegant and gracious era.

Across the street from the Beaufort County Chamber of Commerce (where you can pick up maps, tours, and literature) is the handsome **George Elliott House,** which served as a Union hospital during the Civil War. It was built in 1840 in Greek Revival style, with leaded-glass fanlights, pine floors, and rococo ceilings. The furnishings include some fine early Victorian pieces. *1001 Bay St., tel. 803/524-8450. Admission: $3 adults, $2 children. Open weekdays 11-3, Sun. 1-3.*

Nearby, the **John Mark Verdier House,** an Adam-style structure built around 1790 and headquarters for Union forces during the war, has been restored and furnished as it would have been between 1790 and the visit of Lafayette in 1825. Guided tours are available. *801 Bay St., tel. 803/524-6334. Admission: $3 adults, $2 children under 15. Open Tues.-Sat. 11-3 Feb.-mid-Dec. Closed rest of year and Thanksgiving.*

Built in 1795 and remodeled in 1852, the Gothic-style arsenal was home of the Beaufort Volunteer Artillery. It now houses the **Beaufort Museum,** with prehistoric relics, Indian pottery, Revolutionary and Civil War exhibits, and decorative arts. *713 Craven St., tel. 803/525-7471. Donations requested. Open weekdays 10 AM-noon, 2-5 PM; Sat. 10 AM-noon. Closed Sun., holidays.*

St. Helena's Episcopal Church, dating from 1724, was also touched by the Civil War: It was turned into a hospital and gravestones were brought inside to serve as operating tables. *501 Church St., tel. 803/524-3163. Donations appreciated. Visitors welcome weekdays 8:30-6.*

Part of the 304-acre Historic Beaufort District, **Old Point** includes many private antebellum homes not open to visitors. Some may be open during the annual Fall House Tour, a mid-October weekend, and the Spring Tour of Homes and Gardens, in April or May. The rest of the year, you'll have to content yourself with appreciating the fine exteriors.

Before setting out to explore outlying areas, pause in the **Henry C. Chambers Waterfront Park** to rest and survey the scene. Its seven landscaped acres along the Beaufort River, part of the Intracoastal Waterway, include a seawall promenade, a crafts market, gardens, and a marina. Some events of the popular mid-July Beaufort Water Festival occur here.

Eighteen miles east of Beaufort via U.S. 21 is **Hunting Island,** a secluded domain of ocean beaches, semitropical woodlands, and the photogenic 140-foot-high **Hunting Island Lighthouse,** built in 1859 and abandoned in 1933. If you want to make the effort to climb the spiral staircase—all 181 steps—you'll be rewarded with sweeping vistas of the island, ocean, and marshland. The 5,000-acre barrier island is a popular state park offering three miles of broad swimming beach, hiking, nature trails, and surf, inlet, and lagoon fishing. *Nominal admission per car in summer. For cabin reservations, write Hunting Island State Park, Rte. 1, Box 668, Frogmore 29920, tel. 803/838–2011.*

Heading north from Beaufort on U.S. 21 to Gardens Corner, taking Rte. 17N to Rte. 174, and following that road east to the ocean will bring you to **Edisto Island** (80 mi from Beaufort). Here, magnificent stands of age-old oaks festooned with Spanish moss border quiet streams and side roads. Wild turkeys roam freely in open grasslands. Trawlers dock at rickety piers in an antiquated fishing village that looks like a monochromatic etching in early morning mists. Most of the island's inhabitants are descendants of former slaves, and they preserve many aspects of their African heritage, such as painting doorways and windowsills bright blue to ward off evil spirits.

Edisto Beach State Park, one of the state's most popular, offers three miles of beach with excellent shelling. There are cabins by the marsh and campsites by the ocean. The cabins are basic but clean, and offer full housekeeping facilities. *For information and reservations, contact: Superintendent, Edisto Beach State Park, 8377 State Cabin Rd., Edisto Island 29438, tel. 803/869–2156 or 869–3396.*

What to See and Do with Children

On Hilton Head Island, each major hotel and resort offers some **summer youth activities** or a full-scale youth program. Every summer hundreds of visiting youngsters join island youth in the weekly camps offered by the Island Recreation Center. **Day camp** activities include tennis lessons, beach trips, arts and crafts, games, contests, and special events. **Sports camps** include basketball, boardsailing, golf, racquetball, sailing, soccer, tennis, and volleyball. *Contact: Hilton Head Island Recreation Association, Box 6121, Hilton Head Island, 29938, tel. 803/785–9016.*

Most hotels and resorts offer **baby-sitting** lists. During daylight hours, some **day-care services** welcome drop-ins on an hourly basis for youngsters six months to six years; check the yellow pages; or ask your hotel's concierge or front-desk staff.

Hunting Island State Park (*see* Exploring Hilton Head and Beyond) has playgrounds and is a fine family picnicking site.

Shopping

Malls Major Hilton Head Island shopping sites include **Pinelawn Mall** (U.S. 278 at Matthews Dr., tel. 803/681-8907 or 681-9807), with 33 shops and six restaurants; and **Coligny Plaza** (Coligny Circle, tel. 803/842-6050), with 60-plus shops, restaurants, food stands, a movie theater, and a supermarket.

Antiques **Christina's Antiques Et Cetera** (Hilton Head Plaza, tel. 803/686-2320) features Oriental and European antiques and New Guinea primitives. **Den of Antiquity** (20 mi north of Hilton Head on U.S. 170, tel. 803/842-6711), the area's largest antiques shop, carries a wide assortment of Low Country and nautical pieces. **Harbour Town Antiques** (at Harbour Town, Hilton Head, tel. 803/671-5777) has an impressive collection of American and English furniture, plus unusual pieces of Oriental and English porcelain.

Art Galleries In Hilton Head, the **Red Piano Art Gallery** (220 Cordillo Pkwy., tel. 803/785-2318) showcases works by island artists and craftsfolk. In Beaufort, the **Rhett Gallery** (809 Bay St., tel. 803/524-3339) sells Low Country art by Nancy Ricker Rhett, William Means Rhett, Stephen Elliot Webb, and James Moore Rhett.

Jewelry On Hilton Head, **The Bird's Nest** (Coligny Plaza, tel. 803/785-3737) sells locally made shell and sand-dollar jewelry. **The Goldsmith Shop** (3 Lagoon Rd., tel. 803/785-2538) features classic jewelry, island charms, custom designs, and repairs. **Touch of Turquoise** (The Market on Palmetto Bay Rd., tel. 803/842-3880) sells authentic Indian jewelry, sand-dollar pendants, and more. In Beaufort, **The Craftseller** (210 Scott St., tel. 803/525-6104) showcases jewelry and other items by Southern craftsfolk.

One of a Kind **The Christmas Shop** (Plantation Center near Palmetto Dunes entrance, tel. 803/785-6002) sells Christmas ornaments and trees, plus toys, dolls, and gifts for all seasons. The **Wicker Warehouse** (130 Matthews Dr., tel. 803/686-5511) has baskets, planters, rattan and wicker furniture, straw hats, and more.

Beaches

On Hilton Head Island, the ocean side features wide stretches of gently sloping white sand, extending for the island's entire 12-mile length. Many spots remain secluded and uncrowded. Although resort beaches are reserved for guests and residents, there are about 35 public beach entrances from Folly Field to South Forest Beach near Sea Pines. Two main parking areas are at Coligny Circle, near the Holiday Inn, and on Folly Field Road, off U.S. 278 near the Hilton Head Island Beach and Tennis Resort. Signs along U.S. 278 point the way to Bradley, Burkes, and Singleton beaches, where parking space is limited.

Hunting Island State Park has three miles of broad swimming beaches. **Edisto Beach State Park** on Edisto Island also has nearly three miles of public beach.

Participant Sports

Bicycling There are pathways in several areas of Hilton Head Island (many in the resorts), and pedaling is popular along the firmly packed beach. Bicycles can be rented at most hotels and resorts. One of the oldest rental shops here is **Harbour Town Bicycles** (Graves Plaza, Hwy. 278, tel. 803/785–3546; Sea Pines Plantation, tel. 803/671–7300; and Palmetto Dunes Resort, tel. 803/671–5386).

Fishing On Hilton Head, you can pick oysters, dig for clams, or cast for shrimp. Each year a billfishing tournament and two king mackerel tournaments attract anglers to the island.

Golf Many golf courses on Hilton Head Island are ranked among the world's top 100. Several resort courses are open for public play. Each April, Sea Pines's Harbour Town course is the site of the MCI Heritage Golf Classic, drawing top PGA stars.

Horseback Riding Many trails wind through woods and nature preserves. There are five fully equipped stables in the Hilton Head area: **Lawton Fields Stable** in Sea Pines (tel. 803/671–2586), **Moss Creek Plantation Equestrian Center** (tel. 803/785–4488), **Rose Hill Plantation Stables** (tel. 803/757–3082), **Sandy Creek Stables** near Spanish Wells (tel. 803/681–4610), and **Seabrook Farm Stables** in Hilton Head Plantation (tel. 803/681–5415).

Tennis There are more than 300 courts on Hilton Head. Three resorts —**Sea Pines** (tel. 803/785–3333), **Shipyard Plantation** (tel. 803/785–2313), and **Port Royal** (tel. 803/681–3322)—are rated among the top 50 tennis destinations in the United States. Racquet clubs that welcome guest play on clay, composition, hard-surface, synthetic, and even a few grass courts include **Port Royal Tennis Club** (tel. 803/681–3322), **Rod Laver Tennis** at Palmetto Dunes (tel. 803/785–1152), **Sea Pines Racquet Club** (tel. 803/671–2494), and **Van der Meer Tennis Center** (tel. 803/785–8388 or 800/845–6138). Each April, top professional women's stars participate in the Family Circle Magazine Cup Tennis Tournament at Sea Pines Racquet Club.

Windsurfing Lessons and rentals are available from **Windsurfing Hilton Head** at Sea Pines Resort's South Beach Marina (tel. 803/671–2643) and at Shelter Cove Plaza (tel. 803/686–6996).

Spectator Sports

Polo There are matches every other Sunday during spring and fall at **Rose Hill Plantation** (tel. 803/842–2828).

Dining

All along this stretch of South Carolina coastline, fresh seafood is showcased on menus. But Hilton Head Island is a cosmopolitan community, with restaurants to suit every palate. The most highly recommended restaurants in each price category are indicated by a star ★.

Category	Cost*
Very Expensive	over $25
Expensive	$15–$25
Moderate	$7–$15
Inexpensive	under $7

per person without tax (5% in South Carolina), service, or drinks

The following credit-card abbreviations are used: AE, American Express; CB, Carte Blanche; DC, Diners Club; MC, MasterCard; V, Visa.

Beaufort
Continental

The Anchorage House. The pre-Revolutionary ambience of this 1765 structure is enhanced by period furnishings, candlelight, and gleaming silver and crystal. Sherry-laced she-crab soup, crabmeat casserole, and other Low Country specialties share the menu with such Continental selections as veal piccata and steak *au poivre. 1103 Bay St., tel. 803/524–9392. Jackets suggested at dinner. Reservations suggested. AE, CB, DC, MC, V. Closed Sun., major holidays. Moderate–Expensive.*

Hilton Head Island
Continental

Harbourmaster's. With sweeping views of the harbor, this spacious, multilevel dining room offers such dishes as chateaubriand and New Zealand rack of lamb laced with a brandy demiglaze. Service is deft. *In Shelter Cove Marina, off U.S. 278, across from Palmetto Dunes, tel. 803/785–3030. Jacket required at dinner. Reservations required. AE, CB, DC, MC, V. Closed Sun. and for about a month in winter. Very Expensive.*

★ **The Barony.** An intimate series of softly lighted seating areas with "upscale country French" decor range off the main dining room, which is centered with a display of drop-dead desserts, marzipan flowers, and exotic cheeses and breads, spotlighted by a crystal chandelier. There's glittering crystal and silver, and a quartet of tuxedoed waiters for every table. In addition to the regular Low Country and Continental entrees, elegant low-calorie menus are offered, such as chilled coconut-and-pineapple soup, asparagus salad with quail eggs, sorbet, poached fillet of Dover sole with seafood mousse, and macédoine of fresh fruits with raspberry sauce. *The Westin Resort, Hilton Head Island (formerly Hotel Inter-Continental). 135 S. Port Royal Dr., tel. 803/681–4000. Jacket and tie required. Reservations suggested. AE, CB, DC, MC, V. Closed Mon. Expensive–Very Expensive.*

Fulvio's. A rather elegant, formal atmosphere, reinforced by deft service, prevails in this popular dining room. The menu emphasizes Italian specialties, such as a hearty and luscious *cioppino di frutti di mare*—a tomato-based stew of shellfish and vegetables. *New Orleans Rd. and U.S. 278, in Shipyard Center, tel. 803/681–6001. AE, CB, DC, MC, V. Closed Sun., holidays, first 2 wks in Jan. Dinner only. Expensive.*

Low Country

Old Fort Pub. Tucked away in a quiet site overlooking Skull Creek, this rustic restaurant specializes in such dishes as oyster pie, oysters wrapped in Smithfield ham, Savannah chicken-fried steak with onion gravy, and hoppin' john. *In Hilton Head Plantation, tel. 803/681–2386. Dress: informal. No reservations. AE, CB, DC, MC, V. No lunch Sun. Moderate.*

Seafood

Hemingway's. This oceanfront restaurant serves pompano *en papillote*, trout amandine with herbed lemon-butter sauce, fresh grilled seafoods, and steaks, in a relaxed, Key West–type atmosphere. *Hyatt Regency Hilton Head, in Palmetto Dunes Resort, tel. 803/785–1234. Dress: informal. Reservations suggested. AE, CB, DC, MC, V. Moderate.*

Hudson's Seafood House on the Docks. This huge, airy, family-owned restaurant has its own fishing fleet; catches are rushed straight from the boats to the kitchens. The dining room always seems full, but service is quick and friendly and diners never feel rushed. There's a separate oyster bar, as well as an adjacent family-style restaurant, The Landing. *1 Hudson Rd.,*

on the docks, tel. 803/681–2772. The Landing; 803/681–3363.
Dress: informal. No reservations. AE, MC, V. Moderate.

Lodging

Hilton Head Island is home to some of the nation's finest and most luxurious resort developments. **Sea Pines,** the oldest and best-known, occupies 4,500 choice, thickly wooded acres. Its three championship golf courses include renowned Harbour Town Links, designed by Pete Dye and Jack Nicklaus and one of the top 20 U.S. courses. There's a fine beach, two racquet clubs, riding stables, two shopping plazas, and a 500-acre forest preserve. Accommodations are in luxurious homes and villas fronting the ocean or the golf courses.

Sea Pines's emphasis on preserving the integrity of the island's ecology has set the tone for resorts that have followed. Among them, differences are subtle. In **Shipyard Plantation,** Marriott's Hilton Head Resort caters to groups from 50 to 1,500; its luxuriant garden setting, water sports, and fitness center make it a favorite with family vacationers as well. This plantation also has a wide array of villa condominiums, most overlooking an excellent golf facility with three championship nines. There's a racquet club and a small beach club.

Palmetto Dunes Resort includes the Hyatt Regency Hilton Head, the island's largest resort hotel. It has a concierge floor and extensive meeting space and services, making it especially appealing to groups. A good array of vacation packages attracts families as well. With kitchenettes and all-oceanfront rooms, the Mariner's Inn–A Clarion Hotel (also in Palmetto Dunes) is a great favorite with families and honeymooners. Palmetto Dunes is home of the renowned Rod Laver Tennis Center and has a good stretch of beach and three championship golf courses. In addition to its hotels, there are several luxury rental villa complexes overlooking the ocean.

At **Port Royal Plantation** is the new, super-luxurious Westin Resort, Hilton Head Island (formerly Hotel Inter-Continental Hilton Head Resort). With vast meeting spaces and an emphasis on upscale amenities, it caters to the upscale business traveler and middle-aged to older affluent vacationers. Not that families aren't warmly welcomed, but the atmosphere is a bit more formal than elsewhere on the island. Port Royal has three championship golf courses, which have hosted PGA events, and its racquet club offers play on clay, hard, and grass courts. There are also a few rental homes and a limited selection of villas.

Hilton Head Plantation, a private residential community, is on the northern, "quiet side" of the island. It has no rentals, but two of its golf courses are available for public play.

Not all lodgings are located within the resorts. The high-rise Holiday Inn, for example, occupies a choice patch of beach and is very popular with families and smaller groups. It's easily accessible from the main business area.

Hilton Head Central Reservations (Box 5312, Hilton Head Island, 29938, tel. 800/845–7018) is a good source of detailed information about various island resorts and properties. It represents almost every hotel, motel, and condominium-rental agency on the island.

Rates can drop appreciably in the off-season (on Hilton Head Island, Nov.–Mar.), and package plans are available year-round. The most highly recommended properties in each price category are indicated by a star ★.

Category	Cost*
Very Expensive	over $135
Expensive	$95–$135
Moderate	$50–$95
Inexpensive	under $50

double room; add 7% for taxes

The following credit-card abbreviations are used: AE, American Express; CB, Carte Blanche; DC, Diners Club; MC, MasterCard; V, Visa.

Beaufort
Inexpensive

Best Western Sea Island Motel. At this well-maintained resort inn in the downtown historic district, rooms feature period decor. *1015 Bay St., Box 532, 29902, tel. 803/524–4121 or 800/528–1234. 43 rooms. Facilities: pool, cable TV, restaurant, lounge. AE, CB, DC, MC, V.*

Holiday Inn of Beaufort. This motor inn is conveniently located for visitors to Parris Island or the Marine Corps Air Station. *U.S. 21 and Lovejoy St., Box 1008, 29902, tel. 803/524–2144 or 800/465–4329. 152 rooms. Facilities: heated pool, tennis, cable TV/movies, restaurant, lounge with live entertainment. AE, CB, DC, MC, V.*

Edisto Island
Moderate–
Expensive

Fairfield Ocean Ridge Resort. This is a good choice for vacationers seeking to combine all the resort amenities with a get-away-from-it-all setting. There are accommodations in well-furnished two- and three-bedroom villa units tastefully decorated in contemporary style. *1 King Cotton Rd., Box 27, 29438, tel. 803/869–2561. 110 units. Facilities: pool, wading pool, beach, marina, fishing, tennis, golf, miniature golf, social and recreational programs, children's activities, nature trails, playground, restaurant, lounge, AE, CB, DC, MC, V.*

Fripp Island
Moderate–
Expensive

Fripp Island Resort. The resort encompasses the entire island, and access is limited to guests only. The two- and three-bedroom villas are contemporary in decor. *19 mi south of Beaufort via U.S. 21, 1 Tarpon Blvd., 29920, tel. 803/838–2441 or 800/845–4100. 133 units. Facilities: pools, tennis courts, championship golf course, full-service marina with rental boats, bicycle and jogging trails, laundry, children's program, 3 restaurants. AE, MC, V.*

Hilton Head Island
Very Expensive

Hyatt Regency Hilton Head. At this newly renovated oceanside hotel, the rooms have been lavishly redecorated. Some have balconies. *U.S. 278, in Palmetto Dunes Resort, Box 6167, 29938, tel. 803/785–1234 or 800/228–9000, 800/268–7530 Canada. 505 rooms. Facilities: pools, health club, sailboats, concierge floor, extensive convention facilities, cable TV/movies, coffee shop, dining rooms, lounges, entertainment, dancing. Guests have privileges at 3 18-hole championship golf courses and 25 hard, grass, and clay tennis courts at Palmetto Dunes, plus its 3 mi of private beach. AE, CB, DC, MC, V.*

★ **The Westin Resort, Hilton Head Island** (formerly Hotel Inter-

Continental Hilton Head). Among the island's newest luxury properties, this horseshoe-shaped hotel sprawls in a lushly landscaped oceanside setting. The expansive guest rooms, most with ocean view, are furnished in a pleasing mix of period reproduction and contemporary furnishings. All have comfortable seating areas and desks. Public areas display museum-quality Oriental porcelains, screens, paintings, and furnishings. *At Port Royal Resort, 135 S. Port Royal Dr., 29928, tel. 803/681–4000 or 800/228–3000. 416 rooms. Facilities: pool and ocean swimming, water sports, health club, restaurants (see the Barony in Dining), lounge with live entertainment, pianist in elegant lobby lounge. AE, CB, DC, MC, V.*

Expensive– **Mariner's Inn–A Clarion Hotel.** There's a Caribbean-island feel
Very Expensive to this five-story resort hotel set in an enclave. The grounds are beautifully landscaped. All oceanside, the rooms are spacious and colorfully decorated in a modern style. *In Palmetto Dunes Resort, 21 Ocean Ln., Box 6165, 29938, tel. 803/842–8000 or 800/845–8001. 324 rooms. Facilities: pool, health club, sauna, whirlpool, volleyball, canoeing, fishing, biking, sailing, restaurant, full resort privileges of Palmetto Dunes. AE, CB, DC, MC, V.*

Marriott's Hilton Head Resort. This oceanside hotel has spacious rooms with informally elegant tropical decor and ocean, garden, or forest views. The lobby is highlighted by a dramatic five-story atrium. Pathways wind amid lagoons and gardens to a wide, sandy private beach. *130 Shipyard Dr., Shipyard Plantation, 29928, tel. 803/842–2400 or 800/228–9290. 338 rooms and suites. Facilities: pool, exercise rooms, sauna, rental catamarans, restaurants, privileges at nearby golf and tennis clubs. AE, CB, DC, MC, V.*

Expensive **Holiday Inn Oceanfront Resort.** This handsome high-rise motor hotel is located on a broad, quiet stretch of beach. The rooms are spacious and well furnished in a contemporary style. *S. Forest Beach Dr., Box 5728, 29928, tel. 803/785–5126 or 800/465–4329. 200 rooms. Facilities: outdoor pool, poolside bar, restaurant, lounge with entertainment, beauty salon, boat, children's programs, golf, tennis, marina privileges. AE, CB, DC, MC, V.*

Inexpensive– **Red Roof Inn.** This two-story inn at the center of the island is
Moderate especially popular with families. It's a short drive to the public beaches. *5 Regency Pkwy. (U.S. 278), 29928, tel. 803/686–6808 or 800/848–7878. 112 units. Facilities: cable TV/movies. AE, DC, MC, V.*

The Arts

Community Playhouse (Arrow Rd., tel. 803/785–4878) presents up to 10 musicals or dramatic productions each year and offers a theater program for youths. During the warmer months, there are free outdoor concerts at **Harbour Town** and **Shelter Cove.** Concerts, plays, films, art shows, theater—along with sporting events, food fairs, and minitournaments—make up Hilton Head Island's **SpringFest,** which runs for the entire month of March. For information, contact SpringFest (Box 5278-D, Hilton Head Island, SC 29938, tel. 803/842–3378).

Nightlife

Dancing At the **Battery** (tel. 803/681–4000), in The Westin Resort, Hilton Head Island, at Port Royal Resort, there's entertainment every night except Monday and dancing nightly to a five-piece band. At **Club Indigo** (tel. 803/785–1234), a large cabaret downstairs at the Hyatt Regency Hilton Head, there is dancing and two shows nightly Monday through Saturday. At the **Mockingbird Lounge** (tel. 803/842–2400), in the Marriott's Hilton Head Resort, Shipyard Plantation, there's a dance band at night Monday through Saturday. **Scarlett's** (tel. 803/842–8500), a sophisticated oceanfront night spot at Mariner's Inn, Palmetto Dunes, features smooth jazz nightly. At **W.G. Shucker's** (tel. 803/785–8050), a lively spot on Palmetto Bay Road, there's dancing on the island's largest dance floor. **White Parrott** (tel. 803/785–5126), a locally popular lounge in the Holiday Inn Oceanfront Resort, has nightly entertainment.

Easy Listening **Cafe Europa** (tel. 803/671–3399), at the Lighthouse in Harbourtown, has nightly piano entertainment. **The Gazebo** (tel. 803/681–4000), The Westin Resort, Hilton Head Island's opulent lobby lounge overlooking tropical grounds and the ocean, offers classical entertainment at the grand piano afternoons and early evenings every night but Saturday. **Hemingway's Lounge** (tel. 803/785–1234), adjoining Hemingway's at the Palmetto Dunes Resort, has live entertainment in a casually elegant setting. **The Marsh Tacky** (tel. 803/681–4000), an oceanfront lounge at The Westin Resort, Hilton Head Island at Port Royal, has informal entertainment every night but Sunday. **Playful Pelican** (tel. 803/681–4000), the pool bar at the same location, has a live calypso band Tuesday through Sunday from 1 to 4 PM.

The Heartland

South Carolina's Heartland, between the coastal Low Country and the mountainous Upcountry, is a remarkably varied region of fertile farmland and vast forests of pines and hardwoods, of swamps and flowing rivers. Lakes Murray, Marion, and Moultrie offer some of the best fishing anywhere. They and the many state parks are also popular hunting, hiking, swimming, and camping areas.

At the center of the region is the state capital, Columbia. This is an engaging contemporary city superimposed on cherished historic remnants—a city of restored elegant antebellum and turn-of-the-century mansions, several museums, a vibrant university, a wide variety of dining choices, a lively arts scene, and one of the country's best zoos.

In Aiken, the center of South Carolina's Thoroughbred Country, such champions as Kelso and Pleasant Colony were trained. Here the beautiful scenery is enhanced by splendid homes built in the late 19th and early 20th centuries by wintering wealthy Northerners such as the Vanderbilts and the Whitneys.

Throughout the region, towns like Ninety Six, Sumter, and Camden preserve and interpret the past, with historic re-creations, exhibits, and restorations; and public gardens—such as Edisto Memorial Gardens in Orangeburg, Swan Lake Iris Gardens in Sumter, and Hopeland Gardens in Aiken—provide islands of color during much of the year.

Getting Around

By Plane Columbia Metro Airport is served by American, Delta, Eastern, United, and USAir.

By Car I–77 leads into Columbia from the north. I–26 travels from the Upcountry southeast to Columbia, then continues to Charleston. Beginning at Florence, I–20 travels west to Columbia, then heads southwest, entering Georgia near Augusta. I–95 sweeps northeast–southwest through the eastern edge of the area. U.S. 1 traverses the Heartland from North Carolina to Camden, Columbia, and Aiken before crossing the Savannah River to Augusta.

By Train Amtrak makes stops at Camden, Columbia, Denmark, Dillon, Florence and Kingstree in the Heartland.

By Bus Greyhound-Trailways serves all of South Carolina.

Important Addresses and Numbers

Tourist Information Greater Abbeville Chamber of Commerce, 104 Pickens St., Abbeville 29620, tel. 803/459–4600. Open weekdays 9–5, Saturday 10:30–3:30. Greater Aiken Chamber of Commerce, 400 Laurens St. NW, Box 892, Aiken 29802, tel. 803/648–0485. Open weekdays 9–5. Greater Columbia Convention and Visitors Bureau, State Museum Complex, 301 Gervais St., Columbia 29201, tel. 803/254–0479 or 800/248–4588. Open weekdays 8:30–5, Saturday 10–5, Sunday 1–5. Kershaw County Chamber of Commerce, 700 W. DeKalb St., Box 605, Camden 29020, tel. 803/432–2525. Open weekdays 9–5. Santee Cooper Counties Promotion Commission, U.S. 301 south of SC 6, Drawer 40, Santee 29142, tel. 803/854–2131 or 800/227–8510. Open weekdays 9–5.

Emergencies Dial 911 for emergency assistance.

Dentists Emergency care is available at The Dentist Place in the Columbia Mall (tel. 803/736–5300).

Pharmacies Taylor Street Pharmacy, on Taylor St. at Pickens in Columbia (tel. 803/256–1611), is open 7 AM–midnight daily.

Guided Tours

Orientation Tours Self-guided tour maps and brochures are available at the Abbeville, Aiken, and Kershaw County chambers of commerce (*see* Important Addresses and Numbers). The Aiken chamber also offers a 90-minute tour of the historic district, including homes, gardens, and stables, and will customize tours to suit individual interests.

Special-Interest Tours Historic Columbia Foundation (tel. 803/252–7742) offers historical tours.

Exploring the Heartland

Beginning and ending in Columbia, our tour takes you through the Heartland's historic towns and cities, lovely gardens, Thoroughbred horse country, and a state mega-resort park. This tour covers a large area and should be taken in leisurely segments, with stops along the way to attend equestrian events, visit a winery, canoe through picturesque swamps, or whatever moves you at the moment.

Columbia In 1786, South Carolina's capital was moved from Charleston to Columbia, in the center of the state along the banks of the Congaree River. One of the nation's first planned cities, Columbia soon became a center of political, commercial, cultural, and social activity.

But all of this changed abruptly in early 1865 when General William Tecumseh Sherman and his 60,000 well-equipped Union troops invaded South Carolina with a destructive determination described by a New York newspaper reporter as 50 times worse than the earlier march through Georgia. Two-thirds of Columbia was incinerated; fortunately, the handsome State House, Governor's Mansion, and University of South Carolina campus were among the fine homes and public buildings that were spared.

Our tour begins at the **State House** (Capitol), begun in 1855 of native blue granite in the Italian Renaissance style. Six bronze stars on the outer western wall mark direct hits by Sherman's cannons. The interior is richly appointed with brass, marble, mahogany, artworks, and a replica of Jean Antoine Houdon's statue of George Washington. *Main and Gervais Sts., tel. 803/ 734-2430. Free guided tours every half-hour. Open weekdays 9-4.*

The **Fort Jackson Museum,** Building 4442 on the grounds of the U.S. Army Training Center, displays armaments, heavy equipment from the two world wars, and exhibits on the life of Andrew Jackson. *Tel. 803/751-7419. Admission free. Open Tues.-Sun. 1-4. Closed Mon., holidays.*

The **McKissick Museum** on the University of South Carolina campus features art, history, geology, gemstones, the Bernard Baruch silver collection, and the **20th Century Fox Movietonews Film Library,** where newsreel footage filmed throughout the world from 1919 to 1963 has been preserved. Selected segments can be viewed on the first floor. *Tel. 803/777-7251. Admission free. Open weekdays 9-4, Sat. 10-5, Sun. 1-5. Closed major holidays.*

The **Columbia Museum of Arts and Sciences** showcases the impressive Kress Foundation Collection of Renaissance and Baroque treasures, sculpture, decorative arts, and European and American paintings, with special emphasis on works by Southeastern artists. *1527 Senate St., tel. 803/799-2810. Admission: $2 adults; $1 children 6-12, under 6 free; free for all on Wed. Open Tues., Thurs., Fri. 10-5; Wed. 12-9; weekends 1-5. Closed Mon., major holidays.*

Exhibits at the **South Carolina State Museum,** in a large, refurbished textile mill, interpret the state's natural history, archaeology, historical development, technological and artistic accomplishments. In the onetime water tank of the old mill is the Visitor Center, with exhibits and a 12-projector slide presentation on the region. *301 Gervais St., tel. 803/737-4595. Admission: $3 adults; $2 senior citizens, military, students with ID; $1.25 children 6-17, under 6 free. Open Mon.-Sat. 10-5, Sun. 1-5. Closed Christmas.*

Among the Columbia homes that have been restored and opened to the public is the **Hampton-Preston Mansion,** dating from 1818 and filled with lavish furnishings collected by three generations of two influential families. *1615 Blanding St., tel. 803/252-7742. Admission for this and the following 2 houses is $5 adults, $4.50 members of AAA, $2.50 students; singly, each house is $2 adults, $1.50 members of AAA, $1 students. Tours are given throughout the day.*

The classic columned 1823 **Robert Mills House** (1616 Blanding St., tel. 803/252-7742), was named for its architect-designer who later gained fame as the architect of the Washington Monument. It has opulent Regency furniture, marble mantels, sterling-silver doorknobs, and spacious grounds. Nearby is the **Woodrow Wilson Boyhood Home** (1705 Hampton St., tel. 803/254-7742), displaying the gaslights, arched doorways, and ornate furnishings of the Victorian period.

Riverbanks Zoological Park, among the nation's finest, showcases over 800 animals and birds, some endangered, in natural habitats. Walk along pathways and through landscaped gardens to view such specimens as polar bears, Siberian tigers, and American bald eagles. The South American primate collection has won international acclaim, and the park is noted for its success in breeding endangered and fragile species. There's also a botanical garden, a reptile house, and an aquarium. *Near jct. I-26 and U.S. 76 at Greystone Riverbanks exit, tel. 803/779-8717 or 803/779-8730. Admission: $3.25 adults, $2.50 students over 12, $1.75 senior citizens, $1.25 children 6-12. Open daily 9-4 (until 5 during summer weekends with no one admitted after 4). Taped self-guided tours for the visually impaired and wheelchairs are available.*

From Columbia, drive northeast on I-20 for 32 miles to **Camden.** Dating from 1732, charming Camden is South Carolina's oldest inland community. British General Lord Cornwallis established a garrison here during the Revolutionary War, and the Royals burned most of Camden before evacuating it. Today, the town flourishes as a significant center for the fine arts and for the breeding, training, and exhibition of Thoroughbred horses (*see* Spectator Sports).

Historic Camden, a historic park, re-creates the British occupation of 1780 on the site of the early 19th-century village of Camden. Several house restorations include displays of historic items. Cornwallis had his headquarters at the two-story **Joseph Kershaw Mansion** (ca. 1770), which has been reconstructed and furnished in the style of the period. Nature trails, fortifications, a powder magazine, a picnic area, a farmyard with animals, and a crafts shop are also here. *On U.S. 521, 3 mi north of I-20, tel. 803/432-9841. Admission: $1.50 adults, $1 children. Open Tues.-Sat. 10-5, Sun. 1-5 June-Aug.; Tues.-Fri. 10-4, Sat. 10-5, Sun. 1-5 rest of year. Closed Mon. except when a holiday.*

From Camden, drive southeast on U.S. 521 for 30 miles to **Sumter.** Named for the Revolutionary War hero and statesman General Thomas Sumter, the city was settled about 1740 as the center of a cultivated plantation district. Today it is home to varied industries, lumbering, agricultural marketing and nearby Shaw Air Force Base.

The **Williams-Brice Museum and Archives,** headquarters of the Sumter County Historical Society, are housed in a lovely Victorian Gothic residence dating from 1845. Displays showcase fine period furnishings, Oriental carpeting, vintage carriages, dolls, various historic items. Archival records are valuable for tracing family roots. *122 N. Washington, tel. 803/775-0908. Admission free. Open Tues.–Sat. 10–5, Sun. 2–5 (archives open Wed.–Sat. 2–5). Museum closed Mon.*

Swan Lake Iris Gardens contain numerous varieties of Dutch, Japanese, and other irises, which bloom late May through June. There are plantings for other seasons as well in this glorious setting of ancient cypresses, tall pines, and oaks. Black Australian and white mute swans float among lily pads on a lake. Nature trails, a playground, and a picnic area are available. *W. Liberty St., tel. 803/773-9363. Admission free. Open daily 8 AM–dusk.*

From Sumter, drive south on U.S. 15 and I-95 to U.S. 301, then west to Orangeburg, a total of about 59 miles. Along the way, you may want to stop off at the **Santee State Park,** on Lake Marion, with excellent fishing (*see* Participant Sports), plus golf, tennis, nature trails, and cabin and camping accommodations. (For more information, contact the Santee Cooper Promotion Commission—*see* Important Addresses and Numbers.)

In Orangeburg, **Edisto Memorial Gardens** occupies 110 acres of former swampland along the North Edisto River, noted for its black waters. During late March and early April, azaleas and other seasonal plantings come to bloom among live oaks, crab apple, cypress, dogwoods, and camellias. From mid-April to mid-November, over 300 varieties of roses produce glowing colors. The South Carolina Festival of Roses, with arts and crafts, live entertainment, and golf and tennis tournaments, is held here the first weekend in May. *Off U.S. 301, 7 mi from I-26, Exit 145, tel. 803/534-6211 or 534-6821. Free. Open daily during daylight hours.*

Head south along U.S. 301/601, then west on U.S. 78 to **Aiken,** about 64 miles altogether. Aiken's international fame as Thoroughbred Country began during the 1890s, when wealthy Northerners began wintering here in stately mansions and entertaining themselves with lavish parties and equestrian activities. Many of these mansions—some with up to 90 rooms —remain as testaments to this era of extravagance.

Since those days, the area's horse farms have produced many national champions, which are honored at the **Thoroughbred Racing Hall of Fame** with exhibitions of horse-related artworks, paintings, and sculptures, plus racing silks and trophies. *Tel. 803/649-7700. Admission free. Open Sept.–May, Tues.–Sun. 2–5. Closed Mon. and Jun.–Aug.* The Hall of Fame is on the grounds of the 14-acre **Hopeland Gardens,** with seasonal plantings along winding paths, quiet terraces, and reflecting pools. There's a Touch and Scent Trail with Braille plaques. Open-air free concerts are presented on Monday evenings and theatrical performances on Thursday evenings mid-July–Aug. *Dupree Place, corner of Whiskey Rd., tel. 803/642-7630. Admission free. Open daily 10–sunset.*

The **Aiken County Historical Museum,** devoted to early regional culture, has Indian artifacts, firearms, an authentically furnished 1808 log cabin, a one-room schoolhouse, and a replica of *Best Friend*, the first passenger steam train in the United States. *433 Newberry St. SW, tel. 803/642-2015. Admission free. Open Tues.–Fri. 9:30-4:30, first Sun. of each month 2-5. Otherwise, closed Sat.–Mon.*

About 64 miles from Aiken is **Hickory Knob State Resort Park**—a total vacation experience. To get there, go northwest on SC 19 and U.S. 25 to U.S. 378, drive west to the town of Mc-Cormick, then continue south until you see signs for the park.

On the shore of Clarks Hill Lake, the park offers fishing, waterskiing, sailing, motorboating; a swimming pool; an equestrian center and bridle paths; nature trails; an 18-hole championship golf course, a fully equipped pro shop, and carpet golf; tennis courts; and skeet, trap, and archery ranges. If none of these are to your liking, bring your favorite canine for a training session on the four-mile bird-dog field-trial area. A 60-room lodge, nine duplex lakeside cottages, and campgrounds, plus a restaurant round out Hickory Knob's offerings. *Rte. 1, Box 199B, McCormick 29835, tel. 803/443-2151. Office open daily 7 AM–11 PM.*

Heading Back   Return to McCormick via U.S. 378, then drive northwest on SC 28 and SC 72 to Abbeville, a distance of about 30 miles. This may well be one of inland South Carolina's most satisfying, though lesser-known, small towns. In Abbeville the "Southern cause" was born and died, for here the first organized secession meeting was held and here on May 2, 1865, Confederate President Jefferson Davis officially disbanded the armies of the defeated South in the last meeting of his War Council. The 1830 house where the Council met—the **Burt-Stark Mansion** (313 Greenville, tel. 803/459-2457)—is now a private home open Saturday 1–5, other times by appointment. Admission is $2.

Your first stop should be the **Chamber of Commerce** at 104 Pickens Street (for hours, *see* Important Addresses and Numbers) for an audiovisual presentation and informational materials.

The **Abbeville County Museum** is in an old jail, but even those who lack appreciation for old jails will enjoy the memorabilia, the log cabin restorations, and the gardens. *Tel. 803/459-2740.*

The **Abbeville Opera House** (tel. 803/459-2157) faces the historic town square. Built in 1908, it has been renovated to reflect the grandeur of the days when lavish road shows and stellar entertainers came center stage. Current productions range from light, contemporary comedies to Broadway-style musicals.

About 14 miles away on SC 72 is **Greenwood.** Founded by Irish settlers in 1802, the city received its name from the gently rolling landscape and dense forests. Andrew Johnson, the 17th U.S. president, operated a tailor shop at Courthouse Square before migrating to eastern Tennessee.

The **George W. Park Seed Co.,** one of the nation's largest seed supply houses, maintains colorful experimental gardens and greenhouses. Floral displays are especially vivid during mid-summer. There are guided tours, and visitors may purchase seeds and bulbs in the company's store. The South Carolina Festival of Flowers—with such events as a performing-artists contest, a beauty pageant, private home and garden tours, and live entertainment—is held here annually the second week in July. *On SC 245, 7 mi north of town, tel. 803/223–7333. Free. Open weekdays 8–4:30. Guided tours are given until 2:30 PM; phone ahead for an appointment.*

Drive south and east on U.S. 25 and SC 34, then south on SC 248, a total distance of about 10 miles to the **Ninety Six National Historic Site.** Here the first Revolutionary War battle in South Carolina was fought in November 1775. The site, however, commemorates a more significant engagement in 1781, when Gen. Nathanael Greene's Patriot troops managed to dislodge a force of British Loyalists. The visitor center museum has descriptive displays, and there's a self-guided trail past remnants of the old village, a reconstructed French and Indian War stockade, and Revolutionary-era fortifications. Archaeological digs and historic restoration work are still underway. The nearby town of Ninety Six was along an Indian trade route and derives its unusual name from its distance from the Cherokee village of Keowee in the Blue Ridge Mountains. *2 mi south of town via SC 248, tel. 803/543–4068. Admission free. Open daily 8–5 except Jan. 1 and Dec. 25.*

From Ninety Six, a drive of about 69 miles along NC 242 and U.S. 178/378 takes you back to Columbia (past the fisherman's paradise Lake Murray) and concludes the tour. Those with more time may find it well spent with an excursion into the **Upcountry,** the northwest corner of the state. Beautiful anytime, the 130-mile **Cherokee Foothills Scenic Highway** (SC 11) is especially delightful in spring and autumn, when the Blue Ridge Mountains are carpeted with wildflowers or ablaze with foliage. For more information on the route and sights, *see* Great Itineraries at the front of this guide. The Upcountry has long been a favorite regional family vacation destination, with abundant man-made and natural lakes, and several state parks providing all manner of recreational activities. Also in the area, such comfortable communities as Greenville, Spartanburg, Clemson, Pendleton, and Anderson take justifiable pride in their educational institutions, museums, historic preservation, and cultural accomplishments. For more information on the Upcountry, contact: Discover Upcountry Carolina Association (Box 3132, Greenville, SC 29602, tel. 803/233–2690).

Off the Beaten Track

Historic Brattonsville, 4 miles east of McConnells on SC 322, recreates Heartland lifestyles from the mid-1700s to antebellum times. An 1840 home serves as a visitor center and displays vintage tools and documents. Other structures include a backwoods cabin from the 1750s, a pre-Revolutionary War home with an addition built about 1839, an authentically furnished 1820s homestead and subsidiary buildings. *Tel. 803/ 684–2327. Admission: $2 adults, $1 students. Open Tues. and Thurs. 10–4, weekends 2–5. Tours available on the hour.*

Mepkin Abbey, 13 miles southeast of Moncks Corner off SC 402, is a splendid Roman Catholic monastery on a former rice plantation. Here Henry Luce, famed *Time* and *Life* publisher, and his wife, Clare Booth Luce, playwright, member of Congress, editor, and ambassador, lie buried. The public is welcome to visit the garden grounds and chapel. *Tel. 803/761–8509. Admission free. Open daily 9–4:30.*

The **NMPA Stock Car Hall of Fame/Joe Weatherly Museum** at the Darlington Raceway has the world's largest collection of racing cars, trophies, and memorabilia. Vehicles of such greats as Fireball Roberts, Richard Petty, Buddy Baker, David Pearson and Bill Elliott are on display. You can also experience the sensation of a ride around the Raceway's trick track via a Unocal simulator in Richard Petty's Pontiac. *On SC 34 near junction with U.S. 52 bypass. Tel. 803/393–2103. Admission: $2 adults, under 13 free. Open daily 9–5.*

Andrew Jackson State Park in a district of rolling hills known as the Waxhaws memorializes the 7th President of the United States. He was born in the area, though the exact place is unknown, and both the Carolinas claim him as a native son. Relics of pioneer times are displayed in a museum and one-room log school. A stunning equestrian statue by Anna Hyatt Huntington depicts a youthful Jackson departing his homeland. *On U.S. 521, 8 mi north of Lancaster. Tel. 803/285–3344. Admission free. Park open daylight hours in summer, 9–6 rest of year; museum open weekends 1–5.*

Shopping

Antiques and Flea Markets Many of Columbia's antique outlets are in the Congaree Vista Shopping District concentrated on Huger and Gervais streets, between the State House and the river. Others are across the river on Meeting and State streets in West Columbia. About 70 dealers have established varied and reasonably priced shops, along with flea markets, at the **Old Mill Antique Mall** (310 State St., W. Columbia, tel. 803/796–4229).

Arts and Crafts The spacious, tree-shaded Town Square in Abbeville is lined with attractive gift and specialty shops in restored historic buildings dating from the late 1800s. **Historic Camden** also has gifts and crafts for sale.

Farmer's Market The **State Farmer's Market** in Columbia (Bluff Rd., tel. 803/ 737–3016) is one of the 10 largest in the country. Seasonal fresh vegetables are sold each weekday, along with flowers, plants, dairy products, poultry, and more.

Flower Seeds and Bulbs The **George W. Park Seed Co.** in Greenwood has a retail shop at the colorful test gardens, where you will find a massive assortment of seeds and bulbs for successful gardening (*also see* Heading Back in Exploring the Heartland).

Wines In the retail shop at **Truluck Vineyards** near Lake City (about 40 mi east of Sumter on U.S. 378, tel. 803/389–3400), you're welcome to sample and purchase wines. You can tour the 70 acres of grapevines, the fermentation room, and the cellar. There are also nature trails and a birdwatching path.

Participant Sports

Canoeing A haunting canoe trail leads into a remote swampy depression at **Woods Bay State Park** (from Sumter, take U.S. 378E to U.S. 301N, tel. 803/659–4445), where rentals are available. Self-guided canoe trails traverse an alluvial floodplain bordered by high bluffs at the **Congaree Swamp National Monument** (20 mi southeast of Columbia off SC 48, tel. 803/765–5571), where canoes can be rented.

Fishing **Lakes Marion** and **Moultrie,** formed by power dams on the Santee and Cooper rivers, attract serious anglers eager for catches
of bream, crappie, striped bass, catfish, and large- and small-
mouth bass. Supply stores, fish camps, professional guides,
rental facilities, and overnight accommodations abound in the
area. For information, contact Santee Cooper Counties Promotion Commission (Drawer 40, Santee, SC 29142, tel. 803/854–
2131).

Golf The many fine courses in the area include **Sedgewood** in Columbia (tel. 803/776–2177) and **Highland Park Country Club** in
Aiken (tel. 803/649–6029).

Hiking **Congaree Swamp National Monument** (*see* Canoeing) has 22
miles of trails for hikers and nature lovers and a ¾-mile boardwalk for handicapped visitors. For information on trails in the
Francis Marion National Forest and the **Sumter National Forest,** contact the National Forest Service (1835 Assembly St.,
Columbia 29201, tel. 803/765–5222).

White-water Columbia is one of the few cities located on a navigable white-
Ventures water river. Rafting, kayaking, and canoeing on the Saluda
River offer challenging Class 3 and Class 4 rapids. Guided river
and swamp excursions are also offered. Inquire at the Greater
Columbia Visitors Center in the State Museum (301 Gervais
St., tel. 803/254–0479). In the Upcountry, the Chattooga National Wild and Scenic River, on the border of South Carolina
and Georgia, provides guided rafting, canoeing or kayaking
trips. Contact Discover Upcountry Carolina Association (Box
3132, Greenville, SC 29602, tel. 803/233–2690).

Spectator Sports

Baseball The **Columbia Mets** (tel. 803/256–4110), a Class A affiliate of
the New York Mets, play from mid-April through August.
Home turf is Capital City Park.

Equestrian Events In Aiken, polo matches are played at Whitney Field on Sunday
afternoons September–December, February, and March (tel.
803/648–7874). Three weekends in March are set aside for the
famed **Triple Crown**—Thoroughbred trials of promising year-
lings, a steeplechase, and harness races by young horses
making their debut (tel. 803/648–0485). Camden offers two
steeplechase events: the Carolina Cup in late March or early
April and the Colonial Cup in November (tel. 803/432–6513).

Stock Car Races **Darlington Raceway** (SC 34, 2 mi west of Darlington, tel. 803/
393–5442) is the scene of two stellar racing events featuring top
drivers. NASCAR's TranSouth 500, Winston Cup Series, is
scheduled in mid-April. Labor Day weekend is set aside for the
exciting Southern 500.

Dining

South Carolina Heartland fare ranges from regional specialties
like barbecue and country ham with red-eye gravy to
unselfconscious Continental cuisine. This is a great place to discover a Southern institution—one of the family-style "fish
camps" serving lavish portions of fresh catfish and other
catches from nearby rivers and lakes.

In Columbia, ethnic and specialty restaurants have appeared at a rapid clip in recent years. Costs throughout the region, you'll discover, usually remain pleasingly moderate.

The most highly recommended restaurants in each price category are indicated by a star ★.

Category	Cost*
Very Expensive	over $25
Expensive	$15–$25
Moderate	$7–$15
Inexpensive	under $7

*per person without tax (5% in South Carolina), service, or drinks

The following credit-card abbreviations are used: AE, American Express; CB, Carte Blanche; DC, Diners Club; MC, MasterCard; V, Visa.

Abbeville
Pennsylvania Dutch
★
Yoder's Dutch Kitchen. In the heart of the Sun Belt, here's Pennsylvania Dutch home cooking that's the real thing. There's a daily lunch buffet and (Tues.–Sat.) evening offering many choices, such as smorgasbord fried chicken, stuffed cabbage, Dutch meat loaf, sausage and kraut, breaded veal parmesan, baked chicken and dressing, and plenty of vegetables. Shoo-fly pie, Dutch bread, apple butter, home-made salad dressings, and other house specialties can be bought to go. *U.S. 72, tel. 803/459–5556. No reservations. Dress: informal. No credit cards. Moderate.*

Columbia
American
★
The Chopping Block. This traditional local favorite features delectable prime rib, sautéed mushrooms, king crab feast, chicken and lobster, grilled swordfish, clam chowder, garden fresh veggies, a bountiful salad bar, and a cocktail lounge. A meat cleaver embedded in an antique chopping block at the entrance provides the name. *1021 Briargate Circle, tel. 803/772–2011. Reservations suggested but not required. Dress: informal. AE, DC, MC, V. Expensive.*

Barbecue
★
Maurice Bessinger's Piggie Park. One of the South's best-known barbecue chefs, Maurice has a fervent national following for his mustard sauce-based, pit-cooked ham barbecue. He also serves barbecued chicken, ribs, and baked beans, plus hash over rice, onion rings, hushpuppies, cole slaw, fresh lemonade and orangeade, and home-baked desserts. *1600 Charleston Hwy., tel. 803/796–0220. No reservations. Dress: informal. No credit cards. Closed Sun., major holidays. Inexpensive to moderate.*

Mixed Menu
★
California Dreaming. A splendid example of adaptive use, here's dining in an airy, greenery-bedecked space that is the renovated old Union Train Station. Specialties include prime rib, barbecued baby back ribs, Mexican dishes, and homemade pasta. There's a lounge and a disc jockey. *401 S. Main St., tel. 803/254–6767. Dress informal. No reservations. AE, MC, V. Inexpensive to Moderate.*

Southern
Morrison's Cafeteria. The airy and attractive dining rooms of this popular chain serve basic Southern cookery, featuring

fresh vegetables and homemade breads and desserts. *124 Columbia Mall, 2 Notch Rd., tel. 803/788–9370; Dutch Square Mall, tel. 803/772–9000; Wood Hill Center, 6084 Garner's Ferry Rd., tel. 803/783–3266. No reservations. Dress: informal. MC, V. Closed major holidays. Inexpensive.*

Lodging

In addition to the accommodations listed here, you might seek out chains and bed-and-breakfasts in the area. For a list of B&Bs, write to the South Carolina Division of Tourism (Box 71, Columbia, SC 29202, tel. 803/734–0122) and ask for the pamphlet "South Carolina's Historic Inns, Country Inns & Bed & Breakfast."

The most highly recommended properties in each price category are indicated by a star ★.

Category	Cost*
Very Expensive	over $100
Expensive	$75–$100
Moderate	$40–$75
Inexpensive	under $40

*double room; add 7% for taxes

The following credit-card abbreviations are used: AE, American Express; CB, Carte Blanche; DC, Diners Club; MC, MasterCard; V, Visa.

Abbeville
Moderate
★
The Belmont Inn. Built just after the turn of the century, this Spanish-style structure has been lovingly restored and is a popular overnight stop with Opera House visitors. Rooms are immaculate, comfortably furnished rather than opulent. White spreads cover brass beds, and antique quilts decorate some walls. Package plans are offered that include dinner in the inn's charming restaurant and tickets to the theater. *106 E. Pickens St., Abbeville 29620, tel. 803/459–9625. 24 rooms. Facilities: restaurant, lounge. AE, MC, V.*

Aiken
Moderate-Expensive
Willcox Inn. This newly refurbished inn, built in grand style in the early 1900s, has hosted Winston Churchill, Franklin D. Roosevelt, and the Astors. The lobby is graced with massive stone fireplaces, rosewood pine woodwork, pegged oak floors, and Oriental rugs. The room decor reflects the inn's early days, with floral-print spreads and high four-poster beds. *100 Colleton Ave., Aiken 29801, tel. 803/649–1377. 30 rooms, 6 suites. Facilities: clay tennis court, lawn croquet, dining room, bar. MC, V.*

Inexpensive-Moderate
Comfort Inn. The chain is notable for comfortable, well-maintained accommodations at no-frills prices. This facility is conveniently located for access to Hopeland Gardens, the Masters Golf Tournament, and Thoroughbred Hall of Fame. *2660 Columbia Hwy. (jct. I-20 and U.S. 1), Aiken 29801, tel. 803/642–5692 or 800/228–5150. 78 rooms. Facilities: pool, in-room movies.*

Camden
Moderate
Aberdeen Inn. A graceful historic home (ca. 1810) in the heart of town has been transformed into a bed-and-breakfast inn

(serving a full breakfast). Public areas have antique furnishings, gleaming wide-board floors, and cupboards displaying the owner's impressive glass and china collections. The three guest rooms, also antiques-furnished and all with private bath, have either a double or two twin beds; one has a fireplace. *1409 Broad St., Camden 29020, tel. 803/432–9861 weekdays 9–5, 803/432–2524 evenings and weekends. 3 rooms. Facilities: formal dining room. No credit cards.*

Columbia
Expensive
★ **Claussen's Inn.** This welcome retreat from the downtown bustle is a converted bakery warehouse in the attractive Five Points residential district. Open, airy lobby has Mexican tile floor and rooms, some two-story, are ranged around the lobby. There are eight loft suites, with downstairs sitting room and spiral staircase leading to sleeping area furnished with period reproductions and four-poster beds. *2003 Greene St., Columbia 29205, tel. 803/765–0440 or 800/622–3382. 29 rooms. Facilities: cable TV, whirlpool. AE, MC, V.*

★ **Columbia Marriott.** This upscale downtown hotel is conveniently located near state offices and the University of South Carolina. Public areas and guest rooms are contemporary in feeling, with touches of warmth and elegance characteristic of Marriotts. The Palm Terrace Restaurant is in a spectacular atrium with stunning views of decorative details: Veronique's features evening gourmet dining in an intimate, elegant setting. *1200 Hampton St., Columbia 29201, tel. 803/771–7000 or 800/228–9290. 301 rooms and suites. Facilities: pool, health club, sauna, teleconferencing facilities. AE, CB, DC, MC, V.*

Moderate-
Expensive
Embassy Suites Hotel Columbia. In the spacious seven-story atrium lobby, tastefully designed with skylights, fountains, pools and live plants, overnight guests enjoy sumptuous breakfasts and an early evening manager's cocktail reception—both complimentary. A Piano Lounge and Park Place Restaurant with full luncheon and dinner service are also here. *I–126 at Greystone Blvd. Exit, 200 Stoneridge Dr., Columbia 29210, tel. 803/252–8700 or 800/362–2779. 214 one-bedroom suites. Facilities: indoor pool, health club, sun decks, billiards room, disco, gift shop, 2 cable TVs in each suite along with microwave oven, refrigerator, wet bar. AE, DC, MC, V.*

Inexpensive-
Moderate
La Quinta Motor Inn. At this three-story inn on a quiet street near the zoo, the rooms are spacious and well lit, with a large working area and oversize beds. King Plus rooms have touchtone telephones, remote-control TV, a clock radio, a full-length mirror, and an ottoman. *Junction I–20 and U.S. 176 exit 65, 1335 Garner Lane, Columbia 29210, tel. 803/798–9590 or 800/531–5900. 122 rooms. Facilities: pool, cable TV/movies. AE, DC, MC, V.*

Greenwood
Moderate
Holiday Inn. This chain unit is two miles from downtown and across from a popular shopping mall. *1014 Montague Ave., Greenwood 29646 (U.S. 25 & 72 Bypass), tel. 803/223–4231 or 800/465–4329. 100 rooms. Facilities: pool, cable TV/movies, laundry, restaurant. AE, DC, MC, V.*

Orangeburg
Inexpensive
Best Western Inn of Orangeburg. This two-story downtown motor inn is conveniently located for visiting Edisto Gardens. *475 John C. Calhoun Dr., Orangeburg 29115 (jct. U.S. 601 and 301), tel. 803/534–7630 or 800/528–1234. 104 rooms. Facilities: pool, cable TV/HBO. AE, DC, MC, V.*

Sumter   **Holiday Inn.** This well-maintained motor inn is four miles west
Moderate   of town, near Shaw Air Force Base. *2390 Broad St., Box 6066,
Sumter 29151, tel. 803/469–9001 or 800/465–4329. 124 rooms.
Facilities: pool, tennis and golf privileges, cable TV/movies,
restaurant. AE, DC, MC, V.*

The Arts

Concerts, Opera,   In Columbia, the **South Carolina Orchestra Association** (tel.
and Dance   803/771–7939) represents the South Carolina Philharmonic,
Chamber Orchestra, and Youth Orchestra. The **Columbia Music Festival Association** (tel. 803/711–6303) includes the **Choral
Society, Opera, Opera Guild, Dance Theatre, Brass Band,
Caroliers, and Cabaret Company.**

Theater   Columbia's **Town Theatre** (1012 Sumter St., tel. 803/799–4764),
founded in 1919, is among the nation's oldest theater groups. It
stages six plays a year from September to late May, plus a special summer show. Dramatic presentations are also scheduled
at the **Workshop Theatre of South Carolina** (1136 Bull St., tel.
803/799–4876). The **Abbeville Opera House** (Town Square, tel.
803/459–2157) stages Broadway-caliber productions in an early
20th-century setting.

Nightlife

Most nightlife in the Heartland centers on lounges in hotels,
motels, and restaurants.

Aiken   There's live entertainment at **Jockey's Lounge** in the Holiday
Inn (tel. 803/648–4272).

Camden   **Plums Lounge** at the Holiday Inn (tel. 803/438–9441) provides
pleasant evening unwinding.

Columbia   **Cracker Jacks** (tel. 803/731–5692) features lively beach music
for listening and dancing, occasionally a lusty floor show.
Nitelites Dance Club (tel. 803/252–8700) at the Embassy Suites
Hotel boasts state-of-the-art lighting and showcases a lavish
complimentary hors d'oeuvres buffet during the weekday cocktail time, 5–7:30. Among other capital city nocturnal havens
are **Beau's** (tel. 803/254–3772) in the Radisson Hotel, **Saints**
(tel. 803/731–0300) at Sheraton Columbia Northwest, **Pawley's
Nightclub** (tel. 803/736–3000) in the Holiday Inn Northeast,
and the Columbia Marriott's **Palm Terrace Lounge** (tel. 803/
771–7000). A disco and lounge enliven the scene at **California
Dreaming** restaurant (tel. 803/254–6767).

Orangeburg   There is live entertainment at Rose Anna's lounge in the **Holiday Inn** (tel. 803/531–4600) and at the **Cock 'n' Bull Steak House**
(tel. 803/534–4168).

Sumter   The Holiday Inn's **Plums Lounge** (tel. 803/469–9001) has live
entertainment.

Index

Personal Itinerary

Departure *Date*

Time

Transportation

Arrival *Date*   *Time*

Departure *Date*   *Time*

Transportation

Accommodations

Arrival *Date*   *Time*

Departure *Date*   *Time*

Transportation

Accommodations

Arrival *Date*   *Time*

Departure *Date*   *Time*

Transportation

Accommodations

Personal Itinerary

Arrival *Date* *Time*

Departure *Date* *Time*

Transportation

Accommodations

Arrival *Date* *Time*

Departure *Date* *Time*

Transportation

Accommodations

Arrival *Date* *Time*

Departure *Date* *Time*

Transportation

Accommodations

Arrival *Date* *Time*

Departure *Date* *Time*

Transportation

Accommodations

Addresses

Name	*Name*
Address	*Address*
Telephone	*Telephone*
Name	*Name*
Address	*Address*
Telephone	*Telephone*
Name	*Name*
Address	*Address*
Telephone	*Telephone*
Name	*Name*
Address	*Address*
Telephone	*Telephone*
Name	*Name*
Address	*Address*
Telephone	*Telephone*
Name	*Name*
Address	*Address*
Telephone	*Telephone*
Name	*Name*
Address	*Address*
Telephone	*Telephone*
Name	*Name*
Address	*Address*
Telephone	*Telephone*

Fodor's Travel Guides

U.S. Guides

Alaska
Arizona
Atlantic City & the
  New Jersey Shore
Boston
California
Cape Cod
Carolinas & the
  Georgia Coast
The Chesapeake Region
Chicago
Colorado
Disney World & the
  Orlando Area

Florida
Hawaii
Las Vegas
Los Angeles, Orange
  County, Palm Springs
Maui
Miami,
  Fort Lauderdale,
  Palm Beach
Michigan, Wisconsin,
  Minnesota
New England
New Mexico
New Orleans

New Orleans (Pocket
  Guide)
New York City
New York City (Pocket
  Guide)
New York State
Pacific North Coast
Philadelphia
The Rockies
San Diego
San Francisco
San Francisco (Pocket
  Guide)
The South

Texas
USA
Virgin Islands
Virginia
Waikiki
Washington, DC

Foreign Guides

Acapulco
Amsterdam
Australia, New Zealand,
  The South Pacific
Austria
Bahamas
Bahamas (Pocket
  Guide)
Baja & the Pacific
  Coast Resorts
Barbados
Beijing, Guangzhou &
  Shanghai
Belgium &
  Luxembourg
Bermuda
Brazil
Britain (Great Travel
  Values)
Budget Europe
Canada
Canada (Great Travel
  Values)
Canada's Atlantic
  Provinces
Cancun, Cozumel,
  Yucatan Peninsula

Caribbean
Caribbean (Great
  Travel Values)
Central America
Eastern Europe
Egypt
Europe
Europe's Great
  Cities
France
France (Great Travel
  Values)
Germany
Germany (Great Travel
  Values)
Great Britain
Greece
The Himalayan
  Countries
Holland
Hong Kong
Hungary
India,
  including Nepal
Ireland
Israel
Italy

Italy (Great Travel
  Values)
Jamaica
Japan
Japan (Great Travel
  Values)
Kenya, Tanzania,
  the Seychelles
Korea
Lisbon
Loire Valley
London
London (Great
  Travel Values)
London (Pocket Guide)
Madrid & Barcelona
Mexico
Mexico City
Montreal &
  Quebec City
Munich
New Zealand
North Africa
Paris
Paris (Pocket Guide)
People's Republic of
  China

Portugal
Rio de Janeiro
The Riviera (Fun on)
Rome
Saint Martin &
  Sint Maarten
Scandinavia
Scandinavian Cities
Scotland
Singapore
South America
South Pacific
Southeast Asia
Soviet Union
Spain
Spain (Great Travel
  Values)
Sweden
Switzerland
Sydney
Tokyo
Toronto
Turkey
Vienna
Yugoslavia

Special-Interest Guides

Health & Fitness
  Vacations
Royalty Watching

Selected Hotels of
  Europe

Selected Resorts and
  Hotels of the U.S.
Shopping in Europe

Skiing in North America
Sunday in New York

Help us evaluate hotels and restaurants for the next edition of this guide, and we will send you a free issue of Fodor's newsletter, <u>TravelSense</u>.

Title of this guide:

1 Hotel ❏ Restaurant ❏ *(check one)*

Name

Number/Street

City/State/Country

Comments

2 Hotel ❏ Restaurant ❏ *(check one)*

Name

Number/Street

City/State/Country

Comments

3 Hotel ❏ Restaurant ❏ *(check one)*

Name

Number/Street

City/State/Country

Comments

General Comments

Please complete for a free copy of <u>TravelSense</u>

Name

Number/Street

City/State/Zip

Business Reply Mail

First Class   *Permit N° 7775*   *New York, NY*

Postage will be paid by addressee

Fodor's Travel Publications

201 East 50th Street
New York, NY 10022